APPLICATIONS OF VIRTUAL REALITY

Edited by **Cecília Sík Lányi**

Applications of Virtual Reality
Edited by Cecília Sík Lányi

Published by InTech
Janeza Trdine 9, 51000 Rijeka, Croatia

Publishing Process Manager Jana Sertic

Technical Editor Teodora Smiljanic

Cover Designer InTech Design Team

Additional hard copies can be obtained from orders@intechopen.com

Applications of Virtual Reality, Edited by Cecília Sík Lányi
p. cm.
ISBN 978-953-51-0583-1

For EU product safety concerns:
IN TECH d.o.o., Prolaz Marije Krucifikse Kozulić 3, 51000 Rijeka, Croatia,
info@intechopen.com or visit our website at intechopen.com.

Meet the editor

Dr Cecília Sik Lányi studied Mathematics and Computer Science (B.S.) – József Attila University (1981) - Mathematics and Computer Science (M.S.) – József Attila University (1984). She became Teacher of Mathematics - Berzsenyi Dániel Teacher Training College in 1988. She obtained the degree of Dr. Univ. at the University of Veszprém, Hungary in Physical-chemistry (1993), and the degree of PhD at the University of Veszprém, Hungary in Computer Science (2000). She has worked as a software engineer and as an associate professor for program languages at the University of Pannonia. Currently she is focused on virtual reality and its application, user interface design, computer graphics for informatics engineering students and using multimedia in the education for teacher training courses. PhD and Masters' supervision has an emphasis on multimedia/ virtual reality for the rehabilitation of children with disabilities and patients with mental health issues. She got the "Master teacher" award of the Hungarian Ministry of Education in 2001. She has published more than 300 refereed articles and conference papers, and worked as guest editor for many renowned journals. She was the secretariat manager of EDeAN in 2009. She is the representative of Hungary in IFIP Technical Committee 13: Human-Computer Interaction (TC13).

Contents

Preface

Information Technology is growing rapidly. With the birth of high-resolution graphics, high-speed computing and user interaction devices, Virtual Reality has emerged as a major new technology in the mid $90^{es,}$ last century. An explosion has occurred in our understanding of Virtual Reality, Virtual Environments and in the technologies required to produce them in the last decade. Virtual Worlds and Virtual Environments are produced for people, for users to interact with computer and with complex information sets. It became a commonplace in our increasingly technological world in recent years. These Virtual Reality Applications cover almost all fields of the real life activities. Another standpoint is the ergonomic and psychological concerns that must be investigated, in this way the people will enjoy using Virtual Reality technologies.

Virtual Reality technology is currently used in a broad range of applications. The best known are games, movies, simulations, therapy. From a manufacturing standpoint, there are some attractive applications including training, education, collaborative work and learning.

This book provides an up-to-date discussion of the current research in Virtual Reality and its applications. It describes the current Virtual Reality state-of-the-art and points out the many areas where there is still work to be done. We have chosen certain areas to cover in this book, which we believe will have potential significant impact on Virtual Reality and its applications.

The main features of the book can be summarised as follows:

1. The book describes and evaluates the current state-of-the-art in the field of Virtual Reality.
2. It also presents several applications of Virtual Reality in the fields of learning environments, simulations, industrial application, data mining and ergonomic design.
3. Contributors to the book are the leading researchers from Academia and practitioners from the industry.

This book provides a definitive resource for wide variety of people including academicians, designers, developers, educators, engineers, practitioners, researchers, and graduate students.

We would like to thank the authors for their contributions. Without their expertise and effort, this book would never be born. InTech staff also deserves our sincere recognition for their support throughout the project.

Finally the editor would like to thank her husband Ferenc Sik, her sons András Sik and Gergely Sik for their patience and Professor Janos Schanda, the head of the editor's Laboratory for giving her the freedom of research.

Dr. Cecília Sík Lányi
Associate professor at the University of Pannonia,
Veszprem,
Hungary

1

Virtual Design of Piston Production Line

Zhou Jun[1,2,*], Li Puhong[1,2], Zhang Yanliang[1],
Deng Jianxin[1,2] and Liu Zhanqiang[1,2]
[1]*School of Mechanical Engineering Shandong University, Jinan,*
[2]*Key Laboratory of High Efficiency and Clean Mechanical Manufacture (Shandong University), Ministry of Education, Jinan,*
P.R. China

1. Introduction

Production paradigm has been changing since Henry Ford's "we believe that no factory is large enough to make two kinds of products" (Ford, H. 1926). With their Scion brand Toyota joined the race for offering customers an increasing product variety, a trend which has been characterizing the automotive industry throughout the last decades (Lee, H. et al., 2005). This development has been driven by two factors. On the outside demand, customization is driven by the improved competitive position of companies which address individual customer's needs (Kotler, P.1989). On the inside supply, customization strategies have been significantly promoted - if not was made possible at all-by advances in product design and manufacturing as well as information technology(Da Silveira,G.et al.,2001). Based on these advances it became possible to quickly respond to the customer orders by combining standardized modules and cut down the cost.

As the design of the production line is a complex and systematic project, many scholars advance to apply the computer-aided design to each unit of the production line design. Sang Hyeok Han et al (S.H. Han et al., 2011) used Maxscript in 3D Studio Max for automation of the visualization process, which has been applied to the production line of modular buildings with the output of lean, simulation, and visualization in the form of animation, to automate the visualization process as a post-simulation tool through sharing interactive information between simulation and visualization. Thomas Volling(Thomas Volling&Thomas S. Spengler.2011) provided a model and simulation of the order-driven planning policies in build-to-order automobile production, comprising separate interlinked quantitative models for order promising and master production scheduling and evaluating both models in a dynamic setting. Yong-Sik Kim (Yong-Sik Kim et al., 2006) proposed that virtual reality module uses a commercial virtual manufacturing system instead of expensive virtual reality equipments as the viewer of the immersive virtual reality system on a cluster of PCs and adopts the modified simulation algorithm. GAO Chonghui(GAO Chonhui et al.,2010) constructed the virtual simulation for automobile panels based on analyzing the motion characteristics of automatic press line and extracting the corresponding data of motion. These models took better advantage of computer-aided design technology for

[*] Corresponding Author

production line design, but these methods cannot model for the design process of the whole production line, and cannot complete dynamic analysis of production lines. Because of varieties and quantities of the piston are constantly changing, the above method is difficult to effectively and proactively verify the running condition of piston production lines.

As the part supplier of automobile assembly, piston companies also face the same problems, for example, Shandong Binzhou Bohai Piston Co., Ltd. has more than 70 piston production lines to manufacture those pistons such as car, motorcycle, marine, air compressors, chillers, engineering machinery and agricultural machinery pistons. Those size ranges from Φ30 mm to Φ350mm. However, due to the changing market and customized demand, the annual piston species is up to 800 kinds, some piston production line can change the product twice per month, some even more than five, and the production batch is ranging from small to mass. So it is difficult to quickly make the production planning under those demands with the traditional production line design methods. Therefore, it needs the advancing manufacturing technologies and methods to respond quickly to market changes and customized production.

As for production activities in production lines, it often faces the adjustment of design, and the well-designed production line can reduce operating and maintenance costs, improve equipment capacity factor and the efficiency of the system.

2. Design method of production line

2.1 Traditional design method of the production line

For traditional design method of the production line, it is necessary to provide such information as product type, production output, processes and other system properties to select processing equipments, logistics equipments and various auxiliary equipments, etc. And then, the layout of these devices need to take considerable combined with the structural characteristics of workshop space, and the space between the devices to ensure the maintenance of those devices and safely. The traditional design method includes: determining the cycle time through the layout of entire production; confirming the number of processing equipment with all the processes, synchronizing the processes, assigning the required number of operators, choosing logistics mode, designing the layout and drawing a standard plan charts, and so on. The traditional design method has those shortcomings as following(FAN Xiumin et al.2001; Shao Li et al.,2000):

1. Too complex and design results depending on the experts strongly.
2. Lack of dynamic characteristics description.
3. Not visually display.
4. Difficult to reflect the operational status of the various parts of the system early in the design;
5. Poor to predicate the bottleneck accuracy based on theoretical calculations and easy to waste the resources.

2.2 Virtual design of production line

Virtual design technology is a visualized design method of the production line to establish a visual modelling which can simulate a real production line in the virtual environment. It can provide the model and analysis tool to rapidly design the piston production and improve the design rationality in the end(Shao Li et al.,2000).

Production lines involve multiple objects and actions with discrete, random, complexity, hierarchy and so on. Modelling for production lines is the foundation of virtual design. The traditional simulation model mainly focused on the design of algorithms that can be accepted by the computer, resulting in a variety of simulation algorithms and simulation software (Zhao Ji et al.,2000; S B.Yoo et al.,1994; H.T. Papadopolous& C. Heavey, J. Browne.,1993; Zhang Longxiang,2007). From the 1980s, due to high-level language for computer compiling, structured simulation modelling has been a great progress. Chan and Chan(F.T.S. Chan&H.K. Chan,2004) presented a review of discrete event simulation (DES) applications in scheduling for flexible manufacturing systems (FMS). Ashworth and Carley (M.J. Ashworth&K.M. Carley,2007) had conducted a review that addresses organizational theory and modelling using agent-based simulation (ABS) and system dynamics (SD).Shafer and Smunt(S.M. Shafer&T.L. Smunt,2004), Smith(J.S. Smith,2003), Baines and Harrison(T.S. Baines& D.K. Harrison,1999) targeted the larger domain of operations management and applied the simulation to it. However, most reviews limited themselves to either a single technique (DES or SD) or a single application area where more than one technique is used. However, because the interactivity of the structural simulation modelling is poor, it has not been widely application. With the developing object-oriented technology, object-oriented simulation modelling has been rapidly developed. Object-oriented modelling techniques (OMT) is a software environment applying classes, objects, inheritance, packages, collections, messaging, polymorphism and other concepts, which emphasizes the concept of the problem domain map directly to objects or the interface definition between objects, applies the modelling, analysis and maintenance of the realistic entity, so that the built model is easy to reflect the real objects, and makes the constructed model with re-configurability, reusability and maintainability. And it is easy to expand and upgrade and can reduce the complexity of systems analysis and development costs significantly. Many different OMT methods have been advanced, such as OMT / Rumbaugh, OSA / Embley, OOD / Booch et al (Zhang Longxiang,2007; Par Klingstam& Per Gullander ,1999; Dirk Rantzau et al.,1999).

But when these models are used for dynamic performance analysis on the production line, the modelling is more complex and difficult to describe the dynamic characteristics of the production line quickly and easily, which has greater limitations. QUEST is a virtual integrated development environment applied to queue simulation analysis in Deneb company, which is proper to simulate and analyse the accuracy of the technological process and productivity, in order to improve the design, reduce risk and cost, and make the planned production line meet the design requirements early in the design and implementation, before investing real facilities. Combining the advantages of the QUEST virtual simulation development environment and unified modelling language (UML), this paper presents the simulation, analysis and modelling methods of Virtual Design of Piston Production Line (VD-PPL) to analyse the static and dynamic characteristics of the piston production line.

3. Virtual design of Piston Production Line (PPL)

3.1 The frame of VD-PPL

Due to the characteristics such as multi-objectives optimization, strong resources correlation, large randomness etc., based on system theory and hierarchical design methodology, VD-

PPL theoretical model is divided into five levels: Support, Management, Transaction, Simulation and Decision level levels. Design features and contents about of all levels are shown in Figure 3.1.

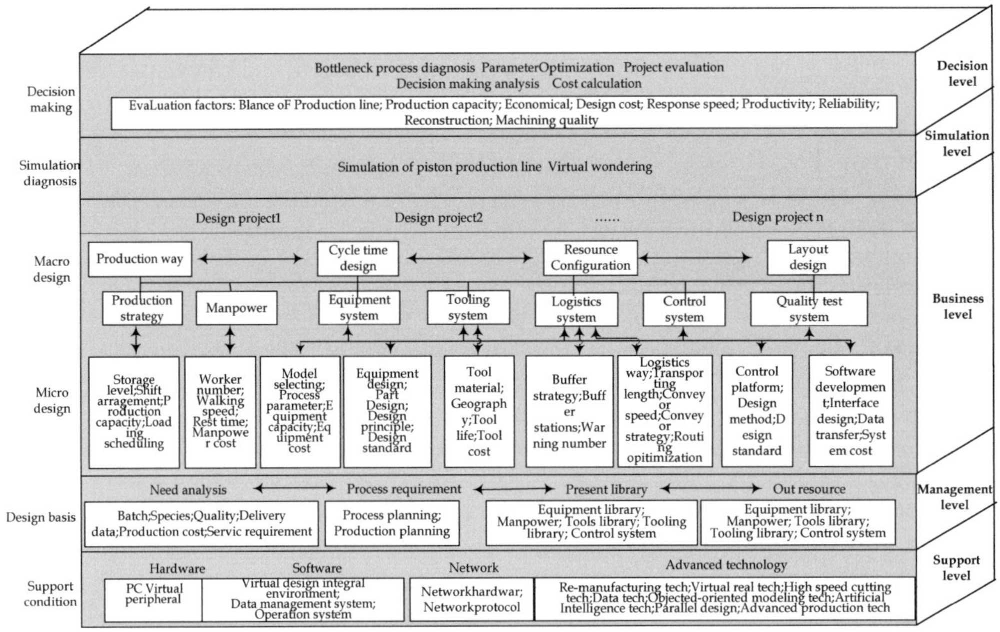

Fig. 3.1. Virtual simulation design frame of reconstructing piston production line

3.2 Object-oriented VD-PPL modeling and simulation analysis

Object-oriented technology is a design method focusing on the concept organization model of real-world mode, which is used with the entity to describe. With object-oriented method, it creates a basic resource library in the complex manufacturing environment of production line, and carries out the analysis and modeling for this library, which cannot only establish a unified framework to describe, design and complete system, but also can better reflect the hierarchy relation between various entities, and establish simulation model to reflect the real production environment. Based on manufacturing environment of production lines, for the piston production line modeling, it is used object-oriented modeling techniques.

3.2.1 Object modelling of Piston Production Line

Modeling for the piston production line not only needs to build three-dimensional geometry of physical entities in a virtual environment, but also needs to define the hierarchy relationships and interactions containing a variety of resource objects. For example, when designing manufacturing processes, it is necessary to define the relationship about of the process and the objects such as machine tools, process parameters, tools and other objects. However this relationship is static without dynamic behavior. Among the above objects, for the machine tools, it has the loading, manufacturing processes, unloading the workplace and other object behaviors (Methods of operation), and interact with other objects by the message passing mechanism. For example, when the simulation of production lines is running, machine tools, buffers area, cutting tools, measuring tools and other objects will interact with each other and the dynamic behaviors will appear.

As it is known, object modeling of piston production line contains three parts: the description of object relations, object behavior and object interaction, which join together to achieve mapping modeling from reality to virtual simulation environment of the piston production line. Therefore, the VD-PPL modeling process is defined as follows:

1. Establish the physical model of VD-PPL

In the simulation environment, make the object model reflect the physical entity of the real piston production line.

2. Establish the logical model of VD-PPL

The logical model contains static logic model and dynamic logic models. Among these, the static logic description the modeling for internal properties of the piston production line, structure and behavior and so on, which reflect the static properties of all objects and relationships of the piston production line.

The dynamic logical is used to describe the dynamics behaviors and dynamic interactions on the piston production line, and to achieve the description of its dynamic characteristics by adding the simulation clock, event controller and other simulation-driving mechanisms, which can reproduce the running condition of description of piston production line to get the simulation results of piston production line.

3.2.2 VD-PPL analysis method

In QUEST, it is applied the model description with the object-oriented techniques, which can make the model reusable and modifiable. But its object model is mainly used for the simulation, and the description of the static object model is not more comprehensive than other object-oriented methods which can be difficult to fully describe the hierarchy and static characteristics of restructuring piston production lines.

UML is one of the modeling language based on Booch, OOSE methods and a variety of OMT methods, which is the product of the unified and standardization of modeling approach. It is proper for all stages of system development, and can establish the static structure and dynamic behavior model of the system. UML is a graphical modeling language, which includes five categories:

1. Case figure

Describe the functions of the system from the viewpoint of the user, and point out the operator of all the functions.

2. Static figure

Include the class diagrams, object diagrams and package diagrams. The class diagram is used to describe the static structure of class in the system, object diagram is a case of class diagram, and package diagram is used to describe the system hierarchy.

3. Behavior diagram

Describe the dynamic model and the interactions of composition objects in the system, including state diagrams and activity diagrams. State diagram is used to describe all possible states of the objects and transfer conditions of the incident state, usually the state diagram is supplement of the class diagram; activity diagram is used to describe the activities and the constraint relationship between activities meeting the requirements of cases, which can be easily expressed in parallel activities.

4. Interactive diagram

Both sequence diagrams and collaboration diagrams are used to describe the interactions between objects. Sequence diagram is used to show the dynamic cooperative relationship between objects, and collaboration diagram emphasizes collaborative relationships between objects.

5. Implementation diagram

It is used to describe the features of the system, including component diagrams and configuration diagram.

Although the use of UML modeling method can well describe the object relations of VD-PPL, the modeling process is complex and model implementation is more time-consuming and difficult when UML is used to describe the complicated and discrete object behaviors and interactive relationship, because of the characteristics of random, discrete and others. QUEST simulation platform based on virtual manufacturing technology, not only supports the physical modeling of resource objects with better virtual visual interface, but also fully supports the simulation of object-oriented discrete/continuous events, which can be the important tools of the simulation and analysis of the production process. Combining the advantages of QUEST and UML, the paper proposed VD-PPL simulation modeling method, as shown in Fig.3.2.

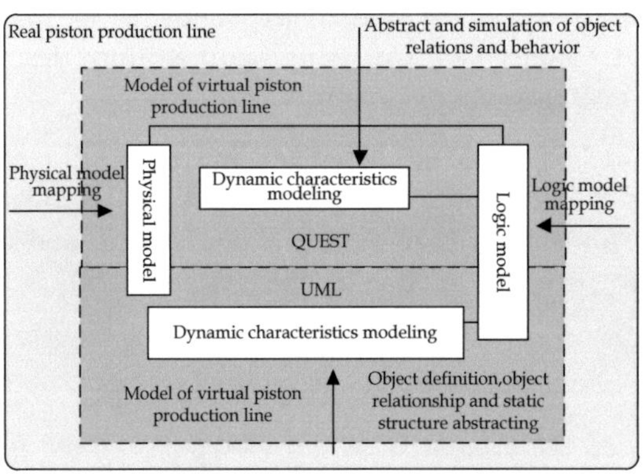

Fig. 3.2. VD-PPL simulation and modeling method based on QUEST+UML

In Fig.3.2, VD-PPL simulation modeling can be divided into two parts: the virtual physical modeling and virtual logical modeling. Virtual physical model is visual appearance of the logical model in a virtual environment, and it focuses on describing the three-dimensional geometry corresponding to the physical entity of the real production line. Therefore, virtual physical model is the foundation of layout design of piston production line and visual simulation. The virtual physical model is divided into virtual static characteristics modeling and dynamic characteristics modeling. Virtual static characteristics modeling includes customization of all the objects on the production line and the description of the relationship between objects, and virtual dynamic model describes the dynamic behavior of the object itself and of interactions between objects. VD-PPL simulation modeling focuses on establishing the virtual logical model of the production line piston.

In VD-PPL modeling process, the contents are established by QUEST as follows: 1) the virtual physical model mapping corresponding to physical entities of the piston production lines; 2). the virtual logical model of VD-RPPL object relationship and object behaviors. Piston production lines describe object definition of the resources, object association and the static structure abstracting and other processes with UML.

3.3 Static properties modeling of Piston Production Line object

For UML modeling methods, the class object is an abstract for some public, private or protective properties and the corresponding behaviors. According to the common features of restructuring piston production line, all the piston production lines can be defined abstractly as a production line class. The production line class can be consider as the base class of VD-PPL modeling, the properties of production line class include the identification of production line, names of production line, maximum machining diameter of piston, minimum machining diameter of piston, and behaviors of the production line class includes getting the costs of production line, accessing the actual production cycle and availability calculation and so on. Fig.3.3 is UML class diagram between the base class of piston production lines and production lines class.

Production line class
-ID: int +Name of production line: char +Model of production line: char -Maximum machining diameter of piston: double -Minimum machining diameter of piston: double -Maximum height of piston: double +Actual cycle: double -Production planning: double -Cost: double -Reconstructing time: double +Layout ID: int -Availability rate of production line: double -Manufacturing products: int
+Getting the costs of production line: double + Getting the actual production cycle: double +Getting constructing time: double +Availability calculation: double +Getting the quantity of manufacturing products: int +Utilization calculation: double

Fig. 3.3. UML classes diagram of piston production lines class

3.3.1 VD-PPL static hierarchical relationship

According to the hierarchical relationships of a piston production line, that physical equipment, process technology, logic control and simulation supporting classes are derived from the production line class. The physical equipment class is corresponding to production entities in the reality, such as processing equipments, logistics equipments and so on. No entity is correspond with the process technology class in the real production line, such as Cycle Process, Load Process, Unload Process, production planning and tasks and other process contents. The logic control class is used to describe the logical relationships between objects, such as AGV control logic, labor control logic, conveyor control logic. The simulation supporting class is applied for describing the interaction process time of production line simulation, events, and data performance statistics and other simulation supporting objects. According to the relationship between base classes and derived classes, the static hierarchy of various objects in VD-PPL design process, as shown in Fig.3.4.

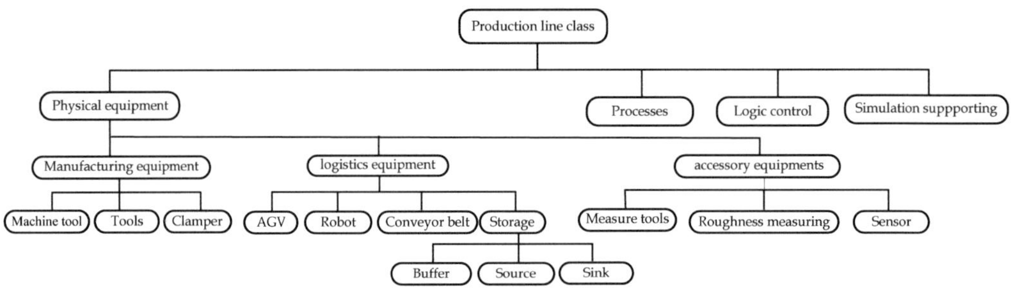

Fig. 3.4. Static hierarchy of piston production line objects

3.3.2 Physics equipment

Attributes of the physics equipment class is divided into physics, processes, function and status attributes. Physical attributes define the static property of resources, such as identity, name, geometry, size, color, accuracy, etc.; Process attributes define the actions completed by relative motion or action of two or more resources, such as utilization, cycle time and so on; Functional attributes define series of a higher level of functional units processes formed by the combination series of processes, on behalf of the ability of resources; State attributes is used to define whether the resource is in using, waiting, idle state or the state of repair, to guide the dynamic dispatch of production resources. The manufacturing equipment class, logistics equipment class, accessory equipment classes are derived from physical equipment class according to their hierarchy.

1. Manufacturing equipment class

Processes equipment mainly refers to the equipment that can complete one or more process technology. The physical attributes of manufacturing equipment include equipment identification, equipment specifications, failure rate, repair rate, etc., and its process attribute also includes equipment utilization, etc.; it is shown in Fig.3. 5(a).

2. Logistics equipment class

Logistics equipment class is responsible for transportation and the storage of the work piece and materials between logistics equipment, such as AGV, conveyor, robot, storage devices

(Source, Sink, Buffer, etc.). Workers (Labor) who complete the transportation and storage of materials can also be treated as abstract logistics equipment. Logistics equipment class is used to describe the properties and methods of equipment and workers that implement the transportation function of the work piece and materials, and it is also used to describe the reconfiguring time, cost, utilization, work piece delivery time of logistics equipment in the process of reorganization objects. According to the definition mode of processing equipment class, the attributes of the logistics equipment class can also be divided into physical, process, functional and state attributes. Especially, the physical attribute includes equipment number, name, size, cost, geometry, size, color and so on. The process attribute includes utilization, delivery times, reconstructing time, delivery speed, acceleration/deceleration, etc. the functional attribute includes the maximum specifications and length of work pieces or materials, the maximum transportation quantities of the work pieces, the maximum work piece capacity and so on. UML class diagram of the logistics equipment is shown in Fig.3.5 (b). AGV, convey, robot and storage classes are derived from logistics equipment class

3. Auxiliary equipment class

Auxiliary equipment is mainly service as the measure and other works to make sure the processes are completed smoothly and accuracy. The auxiliary equipment class is the abstract of such equipment, and its attributes includes device identification, name, size, cost, measure items, measure accuracy, measure time, reconfiguring time and so on; Its behavioral approach is: to get the cost of auxiliary equipment, the reconfiguring time of auxiliary equipment and the measuring time of auxiliary equipment so on. UML class diagram of measure equipment class is shown in Fig.3.5 (c). According to the different measure items, measuring device, roughness measurement, sensor type, and other classes are derived from the auxiliary equipment class.

manufacturing equipment class
+Name: char -No. :long -Quantity: int -Description: char -Productivity:double -ID:int +Name of production line: char +Model of production line: char -Maximum machining diameter of piston: double -Minimum machining diameter of piston: double -Maximum height of piston: double -Minimum height of piston: double -Production planning: double +Actual cycle: double -Cost: double -Reconstructing time: double +Layout ID:int -Availability rate of production line: double -Manufacturing products:int
+Getting the costs of production line: double + Getting the actual production cycle: double +Getting constructing time: double +Availability calculation: double +Getting the quantity of manufacturing products:int +Utilization calculation: double

a) manufacturing equipment class

Logistics equipments class
+Name: char -No. :long -Quantity: int -Description: char -Cost: double -Reconstructing time: double -ID:int +Max. transportation capacity of parts:int +Transportation speed: double +Acceleration: double +Name of production line: char +Model of production line: char -Maximum machining diameter of piston: double -Minimum machining diameter of piston: double -Maximum height of piston: double -Minimum height of piston: double -Production planning: double +Actual cycle: double -Cost: double -Reconstructing time: double +Layout ID:int -Availability rate of production line: double -Manufacturing products:int
+Getting the costs of production line: double + Getting the actual production cycle: double +Getting constructing time: double +Availability calculation: double +Getting the quantity of manufacturing products:int +Utilization calculation: double

b) Logistics equipments class

auxiliary equipments class
+Name of measuring tools: char -No. of measuring tools :int -Specification - Measure accuracy +Measuring ability:char -Quantity: int -Single detecting time:double -ID:int +Name of production line: char +Model of production line: char -Maximum machining diameter of piston: double -Minimum machining diameter of piston: double -Maximum height of piston: double -Minimum height of piston: double -Production planning: double +Actual cycle: double -Cost: double -Reconstructing time: double +Layout ID:int -Availability rate of production line: double -Manufacturing products:int
+Getting the costs of production line: double + Getting the actual production cycle: double +Getting constructing time: double +Availability calculation: double +Getting the quantity of manufacturing products:int +Utilization calculation: double

c) Detecting auxiliary equipments class

Fig. 3.5. Auxiliary equipment classes

3.3.3 Processes class

In order to describe the processes during the piston manufacturing, the process class is acted as base class of VD-PPL process modeling, and those attributes include ID, names, process technology contents; its behavioral approaches are: working hours calculating, efficiency calculating and process, production planning, production scheduling classes and so on can be derived from the process class.

Attributes of the process class contain process ID, name, content, process priority, the number of work piece, number of workers, number of AGV and equipment, average cycle time and distribution of cycle processing time. Those behavioral approaches include defining the work piece priority, logical sequence of process, equipment selecting, working hours calculating, auxiliary process arranging, and so on. According to the classification of process technology, the process class is divided into the initial running process, loading process, recycling processing technology, unloading process, maintenance process classes etc. UML model of process technology class is shown in Fig.3.6 (a).

Attributes of the production scheduling class include ID, name, description of production arrangements, the number of shifts, shifting time, stopping time. Those behavioral approaches contain shift schedule, the calculation of expected stopping time of single work piece, needed equipment between arrange the associated shifts and so on. UML model of the production scheduling class is shown in Fig.3.6 (b).

Attributes of production planning class contain ID, name, and content, description of production plan, production, delivery date, and cost. Those behavioral methods include production cycle calculating UML model of production planning class is shown in Fig.3.6 (c).

Attributes of the process parameters class include ID, names, spindle speed, horizontal-feeding speed, vertical-feeding rate, cutting depth. Its behavioral methods contain machine tools selecting, tools selecting and measuring tools selecting, and so on, they are shown in Fig. 3.6 (d).

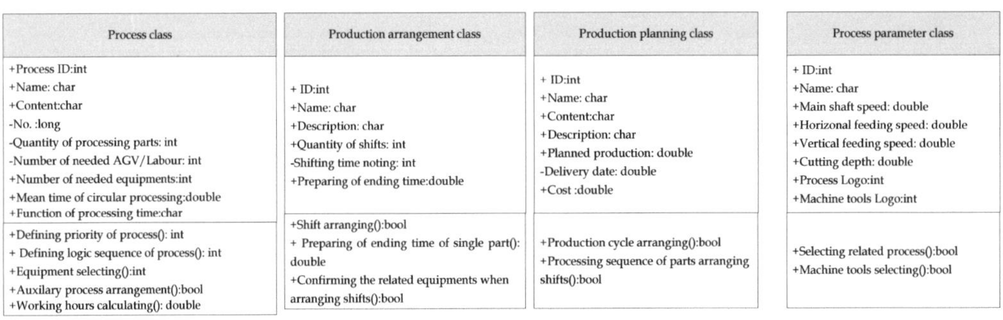

a) process class b) production arrangement class c) production planning class d) process parameters class

Fig. 3.6. UML class diagram of process technology derived class

3.3.4 Logic control class

Logic control is activity on the selection and scheduling functions of production resources, and logic control class is used to be an abstract description of interaction decision-making behavior between the different resource objects in a specific time. Attributes of the logic control class contain the controller ID the number of control objects, logical calculation priority. Those behavioral methods include the definition of initialization logic, processing logic, part routing logic, resource selection logic and other selecting modes. The meanings of the logical models are shown in Table 3.1, and the logical hierarchy relationship of the control class is shown in Fig. 3.7.

Logic mode	Meaning
Initial Logic	Control production resource completes the decision-making process initialization.
Process Logic	Control production resource complete the decision-making of loading process class, recycling processing technology class, unloading process
Part Rout Logic	Control work piece complete the decision-making of routing way from one object to another.
Request Selection Logic	Control the decision-making of resource selecting behavior with process technology.
* Queue Logic	Deal with the sequence of work piece when routing from Buffer object to other production resources.

* Queue Logic is only used for Buffer.

Table 3.1 VD-PPL logic definition

Processing logic is used to define the sequence of processing objects, proportion relations of process objects handling. Routing logic is primarily used to define the model of bottom objects of the work piece. Queuing logic is mainly used to define queuing methods.

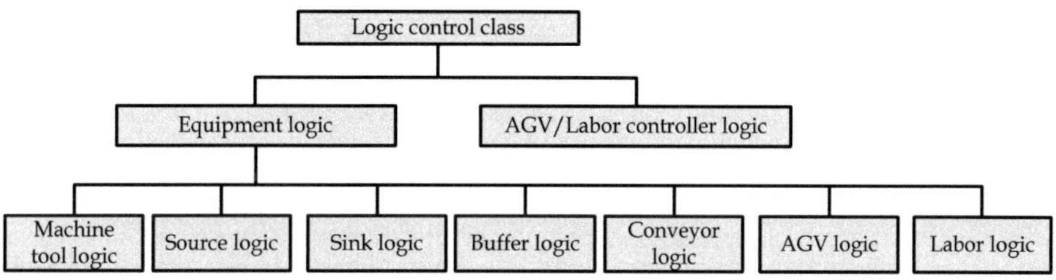

Fig. 3.7. Hierarchy diagram of logic control class

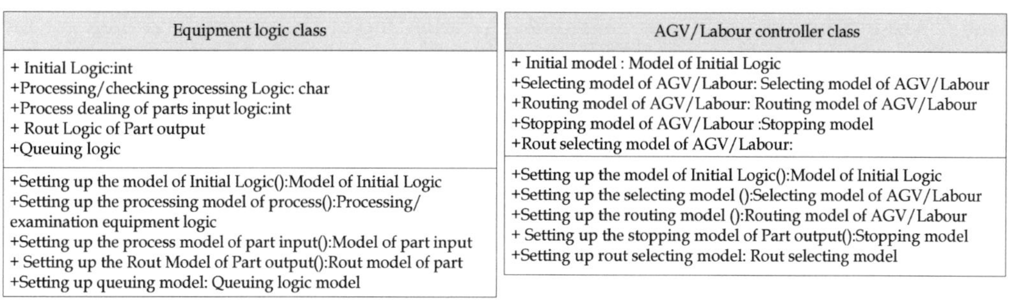

a) Equipment logic class　　　b) AGV/Labour controller class

Fig. 3.8. UML class diagram of equipment logic and AGV/Labor controller logic

The equipment logical device is mainly used in loading the work piece, processing the work piece and unloading the work piece, and the equipment need complete judgment and decision-making. Its UML class diagram is described in Fig.3.8 (a). AGV / Labor control logic means that AGV / Labor controller sends logic instructions to AGV / Labor when the production resources (such as equipment) is set on AGV / Labor , and its UML model is shown in Fig. 3.8 (b).

The piston product line also includes other logic, such as: Initial Logic, Request Input Logic, Part Input Logic, Request Selection Logic, etc.

3.3.5 System interaction class

System interaction class provides function and mechanism of the virtual simulation, and it used to the abstraction supported by dynamic simulation model, including time management, event table handling, creation and elimination of object, generation of random number, data collection and processing of statistics objects, etc., which does not correspond to physical entities in the real production line. Event class, time, etc. is derived from it.

Attributes of event class includes ID, names, events, object identity for demanded resources, corresponding process identifies, the type of events, and occurred time of the event.

Attributes of time class contain ID, names, events, active objects, passive objects, happening time, time to maintain the global simulation, record and order the events recorded according to the event points, determining the next earliest occurrence of future events and happening time and advance simulation clock and so on.

3.4 Dynamic properties modeling

The piston production line is a typical discrete event system. There have been many discrete event systems about dynamics modeling and analysis methods. It contains three types of modeling-logic level, algebra-level and performance level at least. An analysis method of the logic level includes finite automation /formal language method, Petri Net methods and so on. Petri Net methods began to be used for manufacturing system modeling from the early 1980s, which can analyze and describe the dynamic behavior of manufacturing systems well. But, with the system parameters increasing, Petri Net modeling and analysis become more and more difficult. Algebraic methods contain max/min algebra and finite recursion. Min/max algebra applies algebraic methods as a tool to establish the state equation of the time of the incident, according to the running relationship of the system, and then get the processing cycle, utilization and other parameters of the system by eigenvalue analysis. But with the parameters increasing, the state equation will bring out the dimension explosion, solvability variation, and analytical ability weakening. Performance levels contain: queuing network, perturbation analysis, and simulation modeling approach. Queuing theory is generally used for the qualitative analysis of system; perturbation analysis method will generate dynamic disturbance because parameters on the production line is much more, which is more difficult to describe the system dynamic process with tables and dynamic equations. The piston production lines often have uncertain activities, and also affected by constraints of internal/external objects of the system. And these objects are often affected by some other uncertain activities, leading that the variable state of the piston production line presents uncertainties, which will take the larger difficulties for analysis and modeling.

Apply object-oriented modeling method to establish the dynamic model piston production line to simulate and model effectively for dynamic characteristics of piston production line.

3.4.1 Object dynamic model based on UML+QUEST

Before establishing the virtual dynamics model of the piston production line, it is necessary to analyze the object of the piston as follows:

The behavior model of the state changes of all the objects is established based on the object behavior and messaging mechanism with the UML state diagram. Figure3.9 describes UML state diagram of the state changes in the process of the piston machining tool, in which, "⊂⊃"is the state of the machine in the process of machining the piston. "T" is the interactive relationship of states changes.

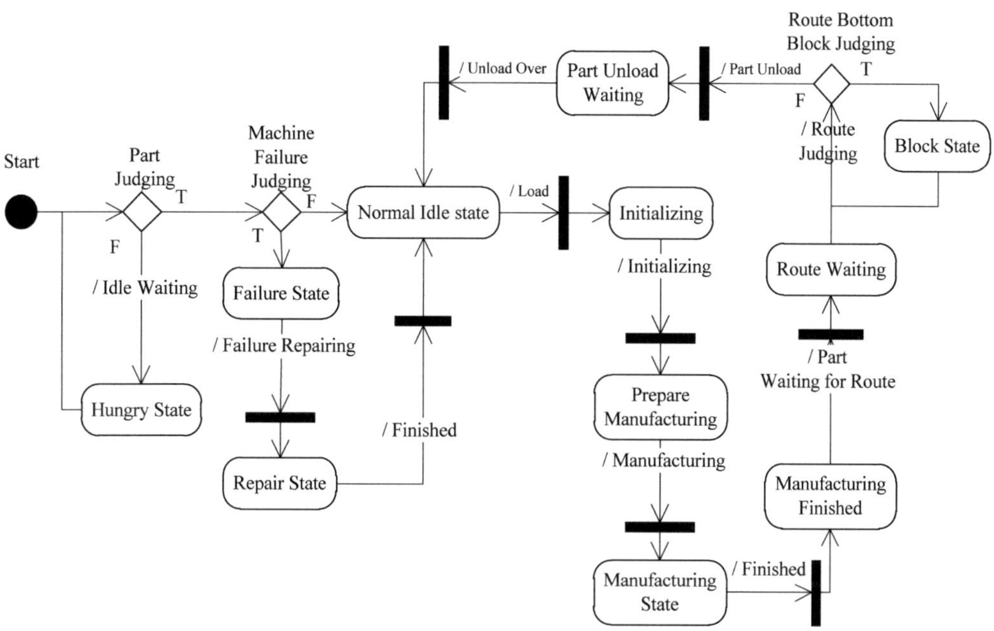

Fig. 3.9. UML state diagram of machine tool when piston is processed

The object relations, behavioral control, object interaction model are established with UML sequence and collaboration diagrams to fully describe the association relationship of various objects during piston processing. Figure.3.10 describes UML sequence interaction diagrams of labor controller, labor, buffer, and machine tool objects.

After analyzing the interaction behavior of dynamic models, in QUEST, virtual dynamic model of PPL is established, and the modeling steps are shown in Fig.3.11.

1. Establishing the physical model

The virtual physical model is the basic task of VD-PPL. The physical model is an abstract description of a real model of the piston production line in a virtual environment. According to the geometry, establish the virtual physical model of the resource objects with three-dimensional geometric modeling functions (or other 3D solid modeling software,

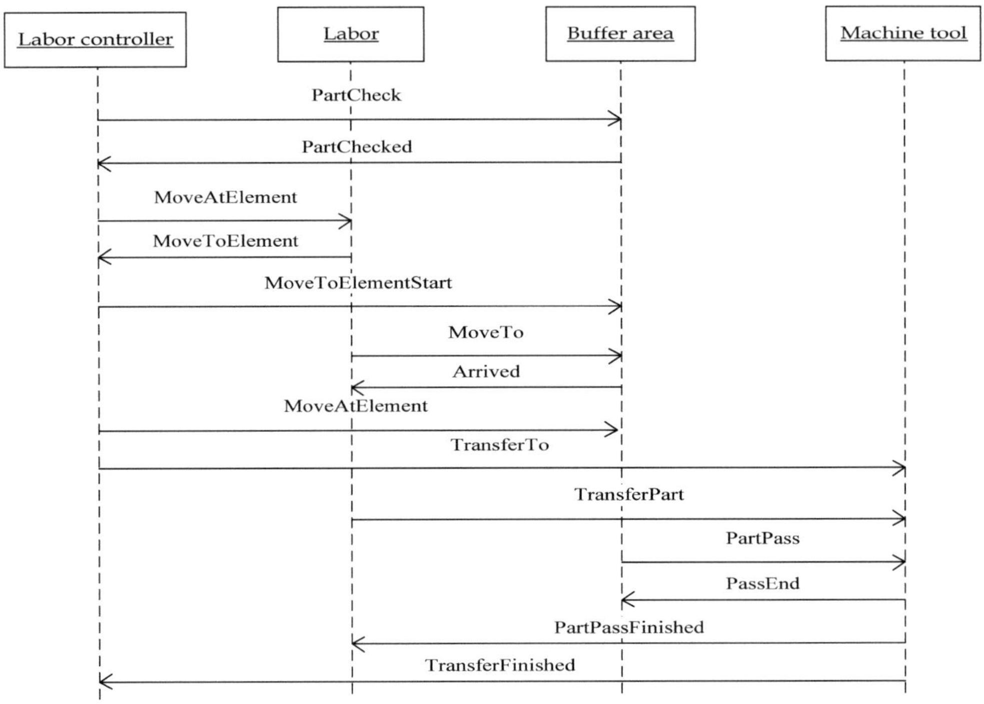

Fig. 3.10. UML sequence interaction diagram of all the objects in the piston conveying

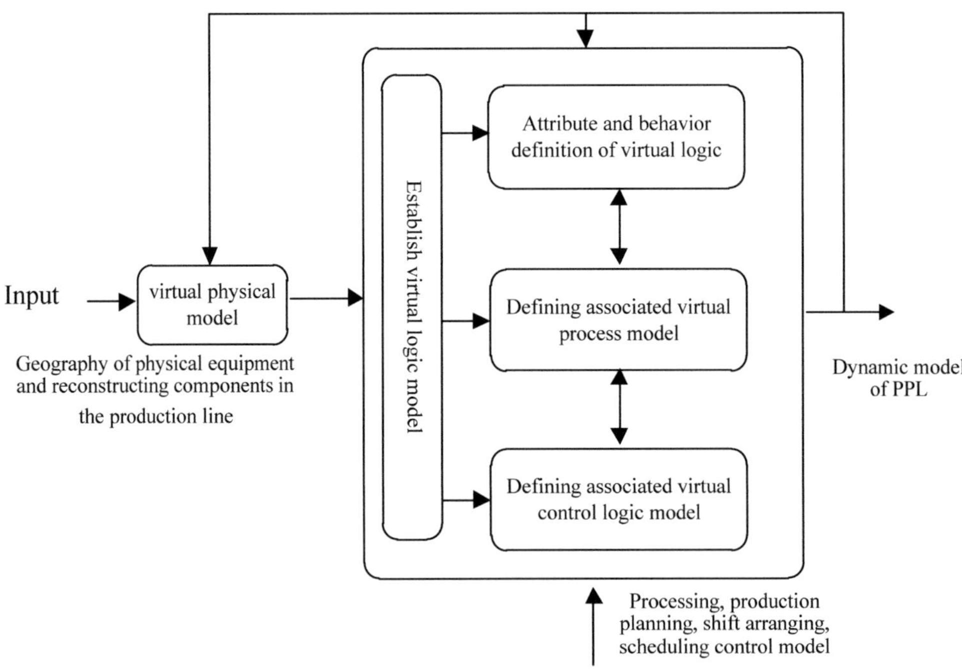

Fig. 3.11. Steps of building virtual dynamic model

transferring to the QUEST integrated environment through the graphical interface). Virtual physical model is established as follows:

1. Make sure all modules of the equipment of the piston production line.
2. According to geometry, shape and size of the equipment, establish the virtual physical model library, which can make the physical model with the function of the reconfiguration and reuse in QUEST environment.
3. According to the physical entity of the resource object, layout the piston production line will be carried out.

2. Establishing virtual logic model of VD-PPL

Abstracting from the virtual physical model to virtual logical model, it needs to complete the following tasks:

1. Complete the abstract definition and description for the attributes and behaviors of virtual physical model. On the one hand, these attributes are used to simulate, on the other hand, are applied with equipment management and reconfiguration of objects.
2. Define the virtual process model associated with the virtual physical model to make the established resource objects with relationship, make the object model with dynamic behaviors, and achieve the function of virtual machining simulation during the production process of piston machining.
3. Define the virtual control logic model associated with the virtual physical model. So that the established model can describe the logic relationship of all the behaviors of objects and make the dynamic behavior of the model occur orderly and circularly.

After finished these steps above, the production line physical model can be changed into the virtual logic model. The virtual model with the process and the logic can be used as visual simulation and dynamically analyze the piston manufacturing process supported by the system simulation strategy and simulation clock.

3.4.2 System simulation strategies of VD-PPL

For the piston production line, there are a variety of objects which are interacted and affected with each other. If the piston production line is virtually simulated, the behaviors of individual object need to be united in the same the simulation clock (simulation time) range, and determine simulation strategies and pushing methods of simulation clock to complete the analysis of the dynamic model. VD-PPL simulation strategies are established based on the advantages of an integrated event scheduling method, activity description method, process interaction method and other simulation strategies. Simulation strategy flow is shown in Fig.3.12.

Changing of the VD-PPL simulation clock time is depended on the simulation step, and simulation time step has the following attributes:

1. It can be a fixed step (The step of controlling simulation speed is fixed), or variable step (Promote the event behaviors, and the simulation clock is pushed forward to the happening point of event directly, the simulation step is variable).
2. Because the changing of the object 's state is random, the step of simulation clock is random too.
3. Between two adjacent events, the simulation clock can overcome these "inactive" period. It can be pushed from the first to the next happening time of event activities occurs.

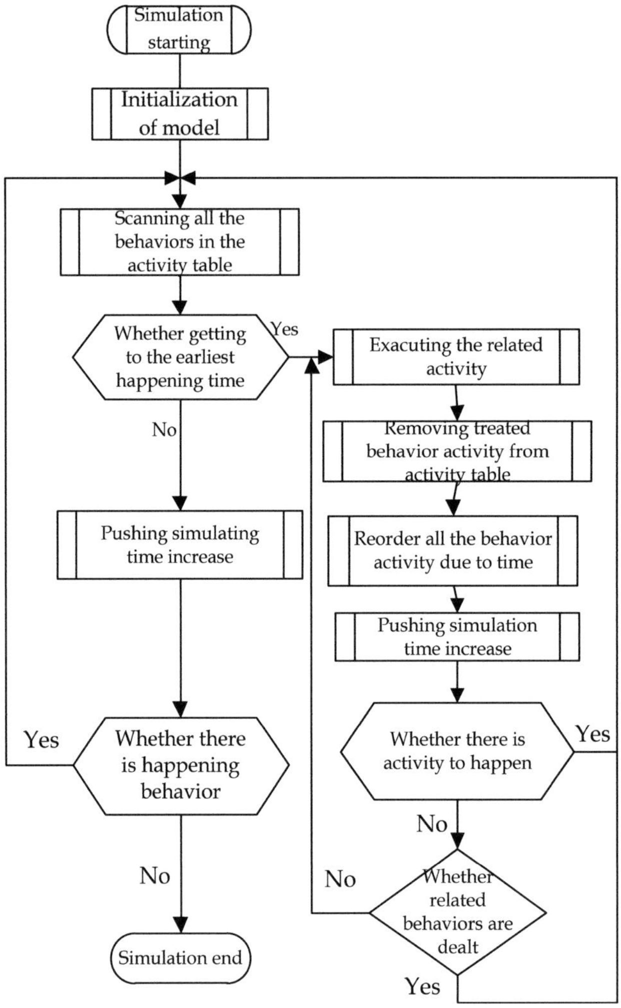

Fig. 3.12. VD-PPL simulation strategies flow

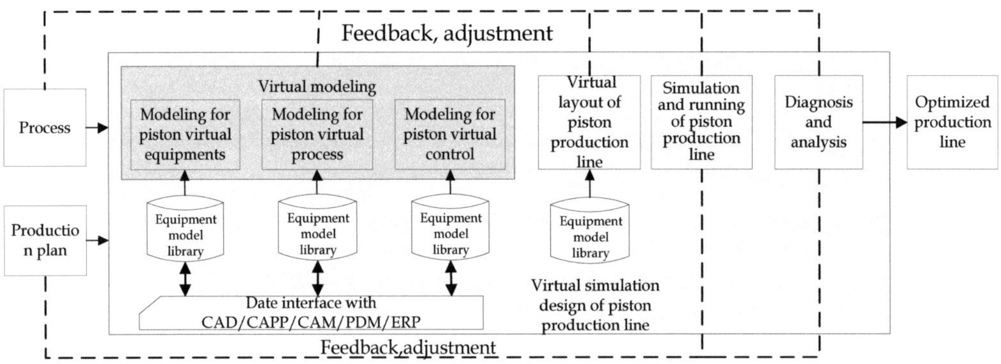

Fig. 3.13. Virtual design procedure of the piston production line

3.5 Virtual design procedure of piston production line

Virtual design procedure of the piston production line is shown in Fig.3.13. Process planning and production planning are the basis for the design process. Under the virtual model of the production line, the virtual layout planning is easy to be built, and if set the simulation clock in the virtual environment, it could get some simulation results which can be used to diagnose the bottlenecks and optimize the related parameters of the production line.

4. An instance of simulation and analysis of piston production line

By analyzing the status of an existing production line and design requirements, complete the virtual modeling, layout, simulation analysis and diagnosis of this line, and thus re-design the line to make the full range of logistics flow unblocked.

4.1 Status of production line and design goals

The line is affiliated to artificial lines, process routing is : finish turning of the spigot→ rough boring of pin hole → finish turning of cylindrical, rough finish and finish turning of the groove of iron hoop→ finish turning the groove of aluminum hoop→semi-finish boring of pin hole → turning of retaining ring groove and outside pin shaft→rough turning of combustion chamber→ fine turning of combustion chamber →fine turning of outside round→ fine turning

Process contents	Equipment code	Number	labor	Shifts	Working Procedure Time (s)
Finish turning the spigot	M1	1	L1,1	1	31
rough boring pin hole	M2	1			43.28 (Double work stations)
Finish turning cylindrical, and	M3	1	L2,1	2	74.3
rough finishing turning of the groove of iron hoop	M4	1			74.3
Finish turning the groove of aluminum hoop	M5	1	L3,1	1	23.24
Semi-finish boring pin hole	M6	1	L4,1	1	76.4 (Double work stations)
Turning retaining ring groove	M7	1	L5,1	1	36
Turning outside pin shaft	M8	1			36
Rough turning combustion chamber	M9	1	L6,1	1	31.3
Fine turning combustion chamber	M10	1			50.26
Fine turning outside round	M11	1	L7,1	1	136.2
	M12	1			136.2
Fine turning roof surface	M13	1	L8,1	1	32
Fine boring pin hole	M14	1	L9,1	2	70.77 (Double work stations)
Rolling pin hole	M15	1	L10,1	1	14.7
Boring decompression chamber of pin hole	M16	1	L11,1	1	73.33 (Double work stations)

Table 4.1. Scheduling of processes on the piston production line

of roof surface→ fine boring of pin hole →rolling of pin hole →boring decompression chamber of pin hole. The parameters of all the processes are shown in Table 4.1.

Because piston species in one production line would be changed 3 to 5 times monthly, for the traditional piston production line, its design method cannot be respond rapidly, and the design of the process time is not balanced and so on, resulting in the serious workpiece products in the line and a serious unbalance labors and machines utilization. Aimed at these problems, ensure the re-design goals: the diameter of piston diameter is between 100 ~ 130mm, monthly production capacity of production line should be not less than 22,000 pieces/ month (two shifts), and cycle should be not more than 47s, the operator should be no more than 9, machine tools should be no more than 16.

4.2 Virtual modelling

According to the real production line, establish the physical models, some typically machines are shown in Fig.4.2 (a-d).

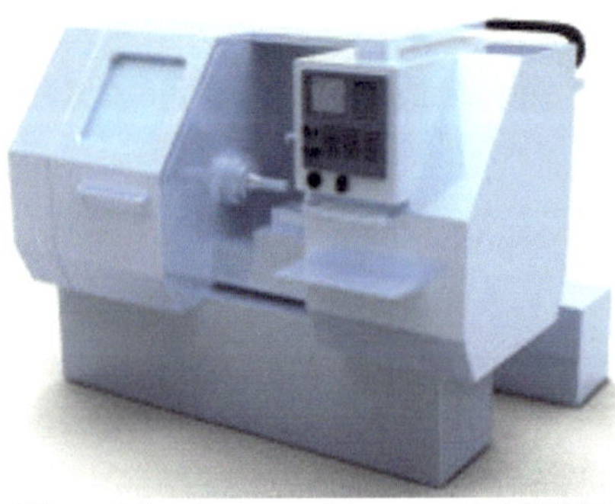

a) Virtual boring machine model BH30

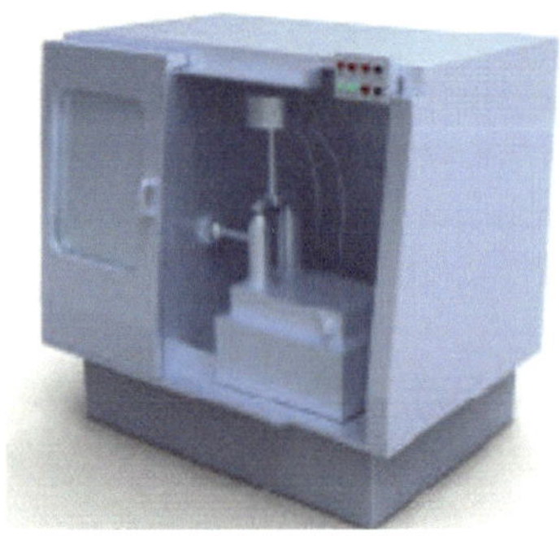

b) Virtual boring machine model BH20

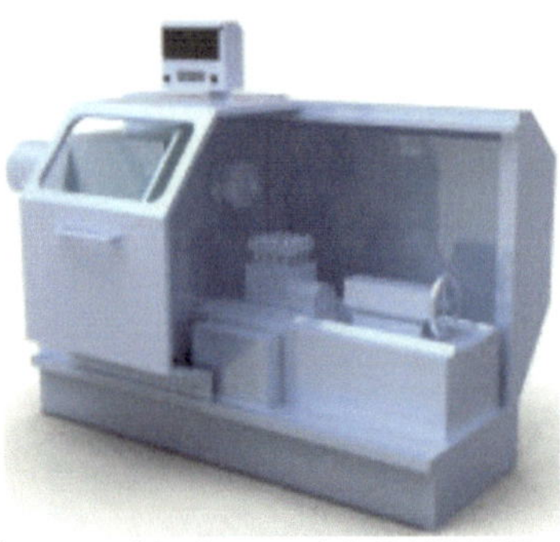

c) Virtual lathe model CAK6250

d) Virtual lathe model CK6146

Fig. 4.1. Physical models of piston line

4.3 Virtual design of piston production line

4.3.1 Virtual design parameters

The layout before optimizing is shown in Fig.4.2, its covers area S= 36772.3 ×5668.1mm^2 = 208.43m^2. The layout of the piston machine is very messy and there are many idle stations in the middle part (These stations are reserved for some special processing procedures, but these machines have been moved to special equipment areas at present.). As the machine pitch is too far, and the machine position is not optimized, resulting in a waste of area in the line, and increasing walking distance and labor intensity.

4.3.2 Process parameters

After the establishment of the virtual physical models, the procedure of definition of the virtual process and control logic is shown in Fig. 4.3–4.7. To realize changes from the virtual physical model to the virtual logical model, because the line does not belong to automated production lines with the central control system, it does not need to create the central control system logic, but it is necessary to define the workers control logic (Labor Control, as shown in Fig.4.8) to control the following actions of the labors:

1. Routes and walking speed of workers, as shown in Fig. 4.9;
2. Rest time and its distribution of workers, as shown in Fig. 4.10-4.11;

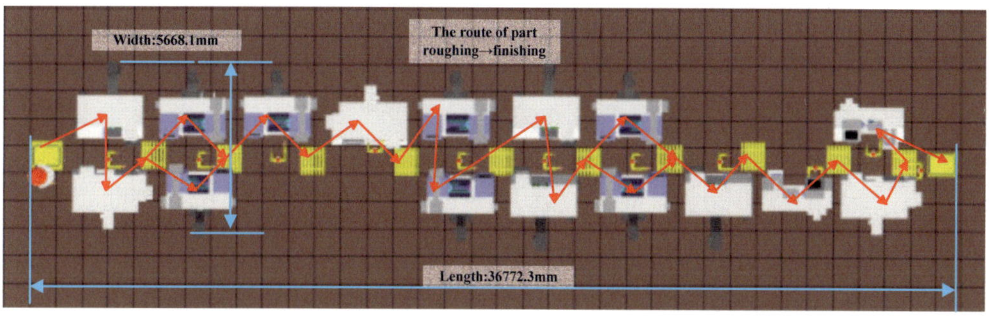

Fig. 4.2. Virtual layout and the connection way of process logic of equipment

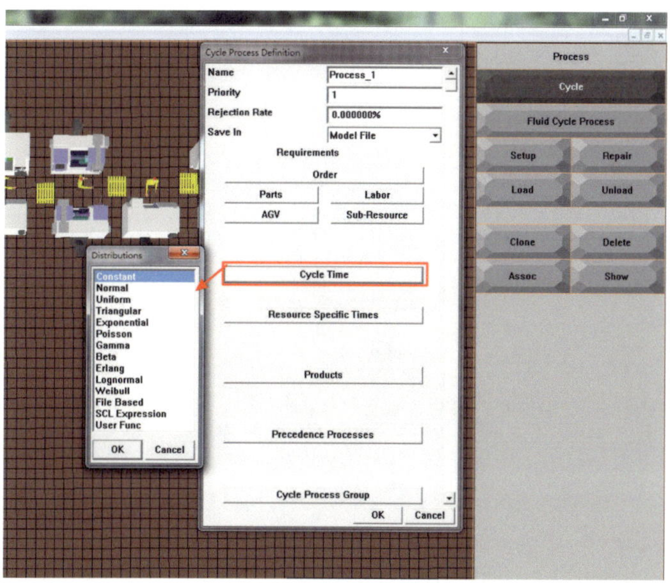

Fig. 4.3. Cycle process logic

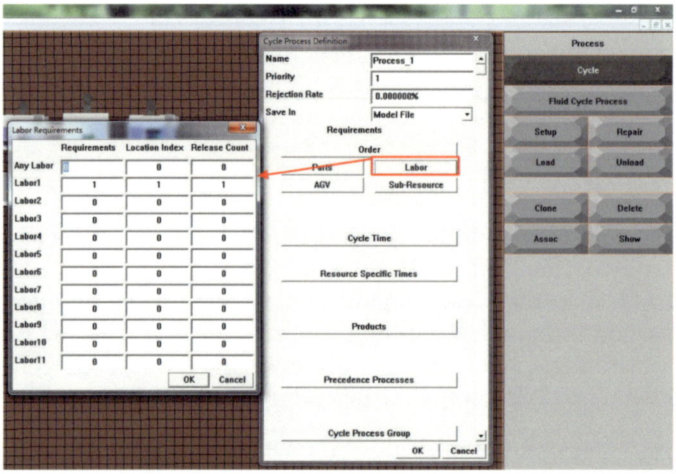

Fig. 4.4. Labor requirements of cycle process

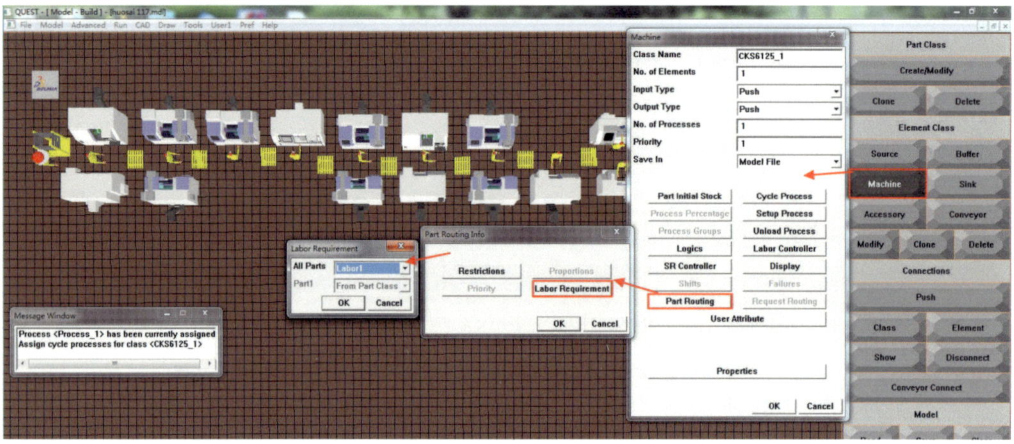

Fig. 4.5. Machine control logic associated with labor

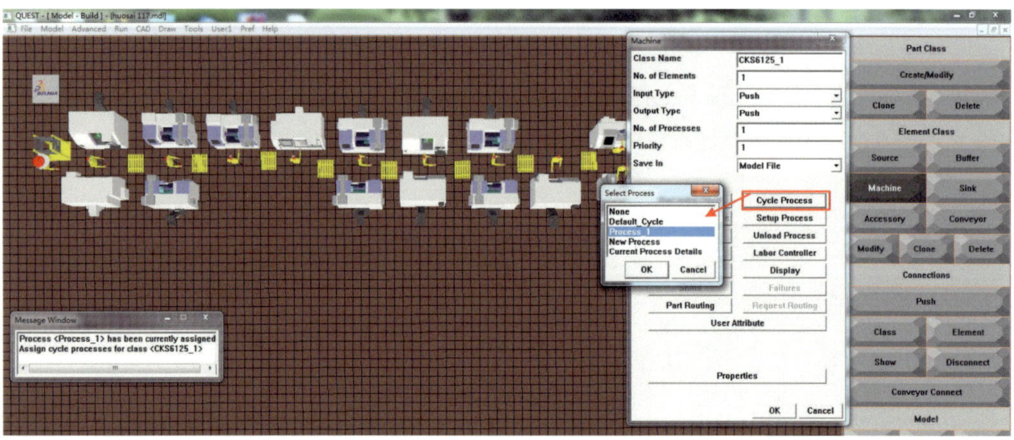

Fig. 4.6. Machine control logic associated with cycle process

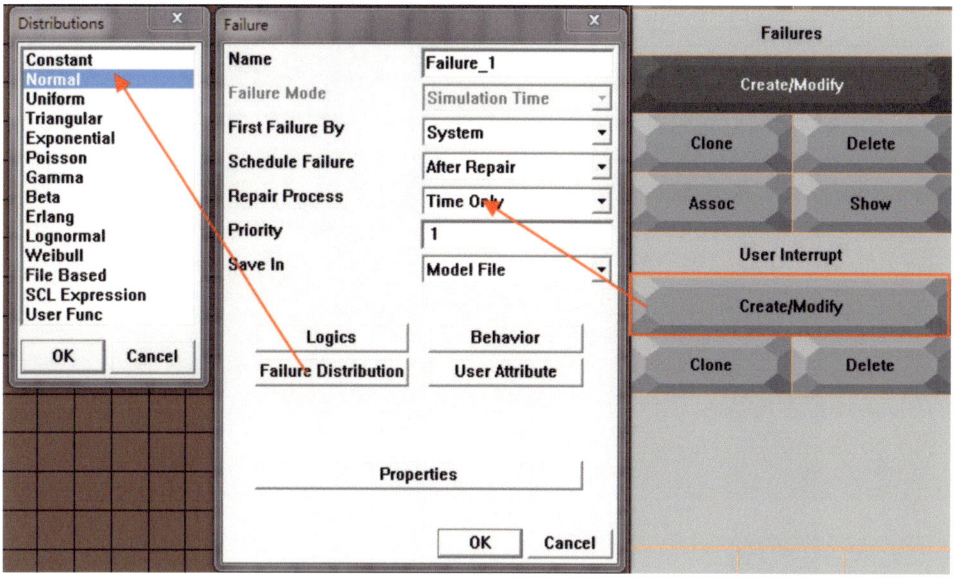

Fig. 4.7. Machine's failures setup

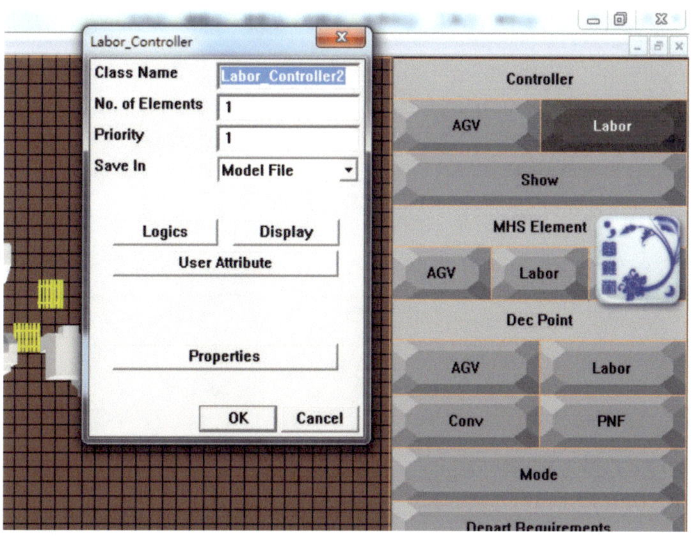

Fig. 4.8. Labor controller logic

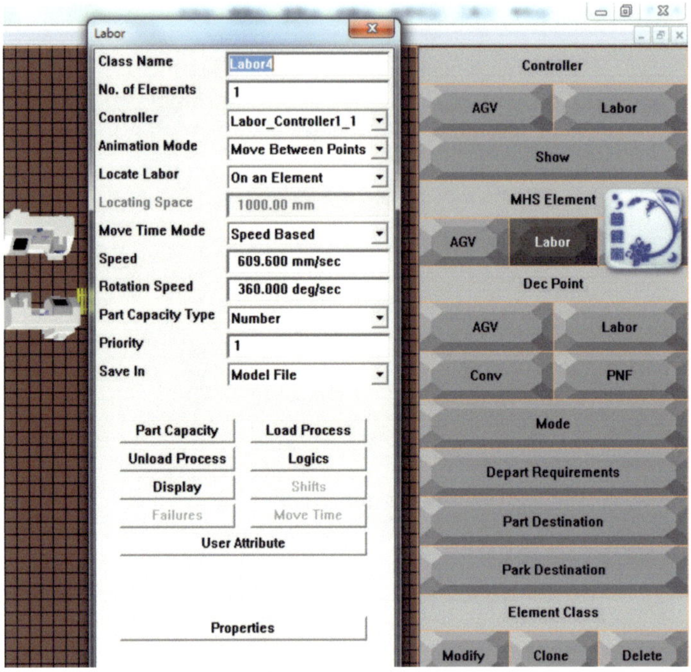

Fig. 4.9. Labor control logic

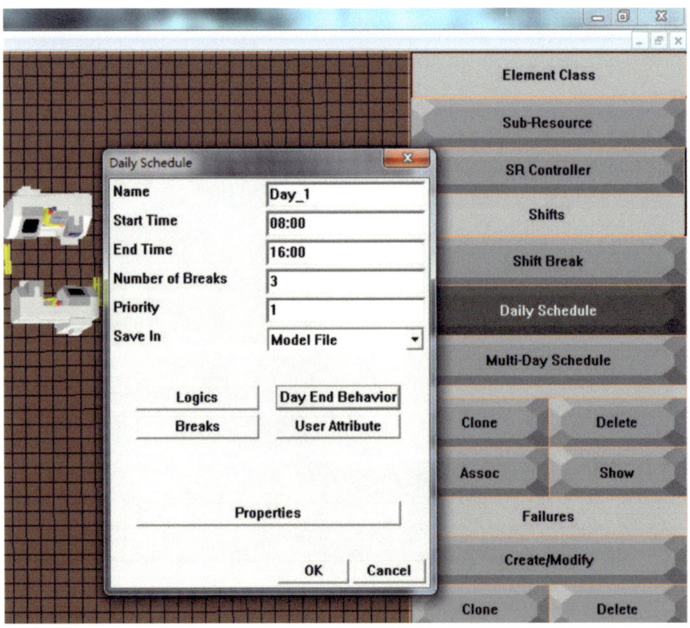

Fig. 4.10. Daily schedule

Fig. 4.11. Shift break

4.3.3 Simulation results

The statistical data after simulation includes output of production line, the work piece of buffer area, processing quantities of equipment, machine utilization, utilization of workers' working hours and walking paths and so on.

1. Work piece in the buffers

The number of the work piece in buffers under different simulation time is shown in Table 4.2. It is known that: The work pieces of B1, B3, B5 and B6 are more serious, with which it is shown that the processes after B1, B3, B5 and B6 are the bottleneck processes. However, only adjusting some parameters to improve some of the bottleneck process may trigger new bottleneck processes, so it is necessary to fully investigate and analyze with output of each machine per shift, machine utilization and labor utilization to provide adjustment strategies for balancing of the piston production line.

Buffer	B1	B2	B3	B4	B5	B6	B7	B8	B9	B10
1 hour	14	0	9	0	0	13	1	1	0	1
1 shift	90	0	58	1	97	85	0	0	0	0
1 week	440	0	270	0	469	436	1	1	0	0

Table 4.2. Accumulation number of parts in buffer

2. Production and cycle time

According to the relationship between the production and time, the cycle time of the entire production line can be calculated. Fig.4.12 shows that the production cycle tends to be stable gradually with simulation time increasing, and it stabilizes at 70.47s. With this value compared with each process time, it is easy to diagnose the bottleneck process of the line.

Figure 4.13 shows the relationship between process time of each machine and the real cycle time, it is shown that: there was a sudden change of output between the processes operated by worker L1 and L2. The same change occurs between the L3 and L4, L5 and L6, L7 and L6, meanwhile, it is also shown that cycle time is different with processes, the process operated by L1 is the smallest, up to about 35s, which means that the process has a greater redundancy. Suddenly changing point of process time happens in fine /rough turning of combustion chamber operated by L6 and finishing turning of cylindrical operated by L7, those processes are mostly near the entire cycle time. It is referred that those processes may be the most serious bottleneck process in the system.

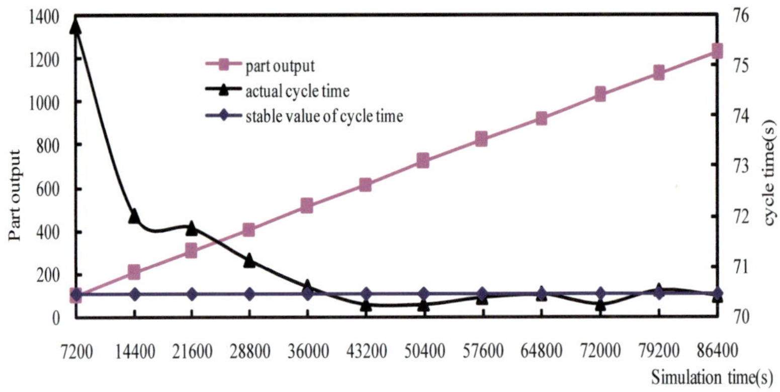

Fig. 4.12. Relationship between simulation time and cycle time

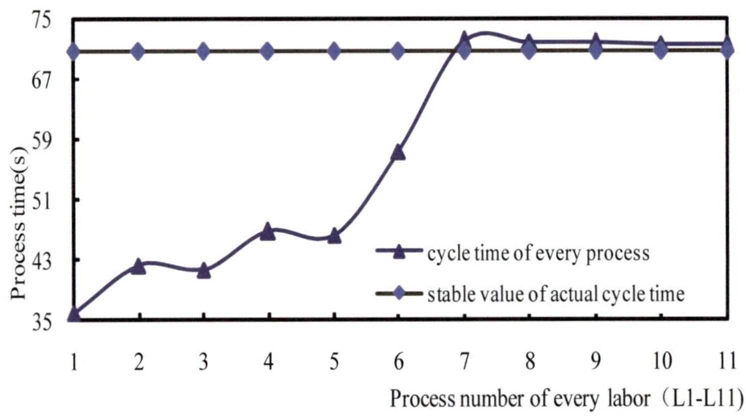

Fig. 4.13. Relationship between process time and actual cycle time of each unit

3. Equipment utilization

Equipment utilization reflects the load of each machine. Under different simulation times, machine utilization is shown in Fig. 4.14. It is known that: when the line is in a steady state, the machine utilization does not change over time on the whole. But the difference of the utilization on each machine tool is much larger, namely: balance of this production line is very poor. The utilizations of M1, M3, M4, M6, M7, M8, M10, M11 and M12 are much higher, and utilization of finishing turning of cylindrical processes machined by M11 and

M12 is the highest, up to 94.6%. Considering the output of the all product line, cycle time, and machine utilization, it can be diagnosed that: the finishing turning of the outside round is the most serious bottleneck process. When adjusting and redesigning the production line, the adjustment should be begun from this process. Constrained by the bottleneck process, utilizations of M13 ~ M16 are relatively low. If adjusting those bottleneck processes, the utilizations of M13 ~ M16 can be significantly improved to carry out the purpose of logistics balance and increasing output of the whole production line.

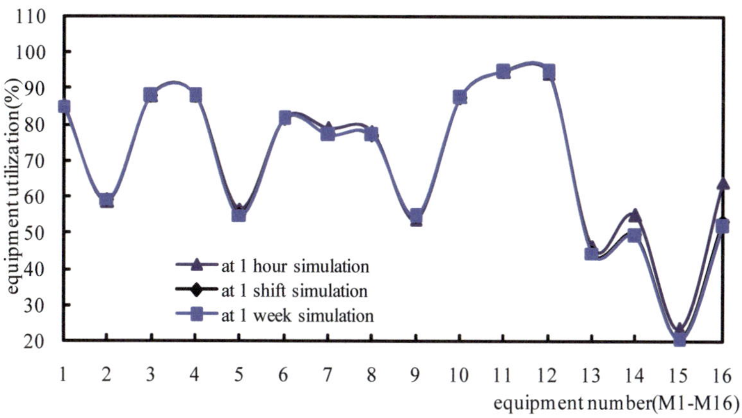

Fig. 4.14. Equipment utilization at different simulation time

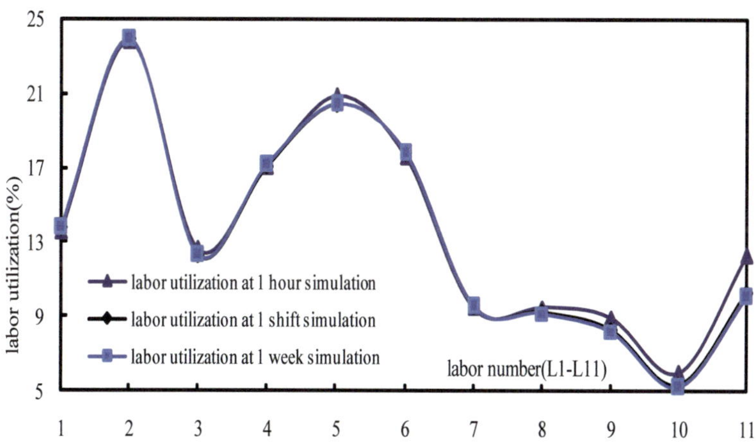

Fig. 4.15. Labor utilization at different simulation time

4. Utilizations of labor

Labor utilizations are shown in the labor intensity during the piston manufacturing. The utilization of each labor at different times after the simulation data is shown in Fig. 4.15.

Fig. 4.15 shows: labor utilization of L2 (responsible for finishing turning iron groove process) is the highest, up to 23.9%, followed by labor utilization of L5. But labor utilization of the bottleneck process operated by L7 (responsible for finishing cylindrical) is lower because the percentage of machine processing time is larger. It leads to decrease the percentage of operating time of labor. During this condition, it is often no longer allowed this labor to operate other machines in order to guarantee machining precision of the bottleneck process. The labor utilization of L10 (responsible for the rolling of the pin-hole process) is lower. It is indicated that the labor has the capacity to operate other machines, to reduce the number of the labor.

4.3.4 Re-design of the production line

Therefore, when redesigning the piston production line, based on the bottleneck diagnosis and analysis with adjusting the process and equipment, or optimizing the layout parameters, it can reduce labor intensity, improve equipment utilization, and reduce the layout area to make the piston production line more balanced.

After re-adjusting the layout, the arrangement of the machine layout is shown in Fig. 4.16. Fig. 4.2 and fig. 4.16 show that: the layout of the optimized piston production line is more compact, which fully takes advantage of the spare station. Optimized layout area S' = 171.603m^2, and the layout area is reduced by 36.827 m^2 than that of before optimization.

Under the same conditions (the same process, the same operating frequency and other parameters) walking paths before and after the optimization are shown in Figure 4.17, it is indicated that: the optimized walking distance of the workers have been shortened at different degree, and the machine arrangement is more compact as well as operating range of the workers is more reasonable. Before and after optimization in this production line, significantly shorter walking paths are: L3 (responsible for finishing turning aluminum tank), L4 (responsible for semi-finishing boring pin hole process), L8 (responsible for the fine turning roof surface process), because the layout optimization is mainly carried out on the machines that they are responsible for it.

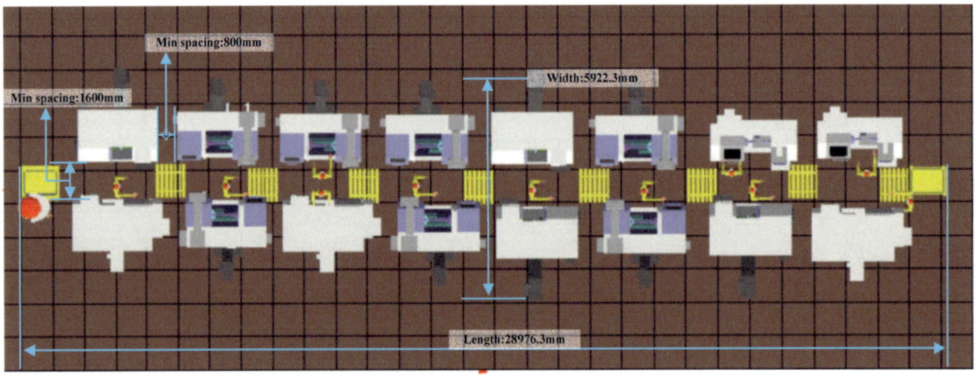

Fig. 4.16. Virtual layout after optimization

Through the analysis for the cycle time, the balance of the process time, utilizations of machines and labors, the most serious bottleneck process in this production line are fine turning of cylindrical, followed by rough and fine turning of the combustion chamber. But the production line's performance is improved evidently, after taking those optimization measures as following:

1. Improve the feed of finishing turning of cylindrical. Increasing the feed of finishing cylindrical to 0.12mm / r, the process can save time 22.7s.

2. Combine the fine and rough turning of the combustion chamber to reduce the auxiliary time, the process can save 9.5s. At this time, the process time of the fine and rough turning of the combustion chamber is 72.06s, but the process needs two devices.

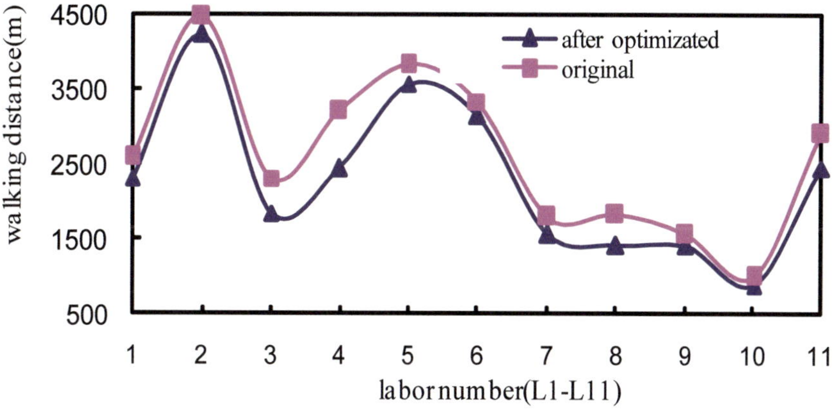

Fig. 4.17. Walking distance of labors before and after optimization

Through above methods, it is modified the virtual dynamic logic model, and simulated the redesign model again, the results could be gained, the piston production per shift in this piston production line increase from 336 to 516, and the most serious bottleneck processes have been weakened. Figure 4.18 and 4.19 show respectively the machine utilization and labor utilization before and after eliminating the bottleneck. It is indicated that: after taking the bottleneck reducing measures, the machine and labor utilization of each process after the bottleneck is improved, reduces the utilizations of machine and labor before the bottleneck to reduce bottlenecks by making the production line in balance direction.

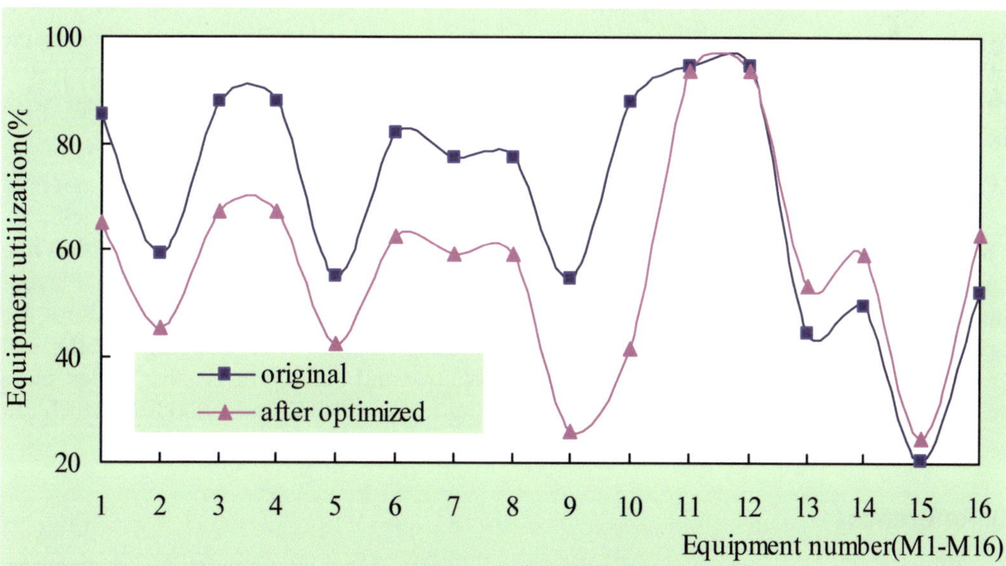

Fig. 4.18. Utilizations of machine tool before and after optimized

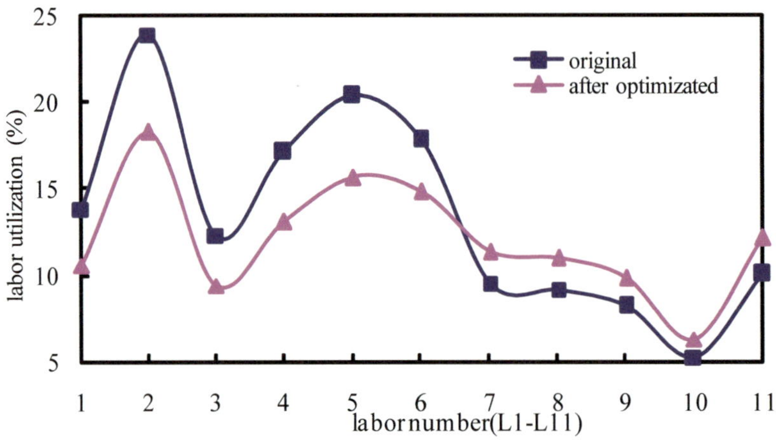

Fig. 4.19. Utilizations of labor before and after optimized

5. Conclusions

Compared to the traditional design method of the production line, virtual design of the production line integrates many advanced technologies, and applies the unified manufacturing process modeling, analysis and dynamic optimization and other advanced design tools to get multiple-objective optimal results. Meanwhile, it is easier to get corresponding design data and decision-making data. Based on those simulation results, it can gain some methods quickly to redesign the real production line's parameters in the early design stage. So, this design method is a prospective powerful tool for the manufacturing planning.

With object-oriented technology, combined with the advantages of QUEST and UML, it is established the simulation model of the piston production line mapping from real to virtual environment with UML class diagram of the physical equipment, process, logic control and system interaction classes. The virtual model of this production line is divided to steps: static modeling is described with the hierarchy of various resources objects in piston production line and other static characteristics, and dynamic modeling defined with behavioral and control logic processes.

With this virtual design method, an instance of this piston production line is used to not only present the virtual design procedure, but also compare those design results quickly with the virtual model. From those simulation results, it is shown that the optimized production line can greatly reduce the labor intensity, improves equipment utilization, decreases the layout area, and makes all processes more balanced. With this method, all design procedures are achieved in a virtual environment with a short design cycle before carrying out the real production line. It is easy to avoid wasting the resource and making the system design more reliable and effective during the beginning planning for the piston production line, which can save the design cost and time to improve the design performance success.

6. References

Da Silveira, G., Borenstein, D.&Fogliatto, F.S.(2001). Mass customization. *International Journal of Production Economics*, Vol.72,No.1, (June 2001),pp.1-13. ISSN 0925-5273

Dirk Rantzau et al..(1999).Industrial virtual reality engineering applications, *The Symposium on Industrial virtual Reality and the 1999 ASME Mechanical Engineering Congress and Exposition (IMECE'99)*, Vol. 5, pp. 49-56 ,Chicago, USA. 1999.

Ford, H., (1926). *Today and Tomorrow (special reprint,1988)*. Productivity Press, ISBN-100915299364 ISBN-13 978-091-5299-36-2, Cambridge.

FAN Xiu-min et al.(2001).Research & Application of Simulation & Optimization Technologies in Virtual Product Manufacturing Planning.*Computer Integrated Manufacturing Systems-CIMS*,Vol.7,No.8(August 2001), pp.41-43,ISSN 1006-5911

F.T.S. Chan, H.K. Chan.(2004).A comprehensive survey and future trend of simulation study on FMS scheduling, *Journal of Intelligent Manufacturing*,Vol.15,No.1,pp.87–102. ISSN 0956-5515

GAO Chonghui et al.(2010).Research and application of virtual simulation of automatic press line for automobile panel. *Forging &Stamping Technology*, Vol.35,No.1(January 2010),pp.146-148,ISSN 1000-3940

H.T. Papadopolous, C. Heavey, J. Browne.(1993).*Queuing theory in manufacturing systems analysis and design* Chapman & Hall. ISBN 978-041-2387-20-3

J.S. Smith.(2003).Survey on the use of simulation for manufacturing system design and operation, *Journal of Manufacturing Systems*,Vol.22,No.2 (March 2004),pp.157–171, ISSN 0278-6125

Kotler, P.(1989). From mass marketing to mass customization. *Planning Review* 17(5), 10–13.

Lee, H., Peleg, B.&Whang, S.(2005).*Toyota: Demand Chain Management*. Harvard Business School Publishing, Boston, MA, Case No.GS-42.

M.J. Ashworth, K.M. Carley.(2007).Can tools help unify organization theory? Perspectives on the state of computational modeling, *Computational and Mathematical Organization Theory*,Vol.13 ,No.1(August 2006),pp.89–111,ISSN 1381-298X

Par Klingstam, Per Gullander.(1999).Overview of simulation tools for computer-aided production engineering *Computers in Industry*. Vol.38,pp.173-186,ISSN: 0166-3615

S.H. Han, et al.. (2012). Automated post-simulation visualization of modular building production assembly line, .*Automation in Construction*. Vol.21, pp.229-236,ISSN:0926-5805.

Shao Li et al.(2000). Virtual integrated design of production line. *Industrial engineering and management*, No.6(June 2000),pp.1-4,ISSN 1006-5429

S B Yoo et al.(1994).An Object-Oriented approach to integrated control of flexible manufacturing systems.*International Symposium on Advances in Intelligent Computer Integrated Manufacturing System*.No.1,pp.383-386

S.M. Shafer, T.L. Smunt.(2004).Empirical simulation studies in operations management: Context, trends, and research opportunities, *Journal of Operations Management*,Vol.22,No.4 (August 2004),pp.345–354, ISSN: 0272-6963

Thomas Volling , Thomas S. Spengler.(2011).Modeling and simulation of order-driven planning policies in build-to-order automobile production. *International Journal of Production Economics*, Vol.131,No.1 (May 2011),pp.183–193. ISSN 0925-5273

T.S. Baines, D.K. Harrison.(1999).Opportunity for system dynamics in manufacturing system modeling, *Production Planning and Control*,Vol.10,No.6 (1999),pp.542–552.

Yong-Sik Kim, Jeongsam Yang&Soonhung Han.(2006).A multichannel visualization module for virtual manufacturing.*Computers in Industry*,Vol.57,No.7 (September 2006),pp.653–662,ISSN 0166-3615

Zhao Ji et al.(2000).On Implementing Virtual Production Line. *Journal of Northwestern Polytechnical University*, Vol.18,No.4(April 2000),pp.518-521,ISSN 1007-5429

Zhang Longxiang.(2007)*UML and System Analysis and Design(2nd edition)*. Post & Telecom Press, BeiJing, ISBN 978-711-5159-52-6

2

Changing Skills in Changing Environments: Skills Needed in Virtual Construction Teams

Willy Sher[1], Sue Sherratt[1], Anthony Williams[1] and Rod Gameson[2]
[1]*The University of Newcastle*
[2]*University of Salford*
[1]*Australia*
[2]*United Kingdom*

1. Introduction

This book focuses on virtual reality. In the context of design, virtual reality is an emerging technology that not only allows designers and other stakeholders to gain a three-dimensional appreciation of the artifact being designed, it also has the potential to significantly alter the manner in which design occurs. Internet-based technologies have made it possible for designers in different locations to collaborate in developing and refining their designs. Virtual reality has contributed to this environment (Maher, 2005) by allowing designers in geographically-dispersed locations to interact with each other. Software applications have been developed to assist and facilitate these collaborative activities (including Shyamsundar and Gadh (2001) and Lau, Mak and Lu (2003)) but comparatively speaking, little research has been conducted into the people-related issues of collaboration via the Internet. Some of these are the issues addressed in this chapter.

Recent developments in virtual communication technologies have the potential to dramatically improve collaboration in the construction industry (Gameson & Sher, 2002). Furthermore, virtual teams "hold significant promise for organizations that implement them because they enable unprecedented levels of flexibility and responsiveness" (Powell, Piccoli, & Ives, 2004, p. 6). Some authors observe that virtual teams are here to stay (Bell & Kozlowski, 2002) and that organisations will be forced to "embrace virtual collaboration to enhance their competitiveness" (Abuelmaatti & Rezgui, 2008, p. 351). Indeed, current research proposes that "(g)lobally disbursed project teams are the new norm in every industry today" (Daim et al., 2012). However, the skills required to work productively in virtual environments have been theoretically defined but not assessed in the real world. Indeed, many of the studies that have been conducted (e.g. Hatem, Kwan and Miles (2011) and Rezgui (2007)) into virtual teamwork have involved tertiary-level students. Abelmaatti and Rezgui (2008) consider that the challenges of virtual teamwork in the real world substantially outweigh the relative ease with which academics can research and develop virtual team solutions. Furthermore, the differences between virtual and face-to-face teamwork means that an overt and explicit effort is needed to design new work processes to make it successful (Nunamaker, Reinig, & Briggs, 2009).

Our studies were part of a project which examined the use of information and computer technologies (ICTs) to facilitate design / construction team interactions. They were funded by the Australian Cooperative Research Centre for Construction Innovation (Maher, 2002) and focused on the early stages of design / construction collaboration where designs for a building are created, developed and revised. Three aspects of collaboration in virtual environments were investigated: (i) the technological processes that enable effective collaboration using these technologies; (ii) the models that allow disciplines to share their views in a synchronous virtual environment; (iii) the generic skills used by individuals and teams when engaging with high bandwidth ICT. The last strand of these investigations was investigated by the authors and is reported on here. Details of the other strands of this project may be found at the project website (Maher, 2002) and other publications (Bellamy, Williams, Sher, Sherratt, & Gameson, (2005) and Sherratt, Sher, Williams, & Gameson, 2010).

2. Virtual teamwork

There are numerous definitions of teams. For this paper teams are defined as a cluster of two or more people usually occupying different roles and skill levels that interact "adaptively, interdependently, and dynamically towards a common and valued goal" (Salas, Shawn Burke, & Cannon-Bowers, 2000, p. 341). At present the term "virtual teams" is used by different authors to mean different things. A more detailed exploration of the various facets of virtual teams is provided by Dubé and Paré (2004) and is summarised in Table 1. A number of other researchers have outlined the characteristics of or factors relating to virtual teams e.g. Berry (2011); Schumacher, Cardinal and Bocquet (2009) as well as the

CHARACTERISTICS		DEGREE OF COMPLEXITY LOW <———> HIGH	
...related to the basics of virtual teamwork	Degree of reliance on ICT	Low reliance	High reliance
	ICT availability	High variety	Low variety
	Members' ICT Proficiency	High	Low
...related to the complexity of virtual teamwork	Team size	Small	Large
	Geographic dispersion (physical proximity)	Local	Global
	Task or project duration	Long term	Short term
	Prior shared work experience	Extensive experience	No experience
	Members' assignments	Full-time	Part-time
	Membership stability	Stable membership	Fluid membership
	Task interdependence	Low interdependence	High interdependence
	Cultural diversity (national, organizational, professional)	Homogeneous	Heterogeneous

Table 1. Key Characteristics of Virtual Teams

variables contributing to effective virtual teamwork (Gaudes, Hamilton-Bogart, Marsh, & Robinson, 2007; Peña-mora, Vadhavkar, & Aziz, 2009). Virtual teams may differ significantly depending upon these aspects and Dubé and Paré suggest that this table could also be used as a diagnostic tool to help assess the level of complexity in a virtual team.

3. Generic skills

There is still much discussion about the core set of knowledge, skills and attitudes that constitute teamwork (Salas, et al., 2000). We sought to contribute to this debate by identifying the skills that transferred from a traditional face to face (F2F) environment and the ones that required refining for virtual environments. Furthermore, we wished to identify if virtual teamworkers needed any new skills. As a starting point, we investigated the generic skills workers acquire and use on a daily basis. Generic skills are defined by Salas et al (2000: p, 344) as "the knowledge, skills and attitudes that a team member possesses when completing a task or communicating with fellow members, whether in a co-located or virtual environment". Generic skills influence both individuals and teams; they are skills which are "...transportable and applicable across teams" (Salas, et al., 2000, p. 344). A review of generic skills (Cannon-Bowers, Tannenbaum, Salas, & Volpe, 1995) was used to identify those which are used by design team members and is summarised in Table 2.

To examine the skills designers use it is necessary to understand the content of their interactions. A number of techniques facilitate such insights including Protocol Analysis and Content Analysis. Protocol Analysis attempts to infer cognitive processes by examining verbal interactions (Ericsson & Simon, 1993) but has been found to be a limited means of identifying non-verbal design cognition. Even where some comparisons are discovered, a large degree of interpretation is required (Cross, Christiaans, & K., 1996). The subjectivity of analysis and the length of time required to complete analysis also call into question the appropriateness of this method.

Content Analysis, according to (Wallace, 1987), involves coding transcripts of communications in terms of frequency analyses because the underlying assumption is that "the verbal content produced by the individual is representative of the thought processes at work in his or her mind" (p. 121).

Several content analysis techniques were used to identify and interpret these thought processes and thereby to investigate the generic skills our participants used. We explored micro-level communication processes because these "can provide valuable insights to managers and researchers alike about how to 'read' the health of teams" (Kanawattanachai & Yoo, 2002: p. 210). We identified quantitative content analysis as an effective means of identifying the generic skills of designers. This necessitated the development of a framework by which our data could be coded. Behavioural marker studies (Klampfer, et al., 2001, Carthey, de Leval, Wright, Farewell, & Reason, 2003) provided a template for our generic skills coding framework. Behavioural markers are observable non-technical "aspects of individual and team performance" (Carthey et al, 2003: p. 411) which are related to the effectiveness of an individual and team. The methods for creating behavioural markers informed the development of our framework. In accordance with Klampfer et al's (2001) recommendations, we devised a system that provided simple, clear markers, used appropriate professional terminology, and emphasised observable behaviours rather than ambiguous attitudes or opinions. The Anaesthetists' Non-Technical Skills (ANTS) (Fletcher, et al., 2003) system was informative and helped shape our coding system. Using the ANTS system allowed us to incorporate the skills in Table 2 into the Generic Skills coding scheme shown in Table 4.

Core Generic Skills	Definition	Sub-skills
Adaptability	The use of compensatory behaviour and reallocation of resources to adjust strategies based on feedback	Flexibility Compensatory behaviour Dynamic reallocation of functions
Shared situational awareness	When team members have compatible mental models of the environment within and outside of the team.	Orientation Team awareness System awareness
Performance monitoring and feedback	Ability of team members to give, seek and receive task clarifying feedback.	Performance feedback Acceptance Mutual performance monitoring Procedure maintenance
Team management: Project management/leadership	Ability to direct and co-ordinate the activities of other team members particularly pertaining to performance, tasks, motivation, and creation of a positive environment.	Task structuring Motivation of others Goal setting Goal orientation
Interpersonal relations	Ability to optimise the quality of team members' interactions.	Conflict resolution Assertiveness Morale building
Co-ordination	Process by which team resources, activities and responses are organized to ensure that tasks are integrated, synchronized and completed within established temporal constraints.	Task organisation Task interaction Timing
Communication	Information exchange between members using the prescribed manner and terminology.	Information exchange Consulting with others
Decision making	Ability to gather and integrate information, use sound judgment, identify alternatives, select the most appropriate solution, and evaluate the consequences.	Problem assessment Problem solving Planning Implementation

Table 2. Integrated skills (as adapted from Cannon-Bowers et al 1995)

In addition to the Generic Skills analysis presented here, three other techniques were used to analyse the data:

1. **Bales's Interaction Process Analysis** (Bales, 1951) - to analyse the interactions between design team members, so that aspects such as decision-making, communication and control could be examined.
2. A **Communication Technique Framework** (Williams & Cowdroy, 2002) – to investigate the techniques which the designers used to communicate.
3. **Linguistic analyses** - to evaluate the communication occurring in teamwork. The approach adopted was derived from systemic functional linguistic theory (Halliday & Matthiessen, 2004).

The aims of this study were to identity and examine the generic skills which facilitate teamwork in three settings, ranging from face-to-face to 3D virtual environments. The teamwork which we studied occurred during the conceptual stages of designing construction projects.

3.1 Data collection

Video and audio recordings of designers collaborating in teams were collected using Noldus Observer Pro (Burfield, Cadee, Grieco, Mayton, & Spink, 2003) to store, code and analyse our data. Noldus is ethnographic video analysis software which facilitates the collection, management, analysis and presentation of observational data. It allows researchers to view video footage and score the frequency of specific behaviours, and to note how these behaviours interact with each other or with independent variables. The advantages of such recordings include: being able to review interactions and behaviours as well as being able to compare different coders' or viewers' interpretations (Guerlain, Turrentine, Adams, & Forrest Calland, 2004).

3.2 Participants

It is often the case that design team members are drawn from different backgrounds/cultures, ages, and experience (Marchman III, 1998), especially in multi-disciplinary design teams collaborating on an entire project. Stratified purposive sampling (Rice & Ezzy, 1999) was therefore used to select a heterogenous group of ten participants. This method of sampling ensured that the diversity of the participants was reflective, as far as possible, of the actuality of design teams in the real world. Participants were both male and female, of varying ages, cultures and had differing levels of experience and influence, ranging from higher management to junior staff. Due to constraints imposed by the funding body, recruitment of participants was limited to organisations within the Cooperative Research Centre for Construction Innovation (CRC-CI). The pool of eligible participants was further constrained by work pressures eventually resulting in participants being recruited solely from the discipline of architecture.

3.3 Task

Data were collected in three experimental conditions:

- **Traditional face-to-face** collaborative design between the design team members (including interactions such as talking and sketching).

- **Virtual design using a shared electronic whiteboard** (incorporating synchronous audio and visual communication) which allowed drawings, images and text to be shared.
- **Virtual design using a high bandwidth 3D virtual world** (Activeworlds-Corporation, 2008) (incorporating synchronous audio communication) which allowed drawings, images and text to be shared. This tool represents team members as "avatars" and allowed them to manipulate 3D representations of a design and to communicate using audio as well as text "chat" facilities.

Designers were grouped into five teams of two and asked to prepare conceptual designs that responded to various briefs. These briefs related to fictional projects on an actual site at Sydney University, Australia. Depending on the session, designers were asked to design an art gallery, a hostel, a library or a dance school for the site. The participants were then given 30 minutes to prepare their designs using one of the three experimental conditions. Prior to each design session the research team spent one to two hours coaching the designers in the capabilities of the whiteboard and 3D virtual world technologies. Once designers were familiar with the hardware and software, they were asked to prepare their designs. Typical characteristics of the virtual teamwork involved in these tasks are presented in Table 3 using Dubé & Paré's (2004) framework.

		DEGREE OF COMPLEXITY LOW <———> HIGH	
Degree of reliance on ICT	Low	Varies	High
ICT availability	High	X	Low
Members' ICT Proficiency	High	X	Low
Team size	Small	X	Large
Geographic dispersion	Local	X	Global
Task or project duration	Long term	X	Short term
Prior shared work experience	Extensive	X	None
Members' assignments	Full-time	X	Part-time
Membership stability	Stable	X	Fluid
Task interdependence	Low	X	High
Cultural diversity	Homo-geneous	Varies	Hetero-geneous

Table 3. Typical characteristics of the virtual teams engaged in this project (adapted from Dubé & Paré, 2004)

All tasks were conducted in an identical sequence (i.e. participants first worked "face-to-face", then used a "whiteboard" and finally designed in the "3D virtual world"). This procedure was prescribed by our research directorate and was designed primarily for the first two strands of our overall research project (Maher, 2002). We are conscious that participants may have become familiar with aspects of the tasks that they were asked to complete, and may also have become fatigued (Pring, 2005). As the designers gained experience of working together, one would assume they would be able to work more effectively over time. If this is so, their final collaboration would have been the optimal one and this would have occurred when they were designing in the 3D virtual world. Conversely, if they had become fatigued or bored, their last task performed would have been the one most affected. It is thus not possible to determine whether sequence affected the outcomes of this research.

3.4 Coding of data

All interactions were coded using the framework shown in Table 4 resulting in 4611 entries. Noldus provided each entry with a time stamp, and allowed entry of a subject code, an observable behaviour and a non-technical skill representative of that observable behaviour (see Figure 1).

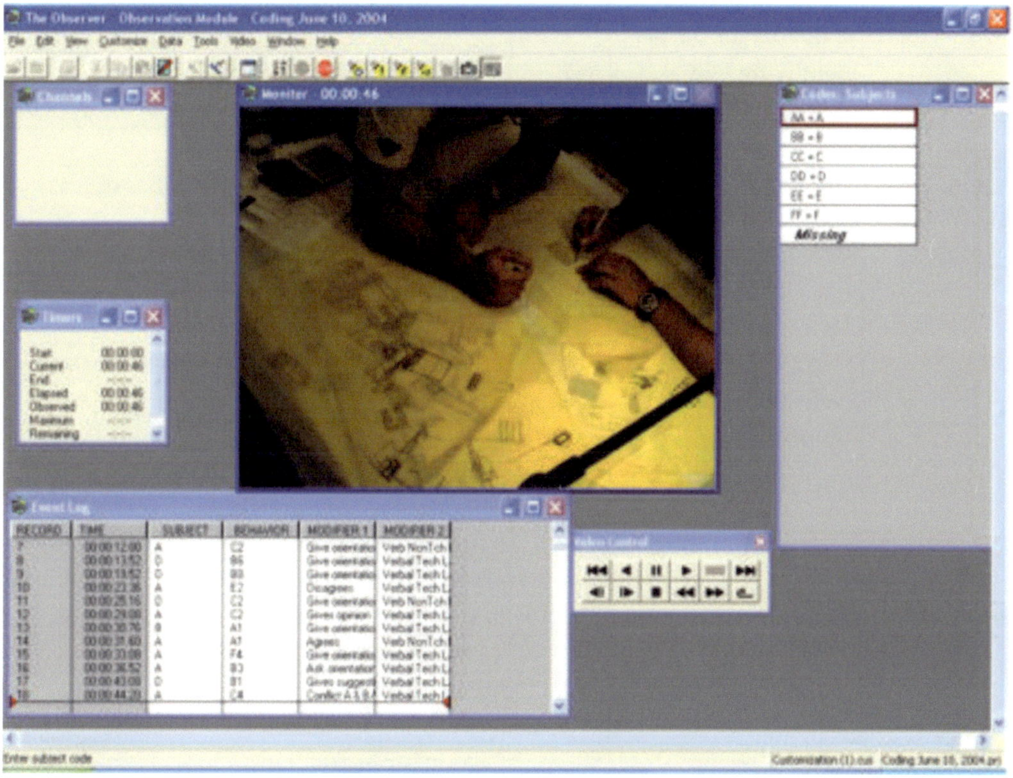

Fig. 1. Screen showing coding of video data in Noldus Observer Pro

The resulting scores were statistically analysed using a repeated measures ANOVA parametric test to establish the differences between participants' performance on the three tasks (traditional face-to-face design, virtual design using a electronic whiteboard, and virtual design using a high bandwidth 3D virtual world) (Riedlinger, Gallois, McKay, & Pittam, 2004). The results of the ANOVA tests were interpreted using Mauchly's Test of Sphericity which examines the covariance of the dependent samples. The data were also examined to determine which shift in condition (i.e. face-to-face to whiteboard or whiteboard to 3D virtual world) was responsible for any significance. SPSS Version 12 was used for all statistical analyses.

Generic skills	Sub-skills	Code	Observable Behaviour
Task Manage-ment	Planning or preparing a task	A11	Outlines and describes the plan/brief for a design
		A12	Reviews a design after changes are made
		A13	Describes actions required once design is completed
	Prioritising tasks	A21	Assigns priority to design tasks to be completed
		A22	Prioritises the segments within design tasks
	Providing direction and maintaining standards for the task	A31	Follows design protocols and briefs
		A32	Cross checks the completion of design tasks
	Identifying and utilising resources	A41	Identifies and allocates resources
		A42	Allocates tasks to team members
		A43	Requests additional resources
Team Working	Co-ordinating activities with team members	B11	Confirms roles and responsibilities of team members
		B12	Discusses design with others
		B13	Considers requirements of others before acting
		B14	Co-operates with others to achieve goals
	Exchanging information	B21	Gives updates and reports key events
		B22	Confirms shared understanding
		B23	Communicates design plans and relevant information
		B24	Clearly documents design
	Using authority and assertiveness	B31	Is appropriately and necessarily assertive
		B32	Takes appropriate leadership
		B33	States case for instruction and gives justification
		B34	Gives clear instructions
	Assessing capabilities	B41	Asks for assistance
		B42	Asks team member about experience
		B43	Notices that a team member does not complete a task to an appropriate standard
	Supporting others	B51	Acknowledges concerns of others
		B52	Reassures / encourages
		B53	Debriefs
		B54	Anticipates when others will need information

Generic skills	Sub-skills	Code	Observable Behaviour
Shared Situational Awareness	Gathering information	C11	Asks for information or artefacts relating to a design
		C12	Checks on the status of a project and tasks
		C13	Collects information regarding a problem
		C14	Cross checks and double checks information
	Recognising and understanding	C21	Describes seriousness or urgency of task
		C22	Pays close attention to advice of fellow member
	Anticipating	C31	Takes action to avoid future problems
		C32	Reviews effects of a change
Decision Making	Identifying options	D11	Discusses design options with clients/other designers
		D12	Discusses various techniques for the design
	Balancing risks and selecting options	D21	Weighs up risks associated with different designs
		D22	Implements chosen design
	Re-evaluating	D31	Re-evaluates chosen design technique after it has been chosen

Table 4. Generic Skills Coding Scheme

Intra-reliability between two raters was established for the generic skills coding scheme on a 35-minute session using Noldus Observer Pro. Point-by-point agreement was 81% and 80% on the frequency of coding strings and frequency and sequence of the coding strings, respectively. These were both at or above the minimum acceptable level of 80% (Kazdin, 1982).

4. Results

4.1 Generic skills

The generic skill *Shared Situational Awareness* increased significantly ($F(2, 8) = 4.903, p < .05$). The Within-Subject Contrasts test indicated a significant difference between face-to-face and whiteboard conditions ($F(1, 4) = 19.478, p < .05$).

For the skill of *Decision Making*, there was a significant decrease ($F(2, 8) = 42.431, p < .001$) in frequency as the design conditions moved from low to high bandwidth conditions. The Within-Subject Contrasts test demonstrated a significant difference between both the face-to-face to whiteboard and whiteboard to 3D virtual world ($F(1, 4) = 120.274, p < .001$ and $F(1, 4) = 8.685, p < .05$ respectively).

For the skill of *Task Management*, the decrease in frequency from face-to-face to whiteboard approached significance ($F(1, 4) = 4.799, p > .1$).

4.2 Observable behaviours

The following five observable skills (see Figure 2) were significantly affected by the experimental conditions:

- A11 ("Outlines and describes the plan/brief for the design" indicative of *Task Management*). There was a significant decrease ($F(2, 8) = 9.021$, $p < .05$) in the incidence of this behaviour from low to high bandwidth levels. The Within-Subjects Contrasts test indicates that the move from face-to-face to whiteboard was significant ($F(1, 4) = 7.943$, $p < .05$).

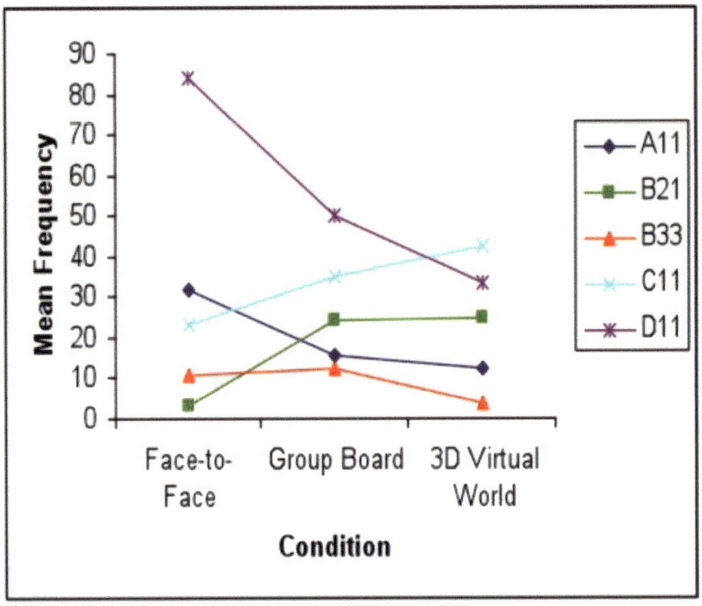

Fig. 2. Frequency of significant observable behaviours A11, B21, B33, C11, D11, in 3 conditions

- B21 ("Gives updates and reports key events", demonstrating *Team Working*). This behaviour increased significantly ($F(2, 6) = 6.343$, $p < .05$) as the design process moved from low to high bandwidth. Furthermore, the difference between *face-to-face* and *whiteboard* conditions was significant ($F(1, 3) = 16.734$, $p < .05$).
- B33 ("States case for instruction and gives justification", also demonstrating *Team Working*). The movement from low to high bandwidth demonstrated a significant decrease in this behaviour ($F(2, 6) = 5.362$, $p < .05$). A significant difference between *whiteboard* and *3D virtual world* was found to be approaching significance ($F(1, 3) = 5.642$, $p = .098$).
- C11 ("Asks for documents and/or information regarding a design" indicating *Shared Situational Awareness*). This increased significantly as the design process moved from low to high bandwidth ($F(2, 8) = 5.526$, $p < .05$). The Within-Subjects Contrasts test showed a significant change ($F(1, 4) = 15.751$, $p < .05$) for the shift from *face-to-face* to *whiteboard* conditions.
- D11 ("Discusses design options with clients/other designers" demonstrating *Decision-Making*). As the design collaborators shifted from low to high bandwidth, the frequency of the behaviour decreased significantly ($F(2, 8) = 25.383$, $p < .001$). In addition, significant differences were also found between *face-to-face* and *whiteboard* and *whiteboard* and *3D virtual world* ($F(1, 4) = 46.24$, $p < .05$ and $F(1, 4) = 8.095$, $p < .05$, respectively).

In addition, two other statistical results from the generic skill Team Working are worth noting:-

- B23 ("Communicates design plans and relevant information" to relevant members). The Within-Subjects Contrasts test indicates that the mean frequency of B23 reduced significantly ($F(1, 4) = 23.774$ $p < .05$) between the *face-to-face* and *whiteboard* conditions.
- B52 ("Reassures/Encourages") was the only observable behaviour that approached significance ($F(2, 8) = 3.462$ $p < .1$). The decrease in frequency of this behaviour between *whiteboard* and *3D virtual world* ($F(1, 4) = 5.956$ $p < .1$) is also approaching significance.

Changes in the incidence of the remaining observable behaviours were non-significant, in some cases due to limited or non-existent data

5. Discussion

This study examined the generic skills of five design teams in three settings: face-to-face and two levels of virtual technology (viz. whiteboard and 3D virtual world). The behaviours underpinning the generic skills designers use during the conceptual stages of a variety of projects were recorded and analysed. The major findings were a significant increase in the frequency of Shared Situational Awareness and a significant decrease in Decision Making as bandwidth conditions increased.

5.1 Shared situational awareness

There was a significant and consistent increase in *Shared Situational Awareness* as the design process moved from low to high bandwidth as well as a significant increase between face-to-face and whiteboard conditions. This generic skill incorporates the sub-skills of gathering information, recognising and understanding as well as anticipating. One of this skill's observable behaviours (C11 "asks for documents and/or information regarding an idea or design") increased significantly as bandwidth increased and also between face-to face and whiteboard conditions. This behaviour is associated with information gathering and involves designers asking questions about a design, a site, an idea or an artefact. Shared goals and shared understandings are considered to be an intrinsic part of the team-building process (Berry, 2011). An increase in the frequency of this behaviour may indicate escalating levels of uncertainty (Gay & Lentini, 1995; Kayworth & Leidner, 2000) and it is conceivable that moving to unfamiliar design environments may have engendered such concerns. Furthermore, designing in 2D is markedly different from designing in 3D. Many designers traditionally work in 2D, and this approach is conveniently facilitated by whiteboard technologies. 3D virtual environments provide additional challenges because few designers have worked in them before. So, not only do 3D environments require designers to exercise their visualisation skills in a more complex way, they require them to use new tools (e.g. avatars, 3D geometric modelling tools etc) to express their conceptual designs. An increase in the incidence of C11 is therefore understandable. From this result, it could be extrapolated that design teams comprised of members from a variety of disciplines would have even greater difficulty in *Shared Situational Awareness*. Berry (2011) has suggested that increased requests for information may be the norm for virtual teamwork, i.e. it may be the normal pattern of communication, reflecting how different the virtual process is from the process of working in a face-to-face team. This increase may be due to the challenge of deciphering the ambiguity of remote communication (Nunamaker, et al., 2009). In addition, Berry (2011) reported that social communication in virtual environments tends to occur more slowly at first. Therefore, even if the amount of communication is similar, the rate may be different. Further research into team communication in these environments may elucidate this issue.

Virtual teams have a greater risk of communication breakdown due to the difficulties of establishing shared context of meaning (Bjørn & Ngwenyama, 2009). This breakdown can cause substantial difficulties as team members struggle to communicate and work with each other. This may also increase project delivery risks (Daim, et al., 2012). This increased need to establish a shared awareness suggests that design collaborators became unsure of their interpretation of communication and so requested additional confirmation. We suggest that design collaborators need to supply more detailed descriptions of what they are proposing or attempting to do and continually relate this to the specific task at hand. Additionally, Nunamaker et al (2009) have also recommended having clear rules and expectations when using certain types of technology and also having a clear definition of effective work completion. Virtual environments make it possible to communicate but the efficiency of such interactions and the level of shared understanding between individuals is not always assured. A way to enrich such communications is to use multiple communication channels or modes simultaneously (Gay & Lentini, 1995; Kayworth & Leidner, 2000). Instead of relying on a single mode of communication it is advantageous to support such communication with artefacts, such as sketches, as designers do in face-to-face situations. Verbal commentary is another way to enhance virtual communication. Where these environments support audio communication, verbal commentary and / or explanation provides valuable supplementary support. Berry (2011) suggests that virtual team members should be encouraged to seek out information when misunderstandings occur. We also recommend that multiple modes of communication be used concurrently to increase shared understanding between design team members in virtual conditions.

5.2 Decision making

There was a significant and consistent decrease in the frequency of *Decision Making* as design processes moved from low to high bandwidth and also between face to face and whiteboard, and between whiteboard and 3D. The sub-skills associated with this generic skill are identifying options, balancing risks and selecting options, and re-evaluating. The behaviour "discusses design options with clients/other designers" demonstrated a similarly significant decrease. The reduced frequency of such interactions suggests that designers using virtual environments more readily accept design proposals as solutions and do not explore as many alternatives as they would have had they been communicating face-to-face. Research on group style characteristics has reported similar findings; virtual teams were described to be less effective at team work, with decision-making being more difficult, resulting in poor decisions (Branson, Clausen, & Sung, 2008). It would seem that, because of the sometimes cumbersome nature of virtual communication, designers working in virtual environments find it more convenient to accept ideas rather than engage in discussions to explore alternative solutions. We therefore speculate that in virtual environments some designers' perspectives may not be offered for discussion, that when they do their ideas may not be acknowledged and / or explored, and that as a consequence, the quality of their solutions may suffer. It is therefore important for designers working in virtual contexts to recognise the potential limitations of their solutions, and to challenge the proposals of their colleagues.

5.3 Other notable results

The generic skill of Task Management demonstrated a decrease between face-to-face and whiteboard conditions that approached significance whilst there was a significant decrease in the behaviour of outlining and describing the plan/brief for the design/s. *Task Management* incorporates the sub-skills of planning or preparing a task, prioritising tasks, providing direction and maintaining standards for the task, and identifying and utilising resources. The management of virtual teams is acknowledged as being challenging (Kayworth & Leidner, 2000) and it may well be that the results apparent here relate to the small team size and personal management style of those involved.

Team Working skills incorporate co-ordinating activities with team members, exchanging information, using authority and assertiveness, assessing capabilities and supporting others. In demonstrating this generic skill, team members increased the frequency of giving updates and reporting key events significantly; however they significantly less frequently stated the case for instruction or gave justification as they worked in higher bandwidth conditions. The change in condition from face-to-face to whiteboard resulted in significantly more updates and reports of key events, as well as significantly fewer design plans and relevant information being communicated to relevant members. In contrast, the move from whiteboard to 3D virtual environments resulted in some changes that approached significance (fewer reassuring or encouraging comments, and more stating of the case for instruction and giving justification). This skill thus appears to present opportunities for further investigations. There are clearly many factors influencing designers' behaviours and further investigations to distil participants' contributions and interactions should provide interesting insights.

6. Limitations

The following are the main limitations of this study:

- Whilst the number of interactions analysed was large, the number of design teams analysed was relatively small (5). Each set of design tasks took 3.5 to 4 hours (including training and preparation) and proved challenging to organise. The fact that only five design teams took part is indicative of the difficulties involved in arranging the sessions. Although the number of teams was relatively small, the use of purposive sampling has permitted an exploration of the diverse nature of design teams.
- The data were collected under laboratory conditions. Because of confidentiality and logistics, it was not possible to video designers working at their normal place of work, nor was it possible to record their work on real-life design projects. Although the designs the participants were asked to work on were fictitious, they represented realistic design projects. It is difficult to determine the relative differences in complexity between the five projects provided.

- Due to the fact that participants were selected from a restricted pool of design professionals, all participants were from one discipline (architecture). Whilst our results may reflect the teamwork culture of the architectural profession, multi-disciplinary design teams may have experienced even more difficulty in exercising generic skills in virtual environments.

7. Implications for future research

An ability to map and measure the generic skills of individuals and teams is crucial for the construction/design industry because it allows specific training needs to be identified. Without a direction, those seeking to improve virtual teamwork may or may not succeed.

Virtual environments do not support non-verbal interactions as effectively as co-located conditions do and this deficiency inevitably leads designers to use different skills and / or skills in a different manner. A number of future research directions stem from this, including further examination of non-verbal interactions, team protocols and the possible impact of prior experience of ICT systems.

It is essential that designers understand the characteristics of the different environments in which they find themselves working. Specific generic skills may be needed for team members to function efficiently and effectively, particularly in virtual, high-bandwidth design environments. By examining the effects of technology on these generic skills, the particular strategies which facilitate and hinder teamwork when different levels of technology are used can be ascertained. These strategies can then be incorporated into the briefing and training sessions provided to construction design teams as they move to make greater use of electronic whiteboards, 3D virtual worlds and other technologies. In this context it is pertinent to note that currently training usually focuses on the use of new software and hardware, rather than on the generic skills that facilitate communication and collaboration. There is clearly a need to raise designers' awareness of the skills required for effective virtual collaboration, and to this end we have developed an interactive CD to assist those new to working in virtual environments (Newcastle, 2008; Williams & Sher, 2007). Additional skills development tools would provide valuable continuing professional development opportunities for design professionals.

8. Conclusions

The major conclusion drawn from our analysis of design collaboration is that there are significant differences for the generic skills profiles between the three operational conditions; face-to-face, whiteboard and 3D virtual world. This was true for the overall design activity of the five teams. As Daim et al (2012) concludes, the basic fundamentals of team building are still valid, but "new dimensions of technology and global economy are making matters complicated and challenging for the managers" (p. 9). While it is clear that the introduction of virtual technologies has implications for designers, the challenges are not solely technical. Ebrahim, Ahmed and Taha (2009) consider that the successful implementation of virtual teamwork is "more about processes and people than about technology" (p. 2663). However, technology has traditionally been the focus of investigation in virtual teamwork without taking into account social and economic considerations

(Rezgui, 2007). In addition, small-medium companies may be at an advantage because they can more flexibly change and adapt to new technology (Rezgui, 2007).

Designers bring with them a range of generic skills acquired over the years from a multitude of different activities. These need to be adapted to the new environments they find themselves working in. This is succinctly summarised by Larsson (2003) who states that since "design involves communication and interaction between individuals and groups in complex social settings, the social character of design is not separated from the technical results" (p. 153). Virtual technologies impact on the way designers work and collaborate and hence impact on the skills that need to be brought to bear. The investigations documented in this chapter contribute to this body of knowledge by identifying the generic skills of design professionals, profiling some of the impacts of different virtual communication technologies on these skills and identifying some goals which need to be addressed if virtual technologies are to be effective and successful. As Carletta, Anderson and McEwan have stated (2000, p. 1250), technologists are less interested in "social and organizational concerns than in equipment mechanics". The performance of virtual teams is far below their potential despite their rapid growth (Abuelmaatti & Rezgui, 2008). Therefore the investigation of these teams takes on a new urgency, particularly as virtual communication has been shown to have advantages over face-to-face interaction during problem-solving (Hatem, et al., 2011). Without taking into account the impact of these new design environments, advanced technologies that allow teams to collaborate at a distance may have a deleterious effect on teamwork and productivity.

9. Acknowledgments

We wish to acknowledge the Cooperative Research Centre for Construction Innovation (CRC-CI), part of the Australian Government's CRC program, who funded this project (Project 2002-024-B), and Tom Bellamy, who was one of our researchers.

Finally, sections of this paper are based on the following publication:

Sher, W., Sherratt, S., Williams, A., & Gameson, R. (2009). Heading into new virtual environments: what skills do design team members need? Journal of Information Technology in Construction, 14, 17-29.

10. References

Abuelmaatti, A., & Rezgui, Y. (2008). Virtual teamworking: Current issues and directions for the future. In L. M. Camarinha-Matos & W. Picard (Eds.), Pervasive Collaborative Networks (Vol. 283, pp. 351-360). Boston: Springer.

Activeworlds-Corporation (2008). Active Worlds Retrieved 28 Sept 2008, from http://www.activeworlds.com/

Bales, R. (1951). Interaction process analysis. Cambridge: Addison-Wesley Press Inc.

Bell, B. S., & Kozlowski, S. W. J. (2002). A typology of virtual teams: Implications for effective leadership. Group and organization management, 27(1), 14 - 49.

Bellamy, T., Williams, A., Sher, W., Sherratt, S., & Gameson, R. (2005). Design communication: issues confronting both co-located and virtual teams. Paper presented at the 21st Association of Researchers for Construction Management

(ARCOM). Berry, G. R. (2011). Enhancing Effectiveness on Virtual Teams. Journal of Business Communication, 48(2), 186-206.

Berry, G. R. (2011). Enhancing Effectiveness on Virtual Teams. Journal of Business Communication, 48(2), 186-206.

Bjørn, P., & Ngwenyama, O. (2009). Virtual team collaboration: building shared meaning, resolving breakdowns and creating translucence. Information Systems Journal, 19(3), 227-253.

Branson, L., Clausen, T. S., & Sung, C.-H. (2008). Group Style Differences Between Virtual and F2F Teams. American Journal of Business, 23(1), 65-70.

Burfield, I., Cadee, N., Grieco, F., Mayton, T., & Spink, A. (2003). The observer: Reference manual ver 5.: Wageningen, Neth: Noldus Information Technology.

Cannon-Bowers, J., Tannenbaum, S., Salas, E., & Volpe, C. (1995). Defining competencies and establishing team training requirements. In R. A. Guzzo & E. Salas (Eds.), Team effectiveness and decision making in organisations (pp. 333 - 380). San Francisco, CA: Jossey-Bass.

Carletta, J., Anderson, A. H., & McEwan, R. (2000). The effects of multimedia communication technology on non-collocated teams: a case study. Ergonomics, 43(8), 1237 - 1251.

Carthey, J., de Leval, M. R., Wright, D. J., Farewell, V. T., & Reason, J. T. (2003). Behavioural markers of surgical excellence. Safety Science, 41(5), 409-425.

Cross, N., Christiaans, H., & K., D. (1996). Introduction: The Delft protocols workshop. Analysing Design Activity. Chichester: John Wiley and Sons.

Daim, T. U., Ha, A., Reutiman, S., Hughes, B., Pathak, U., Bynum, W., et al. (2012). Exploring the communication breakdown in global virtual teams. International Journal of Project Management(0). Volume 30, Issue 2, February 2012, Pages 199-212

Dubé, L., & Paré, G. (2004). The Multifaceted Nature of Virtual Teams. In D. J. Pauleen (Ed.), Virtual teams: projects, protocols and processes: Idea Group.

Ebrahim, N. A., Ahmed, S., & Taha, Z. (2009). Virtual teams: a literature review. Australian Journal of Basic and Applied Sciences, 3(3), 2653-2669.

Ericsson, K., & Simon, H. (1993). Protocol analysis: Verbal reports as data (Revised version). Cambridge: MIT Press.

Fletcher, G., Flin, R., McGeorge, P., Glavin, R., Maran, N., & Patey, R. (2003). Anaesthetists' Non-Technical Skills (ANTS): evaluation of a behavioural marker system{dagger}. Br. J. Anaesth., 90(5), 580-588.

Gameson, R., & Sher, W. (2002). An investigation into perceptions of project team dynamics and the utilisation of virtual environments, Association of Researchers in Construction Management (ARCOM) (Vol. 1, pp. 177 - 186). Northumbria University, UK.

Gaudes, A., Hamilton-Bogart, B., Marsh, S., & Robinson, H. (2007). A framework for constructing effective virtual teams. The Journal of eWorking, 1(2), 83-97.

Gay, G., & Lentini, M. (1995). Use of Communication Resources in a Networked Collaborative Design Environment. Journal of Computer-Mediated Communication, 1(1), 0-0.

Guerlain, S., Turrentine, B., Adams, R., & Forrest Calland, J. (2004). Using video data for the analysis and training of medical personnel. Cognition, Technology and Work, 6, 131 - 138.

Halliday, M. A. K., & Matthiessen, C. M. I. M. (2004). An Introduction to Functional Grammar (3rd ed.). London: Hodder Arnold.

Hatem, W. A., Kwan, A. S., & Miles, J. C. (2011, July 6th - 8th). A comparison of face to face and computer mediated collaboration Paper presented at the 2011 eg-ice Workshop, University of Twente, The Netherlands.

Kanawattanachai, P., & Yoo, Y. (2002). Dynamic nature of trust in virtual teams. The Journal of Strategic Information Systems, 11(3-4), 187-213.

Kayworth, T., & Leidner, D. (2000). The global virtual manager: a prescription for success. European Management Journal, 18(2), 183-194.

Kazdin, A. (1982). Single-case research designs. New York: Oxford University Press.

Klampfer, B., Flin, R., Helmreich, R., Hausler, R., Sexton, B., Fletcher, G., et al. (2001, 5 - 6 July 2001). Enhancing Performance in High Risk Environments: Recommendations for the use of Behavioural Markers. Paper presented at the Behavioural Markers Workshop, Swissair Training Centre, Zurich.

Larsson, A. (2003). Making sense of collaboration: the challenge of thinking together in global design teams. Paper presented at the GROUP '03 Conference.,

Lau, H. Y. K., Mak, K. L., & Lu, M. T. H. (2003). A virtual design platform for interactive product design and visualization. Journal of Materials Processing Technology, 139(1-3), 402-407.

Maher, M. L. (2002). Team Collaboration in High Bandwidth Virtual Environments Retrieved 6 Sept 2008, 2008, from http://www.construction-innovation.info/index.php?id=63

Maher, M. L. (2005). Collaborative Processes: Research Report on Use of Virtual Environment. Brisbane: Cooperative Research Centre for Construction Innovation.

Marchman III, J. F. (1998). Multinational, Multidisciplinary, Vertically Integrated Team Experience in Aircraft Design. International Journal of Engineering Design, 14(5), 328 - 334.

Newcastle, U. o. (2008). Training and CPD Retrieved 13 Oct 2008, 2008, from http://www.construction-innovation.info/index.php?id=1107

Nunamaker, J. F. J., Reinig, B. A., & Briggs, R. O. (2009). Principles for effective virtual teamwork. Communication of the ACM, 52(4), 113-117.

Peña-mora, F., Vadhavkar, S., & Aziz, Z. (2009). Technology strategies for globally dispersed construction teams ITcon: Special Issue Technology Strategies for Collaborative Working, 14, 70-80.

Powell, A., Piccoli, G., & Ives, B. (2004). Virtual teams: a review of current literature and directions for future research. SIGMIS Database, 35(1), 6-36.

Pring, T. (2005). Research Methods in Communication Disorders. London: Whurr Publishers.

Rezgui, Y. (2007). Exploring virtual team-working effectiveness in the construction sector. Interacting with Computers, 19(1), 96-112.

Rice, P. L., & Ezzy, D. (1999). Qualitative Research Methods: A Health Focus. South Melbourne (Australia): Oxford University Press.

Riedlinger, M. E., Gallois, C., McKay, S., & Pittam, J. (2004). Impact of social group processes and functional diversity on communication in networked organizations. Journal of Applied Communication Research, 32(1), 55 - 79.

Salas, E., Shawn Burke, C., & Cannon-Bowers, J. A. (2000). Teamwork: emerging principles. International Journal of Management Reviews, 2(4), 339-356.

Schumacher, M., Cardinal, J. S.-l., & Bocquet, J.-C. (2009). Towards a methodology for managing competencies in virtual teams - a systemic approach. Paper presented at the IFIP AICT 307 - PRO-VE 2009.

Sherratt, S., Sher, W., Williams, A., & Gameson, R. (2010). Communication in construction design teams: Moving into the virtual world. In R. Taiwo (Ed.), Handbook of Research on Discourse Behavior and Digital Communication: Language Structures and Social Interaction. Hershey, PA: IGI Global.

Shyamsundar, N., & Gadh, R. (2001). Internet-based collaborative product design with assembly features and virtual design spaces. Computer-Aided Design, 33(9), 637-651.

Wallace, W. (1987). The influence of design team communication content upon the architectural decision making process in the pre contract design stages. Edinburgh: Department of Building. , UK, Heriot-Watt University.

Williams, A., & Cowdroy, R. (2002). How designers communicate ideas to each other in design meetings. Paper presented at the Design 2002, International Design Conference.

Williams, A., & Sher, W. (2007, 12 - 15 Nov). The Alignment of Research, Education and Industry Application. Paper presented at the IASDR 07: International Association of Societies of Design Research, Hong Kong Polytechnic University.

3

Virtual Garment Creation

Ausma Viļumsone and Inga Dāboliņa
Riga Technical University
Institute of Textile Material Technologies and Design, Riga
Latvia

1. Introduction

The use of new information technologies and software provide the possibility to solve problems connected with raising work efficiency in the company (Hannelore, 1999). The first information on using information technologies in the sewing industry, particularly in construction designing, turned up in the beginning of the 70-ies of the XX century, but first publications on computer aided designing software - only in the 90-ies of the XX century. At present most of the companies use computer aided software.

Modern computer aided designing software provides the possibility to avoid small operations and manual work, to raise precision, productivity and organize information flow (Beazley, 2003). The usage of garment designing systems excludes the time consuming manual preparation of patterns, creation of layouts and relocation of written information. The computer systems are meant for the execution of every single process and the integration of all processes into one joint flow, for the organization of logistics and the mobility of work tasks.

The computerization of different processes in the garment industry is necessary to reduce the costs of a product and raise the competitiveness (Kang, 2000).

Computer systems allow making two dimensional as well as three dimensional product illustrations and visualizations (D'Apuzzo, 2009; Lectra, 2009). It is possible to create computer aided garment constructions, as well as gradations, and create a virtual first pattern of the model - such computer aided operations significantly decrease the time consumption and cost necessary to design a product. The costs of the product itself can be calculated with the help of the product management systems following the development parameters, the layout of patterns, textile expenditure, model complexity and specification, as well as previous experience of the company stored in a data base.

Although computer systems significantly facilitate the development of a product, the knowledge and skill of the user are still very important. One of the most important garment creation stages is constructing.

Constructing is the reproduction of a spatial model (clothing) on a plane (construction); this transformation has to be reflexive when joining the parts of the construction a garment is originated. The creation of the drafts of the construction is the most complicated and responsible stage of garment designing, because a non-existent complicated spatial shape product surface layout has to be created (drawn) (Vilumsone, 1993; Koblakova, 1988). One of the most topical problems in garment designing has always been the search of garment designing methods scientifically reasoned, precise and as little as possible time and labour consuming. Several factors depend on a precise development of garment surface layout - material expenditure, garment set quality, labour intensity level, the aesthetical and hygienic characteristics of the finished product.

The traditional mass production ever decreases the volumes of series, the production becomes more elastic and the choice of goods expands; the wear time decreases. Along with the serial production, individual production becomes more and more popular. The current economic situation shifts the search for labour more and more to the East, but the creation of individually oriented products could make it possible to maintain working places and production units in Europe. People will be willing to pay more for this type of clothing and receive it in a possibly short term. Thereby the promotion of individualized production is affected by social and economic aspects.

The non-contact anthropometrical data acquisition methods are currently used to solve the problem of acquiring the clients' measures for individualized production, yet still the spread of individualized production is limited by the uniformity of assortment, the labour intensity of designing, the uncertainty of the result of the construction and the complexity of the constructing tasks creating an individual product for each customer (D'Apuzzo, 2008; Fan, 2004).

In its turn the potentialities of the virtual reality are used to create e-store offers that are more attractive to customers, create virtual twins, model fitting and the reflection of garment individualities.

2. Computer aided garment designing

Computer aided designing software (AceApparel; Assol; Assyst; Audaces; Bernina; Comtense; FashionCad; Gemini; Gerber; Grafis; InvenTex; Jindex; Lectra; Leko; Optitex; PadSystem; RichPeace; Staprim; WildGinger; TanyaGeo) not only provide the possibility to speed up the process of putting a new model into production and improve the quality of the products, but also to reduce material costs and labour intensity, ensuring an elastic change of the assortment. Most of the systems are made by the module principle in which separate garment designing stages are implemented (Razdomahins, 2007). The systems are constantly being developed according to the improvements of in production conditions, the implementation of new technologies as well as the optimisation of the designing process.

When introducing CAD/CAM systems, some main aspects have to be taken into consideration: costs of software, equipment, technical supply and training, the suitability to the particular production conditions, the safety of exploitation and improvement possibilities (Vilumsone, 1993; Pavlovskaya, 2009). Although the implementation of systems is an expensive process, the advantages compensate the high costs and difficulties that arise during the implementation.

Modern computer aided designing systems allow performing different designing stages including traditional 2D designing, as well as the imitation of a 3D garment, 3D virtual fitting.

Modern 2D CAD/CAM systems perform constructing in three ways:

Type 1 The construction is designed manually, but the production preparation is performed using computer technologies (manually prepared patterns are entered into the system with a digitizer).

Type 2 Manual work is completely excluded. The whole designing and preparation process is computer aided.

Type 3 Part of the designing stages are computer aided, without human help, but the rest is an interactive process.

The use of any kind of computerization has indisputable advantages: improved production quality, higher productivity, humanization of the working process, more elastic production, process control, the possibility to link the production with the desires of the customer (rapid response). Nevertheless each system can be improved. For a 3D imitation of a garment to adjust a parametric mannequin to the individual measures of a human body additional projection body measures have to be considered (at present only the height is integrated, but the width characterizing the configuration of transversal planes is necessary too.

The latest tendency in the CAD/CAM development is the creation of 3D designing. There are several reasons for the implementation of 3D designing:

- plane-like garment designing methods do not provide an absolute conformity of the garment with the expectations;
- the construction of garments in opposition to the object (garment) to be designed is a plane-like process - it does not provide a preview of the product. In its turn the preparation of patterns is an expensive and time consuming process;
- the 2D visualizations of the garment do not provide the evaluation of the characteristics of textile materials.

Although 3D designing where it is possible to create a layout of plane details by a 3D shape drawing already exists, such systems have several disadvantages: a limited assortment and shape of garment, segmentation.

Depending on the practicable task, 3D systems can be divided as follows:

Type 1 Imitation of the garments' appearance - the system allows changing the 3D sketch or photograph to evaluate the appearance of the garments' model with visually different types of textile materials;

Type 2 Garment imitation - the systems allows performing a virtual fitting, evaluate the external appearance, shape, set, proportions of the garment (the garment is created in 3D by joining patterns constructed in a plane, creating an imitation of the garment with the intention to ascertain the conformity of the outer appearance to the expectations);

Type 3 Garment designing - the system allows creating the shape of a garment, identify (define) dividing lines, create patterns in a 3D environment following a layout in a plane.

The apparel appearance imitation systems are suitable mainly for making catalogues and specialist communication to verify the visual conformity of the textiles with the particular model. To create the reality of the apparel perception a shading/lustre of a photograph/sketch. A new fabric is spread over the fabric in the image in a way that the direction of the pattern conforms with the pattern direction of the fragment defined with the help of a net structure (Figure 1). In case of a complicated model the preparation of the image for fabric "spreading" can be quite labour-intensive. Nevertheless it pays off since after that a large variety of patterns and colours can be tested within a very short period of time.

Fig. 1. Imitation of the garments' appearance KOPPERMANN Tex Design

There are several other 3D designing elaboration foreruns and finished elaborations, the usage of which is limited by different factors - assortment, segmentations of products, the fiction of 3D designing - all changes are made in a 2D environment (Viļumsone, 2007).

A structural scheme of the production process (Fig.4.), identifying the processes of typal production with the goal to determine the mutual relationship of the production preparation processes and the structure of the informative and software means, has been developed; it has been concluded that no matter what level CAD/CAM system is used, their usage provides a faster development of the product and shortens the working process. A complete 3D designing process would exclude different working stages connected with constructing and constructive modelling, 3D imitation and creation of a virtual prototype.

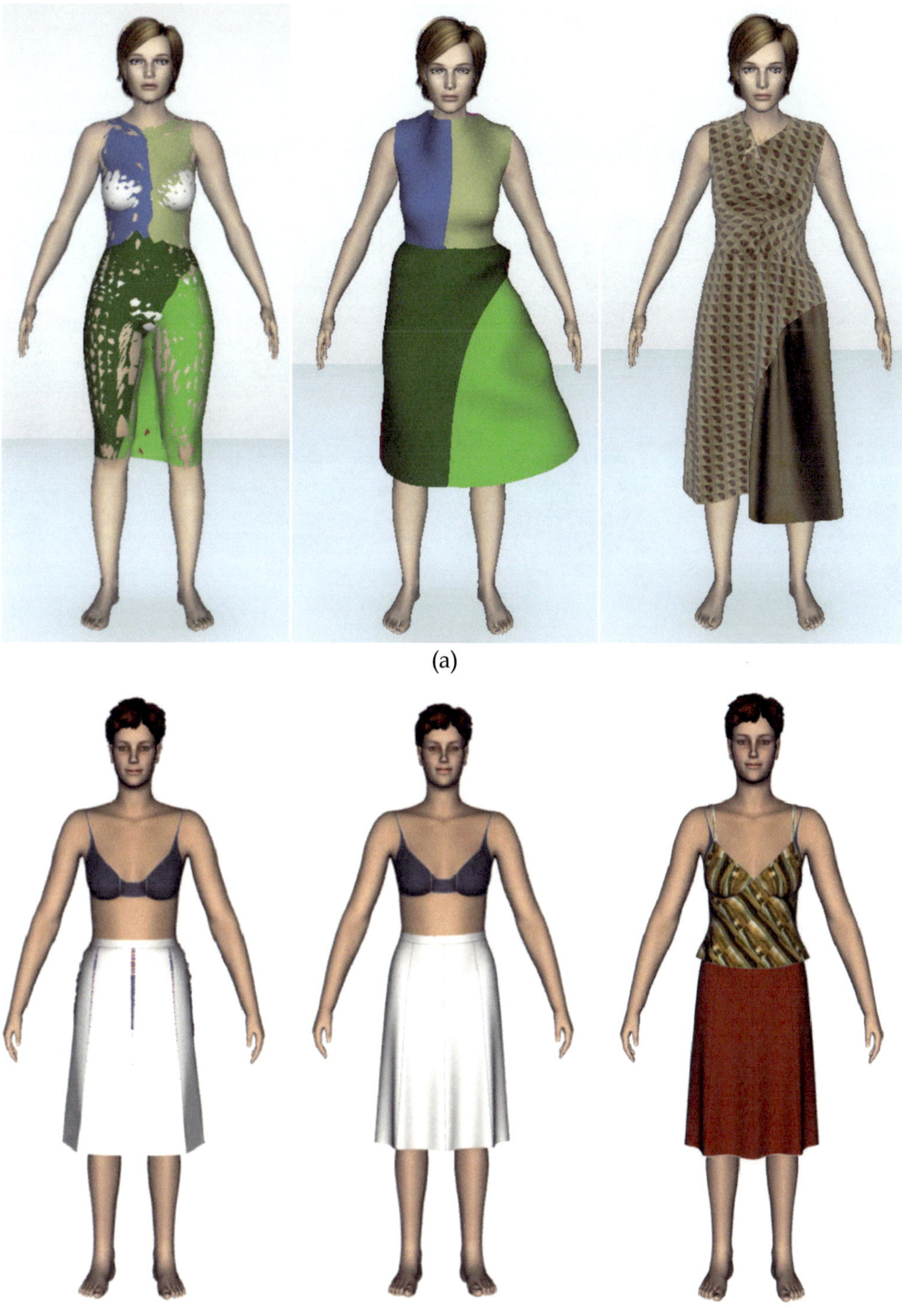

(a)

(b)

Fig. 2. Garment imitation a) LECTRA 3D Fit, b) BERNINA My Label

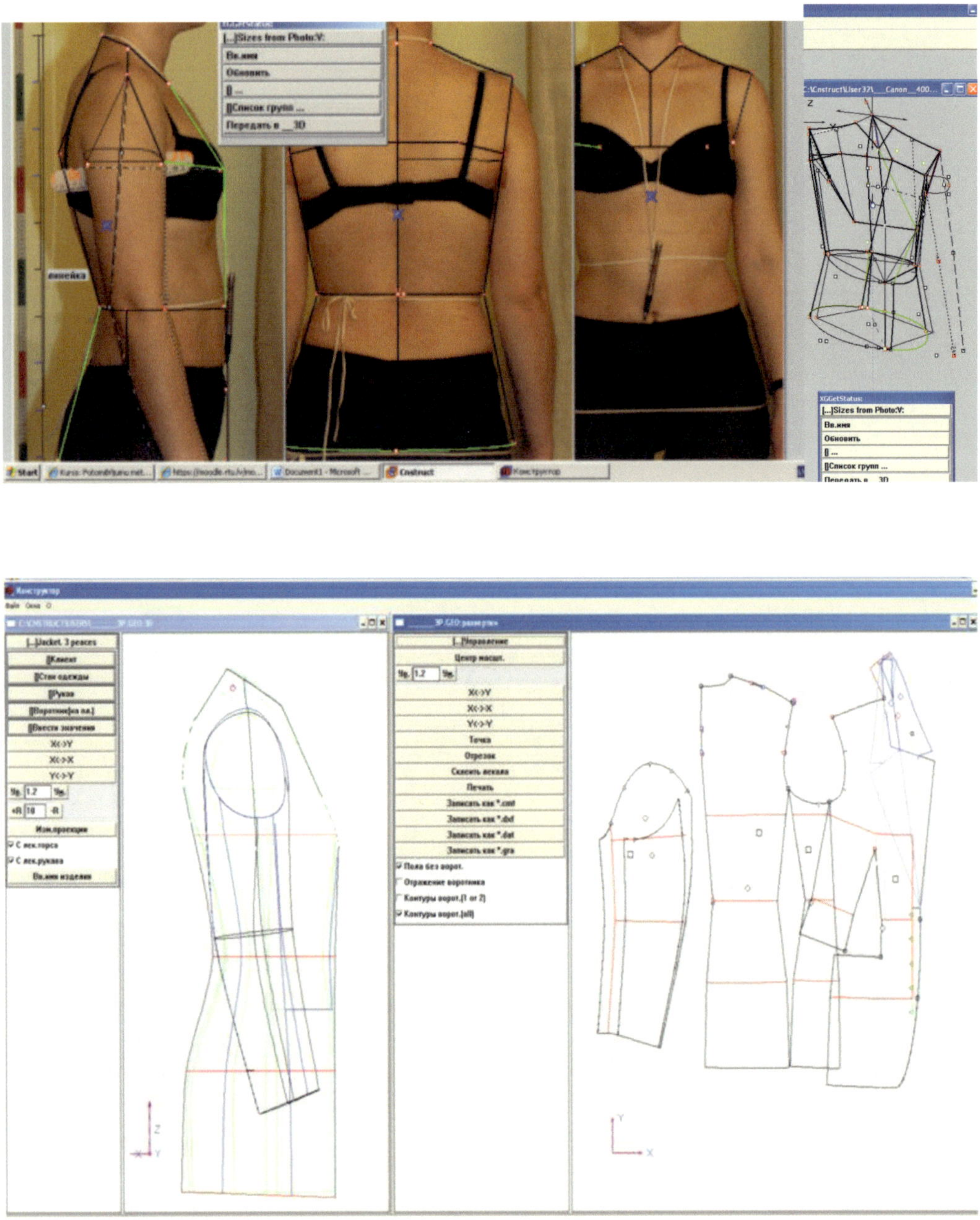

Fig. 3. Garment designing 3D CAD STAPRIM

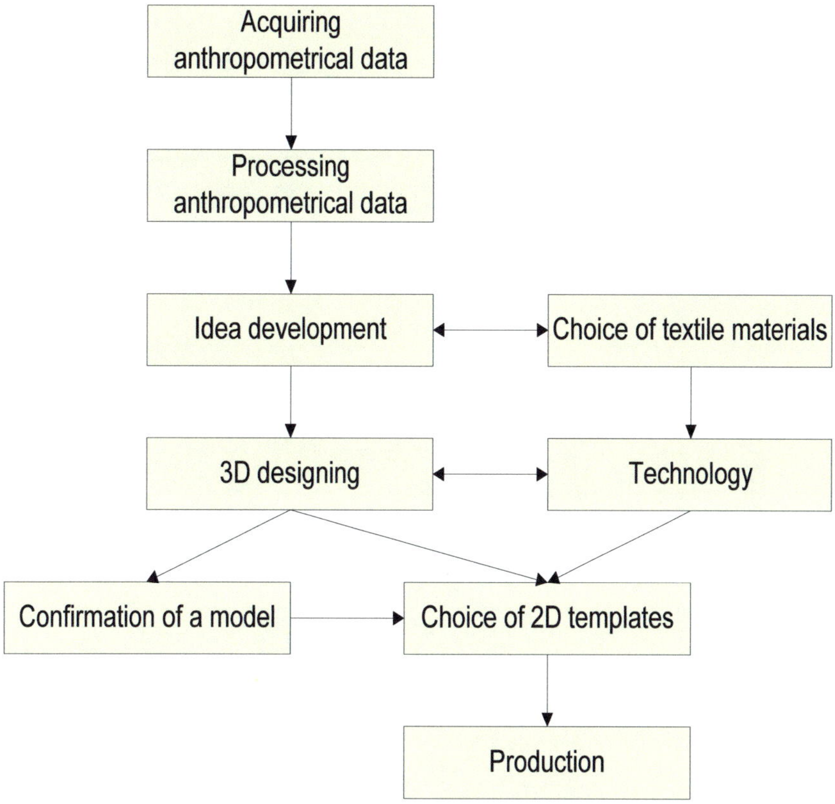

Fig. 4. The 3D process of garment designing

3. A comparison of the existent 3D designing systems

When developing 3D apparel designing systems three mutually connected tasks are being solved: the development of a virtual mannequin, the creation of a 3D shape of a garment model and the 2D layout of details (Winsborough, 2001; Yan, 2007). There are two sequences possible for these tasks. Systems, like Optitex (OptiTex CAD/CAM), that imitate garments, use 2D templates that are sewn together virtually. In its turn 3D designing systems create the surface of a garment in relation to a mannequin and acquire the layout of details afterwards (Staprim CAD/CAM). In addition problems connected with the qualities of the textiles. The imitation of the physical qualities of fabrics (elasticity, drapery etc.) when placing parts of a garment onto a 3D mannequin influence the correct set of a garment and the visual perception of a model (Szabó, 2008). The visual qualities of a fabric - colour, pattern, texture - are very important for a wholesome perception and evaluation of an apparel model.

The comparison table of the existent 3D designing systems examines the best known systems which offer 3D designing: Optitex (Israel; http://www.optitex.com/), Staprim (Russia; http://www.staprim.com/), Lectra (France; http://www.lectra.com), Assyst (Germany; http://www.human-solutions.com), Gerber (USA; http://www.gerbertechnology.com/), Assol (Russia; http://www.assol.org/), Bernina (Switzerland; http://www.berninamylabel.com/).

#	Parameter	Description		Optitex	Staprim	Lectra	Assyst	Gerber	Assol	Bernina
1.1.	MANNEQUIN	sex	feminine one type	x	x			x	x	x
1.2.			feminine several types			x	x			
1.3.			masculine	x		x	x	x		
1.4.		parametric		x	x	x	x	x	x	x
1.5.		individualization	traditional measurements	x	x	x		x	x	x
1.6.			projection measurements		x					
1.7.			integration from 3D scan			x	x	x	x	
1.8.		imitation of movements	virtual movement	x						
1.9.			change of current postures			x	x	x		
2.1.	CREATION OF GARMENT SHAPE	designing of apparel parts on a 3D mannequin		x					x	
2.2.		definition of an intermediate layer (ease allowance)	projection distances		x				x	
2.3.			traditional ease allowances		x					x
2.4.		usage of finished apparel parts	3D construction templates		x				x	x
2.5.			„sewing" and "try on" using 2D templates	x		x	x	x		
3.1.	CORRECTION OF GARMENT SHAPE	in plane, checking 3D		x		x	x	x		x
3.2.		3D, automatical changes in plane		x		x	x	x		
3.3.		changing numerical parameters			x		x		x	x

#	Parameter	Description		Optitex	Staprim	Lectra	Assyst	Gerber	Assol	Bernina
4.1.	VISUAL CHARACTERISTICS OF A GARMENT	fabric characteristics	elasticity	x		x	x	x	x	
4.2.			drapery	x		x	x	x	x	
4.3.			structure	x		x	x	x	x	
4.4.			stiffness control			x	x	x		
4.5.		visual characteristics of the fabric	colour/ pattern	x		x	x	x	x	x
4.6.			Size of pattern			x	x	x	x	
4.7.			texture			x	x	x	x	
4.8.		placement of decorative elements		x		x	x	x	x	x
5.1.	EASE CONTROL	colour code		x		x	x	x		
5.2.		numeric evaluation		x	x	x	x	x		

Table 1. Comparison table of the existent 3D designing systems

The comparative table shows that despite the fact that most systems strive to use some of the 3D designing and/or fitting stages, most of the systems are made for 2D pattern fitting, whereas the actual indications of 3D designing would be the creation of garment patterns on the surface of a 3D mannequin and defining ease allowances by setting projection space between the garment and the mannequin. The systems reviewed in the table can be shortly described as follows:

- Using OptiTex 3D Garment Draping and 3D Visualization software system - designers, pattern makers, and retailers can visualize patterns, change the texture, colors, add/remove logos and buttons, instantly in 3D. It is possible to use modeling system software, analyze fabric behavior, proof-fitting assumptions, the product development process. It also provides a tool for sales and merchandising, allowing users to create 3D catalogs.
- In the 3D CAD system Staprim the patterns of clothes are created automatically by laying out the surface of the constructed model from three photoes on a plane (Viļumsone, 2008; Razdomakhin 2003 & 2006). This allows to solve a number of essentially important engineering problems, for instance: to set high quality of the layout of a product on a human body; to carry out maximum computerization of processes of clothes designing from the idea up to the layout of patterns; to estimate the created (virtual) model of a product before the manufacturing stage by rendering the image on a screen, etc. The computerization of the process from the idea to a layout of a

pattern is solved by means of merging 3D CAD Staprim with traditional 2D CAD Comtense (Russia; http://www.comtense.ru/). The Comtense ensure development of production patterns comprises: pattern creation, modeling, grading, marker making, plotting, and CNS-cutter control file generation.

- Lectra and its consultants accompany apparel businesses in the design, engineering, and manufacturing of their products. CAD application software for product design, pattern-making, and 3D-prototyping addresses collection development from drawing board to cutting room. Developed especially for fashion, Lectra Fashion PLM meets the needs of the entire apparel development chain from brands, to suppliers, to retailers. Lectra Modaris is a solution for flat pattern making, grading, and 3D virtual prototyping. Modaris simulates virtual samples by associating flat patterns, fabric specifications, and 3D virtual mannequins.
- The Human Solutions GmbH has taken over all software products, software-related services and the software-related hardware supplies of the former Assyst GmbH from that company's insolvency estate. At present the cooperation between Assyst and Human Solutions has grown into a successful virtual fitting and prototyping system allowing more than just integrating individually scanned mannequins and fitting the chosen apparel model on it. It is also capable of a realistic analysis and reproduction of the characteristics of a model, seam allowance placement - constructively technological individualities. It is also possible to imitate and virtually control the fastener, pocket openings, cuffs, flaps and other covering details of a garment model.
- Gerber Vstitcher software is created in collaboration with Browzwear Int. Ltd. (Israel; http://browzwear.com/). Software is a 3D design and visualization system, it transforms two dimensional patterns into three dimensional garments. It interfaces seamlessly with Gerber's AccuMark pattern design, grading and marker making software, enabling a transformation of 2D patterns into 3D garments. Virtual samples can be used for internal design reviews before the factory creates actual samples. They also minimize the need to send physical samples through the mail, saving time and reducing costs. It is possible to simulate texture, draping and fit of garments by displaying them on a virtual human body form based on pattern created in 2D, fabric and texture data. Maintain fit consistency throughout the development process.
- Assol is an apparel designing system that, in cooperation with AutoDesk, have created a garment designing module on the basis of AutoCAD which provides the parametric designing of garment templates, as well as a parametric gradation of templates, usage of different mannequins (parametric and digitized) for 3D designing and the designing of 3D garments for limited assortments. The usage of AutoCAD as a base allows for a more elastic connection of software and hardware.
- Bernina My Label is pattern-making software with integrated 20 different styles based on parametrical mannequin which can be changed for individual measurements. It is possible to change wearing ease and make slight design details, like making a skirt longer, collar wider, etc. Once the measurements are entered, a 3D model is generated using Optitex imaging software. After individual mannequin is created and saved, garments may be selected and simulated on the model. If the garment is too tight or too loose, it is possible to vary the style properties. Wearing ease is included and it can be changed.

A more rapid development of 3D imitation systems is driven by the fact that the new “fitting” module is being developed as an addition to the existent traditional CAD system template designing, gradation, layout and other modules. The designers of the systems have the possibility to continue to improve the existent approbated modules and develop the new ones. It does not require the development of a basically new template designing process, namely, it allows to use the pattern making and gradation methods that have developed for centuries and which are relatively successfully used by companies to create the contours of the garment details of a particular assortment despite the specific weight of uncertainties and subjective solutions. As all creative processes the creation of the shape of a garment (both, in2D or 3D) is very complicated to formalize. The contours of details intuitively drawn or manually developed in the pin up process by skilful designers or constructors are entered into the computer system for further processing. The necessity for a digitizer module to be included into industrial CAD systems is determined by the inability to precisely forecast the shape of a garment using 2D template systems.

The virtual fitting of a model is visually very attractive for the designer as well as for the consumer thanks to the imitation of the physical individualities of textiles as well as the imitation of patterns, colour and texture. The effect of reality is becoming more and more convincing. The designers of the systems offer new and more convenient tools. Some have even implemented movements of a mannequin. Nevertheless the virtual "sewing" function procedures of more complex models have to be improved on almost all existent systems. The main problems are connected with defining the connectable layers, determination of tuck-up and roll-up parts of a garment, characterization of the multi-colouristic qualities of a fabric, the thickness of layers and the position of padding.

So far the 3D designing systems have coped better with designing products and developing layouts of details for close fitting models, where the apparel is smaller (or the same size) than the given layout of a mannequin's surface. As an example CAD Assol and Optitex can be mentioned.

Research on creating the surface of a garment in a particular distance from the surface of a mannequin is being carried out to be able to design a broad assortment of apparels. Since 1995 the STAPRIM software is on the CAD system market. The developers of this system were the first to be able to define projection spaces between the surface of the garment and the mannequin and connect them with traditional tailor measurements as well as transfer them into standard and individual patterns. Though the carcass type representation of the mannequin and garment does not produce the realistic sense characteristic to the "fitting" systems, but it is informative and the automatically acquired detail contours are mutually perfectly coordinated and ensure the set visible in the virtual image.

Such a system could be very suitable for the creation of different uniforms, since it allows creating well set constructions for different individual figures, but the result provided by the system is a basic construction and does not foresee full designing of special features of a model. Importing this construction into any other system the model construction and pattern designing process has to be started anew. Therefore it is advisable to develop an algorithm providing the in heritage of detail size and shape of individual figures up to the level of finished patterns (as it is, for example, in the software GRAFIS).

The developers of CAD Assol (Russia) also notify of the existence of such a module. In their informative materials they demonstrate examples of all types of 3D CAD apparels, developed by means of AutoDesk.

Which company CAD system is better? It is wrong to state the question in this way, and not just because it wouldn't be correct. All CAD systems, i.e. the CAD of various companies are actually identical. All of them computerize the same or almost similar plane-like methods for creating patterns of clothes. This is the circumstance and it is difficult to disagree. As to the layout of patterns there are some distinctive features between the systems, but they are never long-term considering the constant development of the software of all companies. Certainly there are differences in the choice of toolkits as solutions of some parts of the system, but in some period of time similar solutions appear on other systems. The preference is given by the user who studies the systems of various companies and chooses the most convenient one for the particular assortment and for him-/ herself. Certainly the greatest and maybe even the crucial impact are given by the price policy of different companies. But it is not that simple again. We cannot say that everything that is more expensive is better. Just as we cannot say the contrary - that everything that is cheaper is worse (Razdomakhin, 2006).

4. Possibilities of acquiring anthropometrical data

Since a virtual mannequin is necessary as the basis of any 3D CAD apparel system, great attention is paid by the scientists to its development and processing (Scharrenbroich, 2009).

There are two types of human body measurement acquiring methods:

Type 1 manual anthropometry methods (contact methods);

Type 2 optic anthropometry methods (non-contact methods).

Anthropometrical data (Fig. 5.) can be acquired with different tools (3D Ouest; 3D-Shape; 4D Culture; Bodymetrics; Cyberware; Digimask; GFai; Hamano Engineering; Human Solutions; InSpeck; Intellifit; Singular Inversions FaceGen; Telmat; VisImage Systems; Vitronic Stein Bildverarbeitungssysteme; Wicks and Wilson; XX Production online). Traditional methods use different manual tools (measuring tape, anthropometer, etc.). As the technologies develop, new tools are created and/or the existent ones are improved. The electronic measuring tape can be considered as an improvement of the electronic measuring tape, but its use for anthropometry is doubtful. It has been proved by an experiment that when using the electronic measuring tape, more than half of the measures taken were wrong.

Photo measuring methods are fast and effective, but the processing of data is time consuming and labour intensive. A relatively new tool (approximately since 1980 (Fan, 2004)) in anthropometry is the 3D scanner.

Considering the advantages of 3D scanning, the scanning technologies are being developed and improved. Most of the scanners can not only create a 3D image of the human body, but also read the x, y and z coordinates thereby acquiring precise information about the human body and its volumes (Hwang, 2001; Rupp, 2005; D'Apuzzo, 2003; Sanyo Electric Co.).

A human body surface reproduction dot cloud is created from the coordinate readings, which can be used as a virtual mannequin or only the coordinates themselves can be used. A virtual reproduction of the human body can be used in garment production, car production, engineering and medicine.

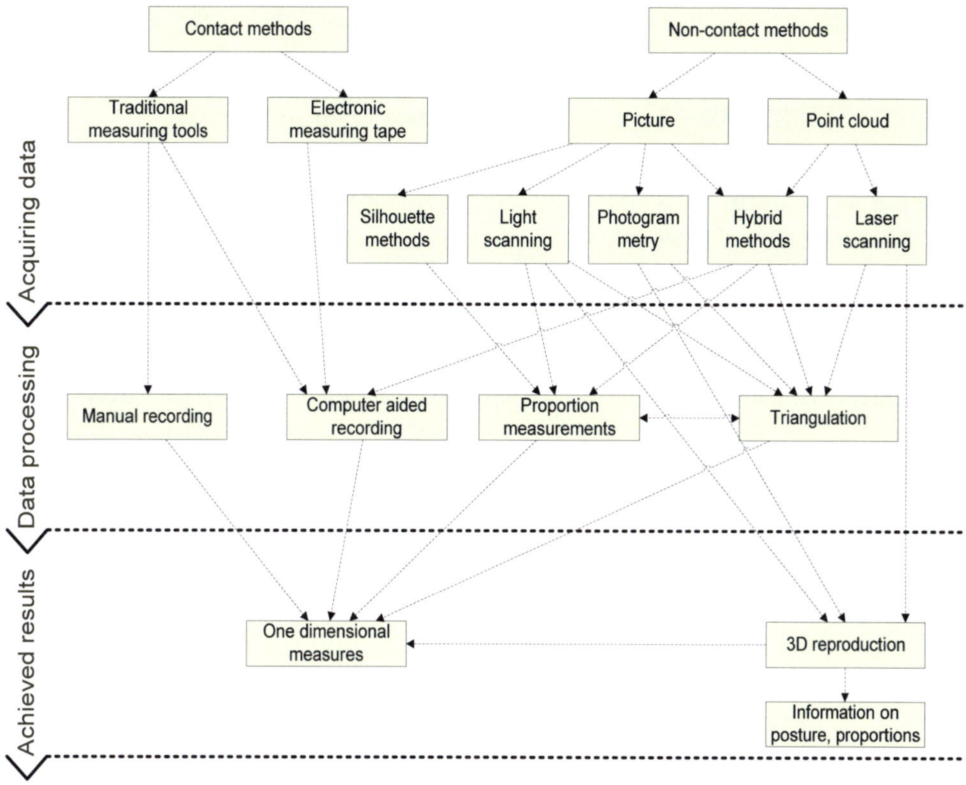

Fig. 5. Types of anthropometrical data acquisition

Any scanning device is equipped with optic (light) appliances to ensure non-contact measuring. Such optic measurement acquisition devices can be divided into categories: photogrammetry, silhouette methods, laser scanning, light projection, electromagnetic wave and hybrid methods (Vanags, 2003; Winsborough, 2001; Xu, 2002; Youngsook, 2005; D'Apuzzo, 2008).

Each method has its advantages and disadvantages (Wen, 2007; Devroye, 1998). In spite of the fact that laser scanning has been recognized as the most precise method and the gathered results are the most extensive (human body measurement data, a 3D virtual mannequin, a reflection of the actual texture, surface relief measurements, etc.), the light projection method is used more widely in the garment production industry since the equipment is much more cheaper than a laser scanner.

There is still not enough research and results as to use virtual mannequins for 3D garment designing. Mostly 3D scanning results are used to generate measures used in tailoring to use them in traditional or computer aided constructing methods (DOI, 2005; Dāboliņa 2007; Dekker, 1999; D'Apuzzo, 2008).

5. Limitations of human body 3D scanning

3D scanning of the human body can be used successfully in computer aided garment designing and individualized production (Buxton, 2006; CAD Modelling Ergonomics;

FitMe.Com; Hamamatsu Photonics K.K.; Hwang, 2001). Nevertheless the scanners have to be improved considerably - the data acquisition time has to be shortened, the way of displaying the scanned data has to be improved, the 3D scanner software has to be improved, etc (ISPRS, 2009; Istook, 2001; Simmons 2004; D'Apuzzo, 2003).

The scanning technologies are being improved constantly, the price has falls considerably comparing to previous developments, and nevertheless each system has individual imperfections (Siegmund, 2007; Sungmin, 2007).

Although it is possible to enumerate the deficiencies of each system, their data precision is sufficient so that 3D scanners can be considered as appropriate for anthropometrical data acquisition for garment designing.

Two researches connected with the limitations of 3D scanning have been described:

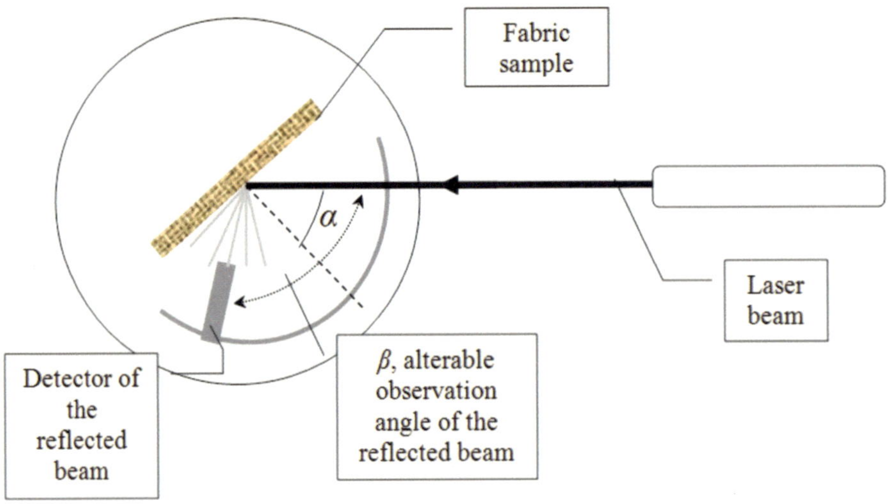

Fig. 6. Scheme of the reflection study experiment

The scanning systems for human body measure acquisition use different data acquisition ways: dynamic range (lights and darks), laser beams, etc. The experiment determines the laser beam reflective abilities of different textile materials and the curve characterising the reflectivity has been compared to the Lamberts' law diffuse reflectivity curve (Dāboliņa, 2008).

Studying the light reflections from different fabrics, essential deviations from the Lambert law were observed. Such deviations come from the geometry of the fabric surface (relief, texture, trim). Insignificant deviations from the standard curve can be observed on very smooth (bright) surfaces and uneven (relief) surfaces. Decorative elements - embroidery, applications can cause a too bright and uneven surface causing deviations from the standard division in these areas. If the underwear is decorated with crystals or other very bright materials, the reflection curve is very uneven with several extreme points. The reflectivity of different textile materials depending on the decoration varies from diffuse to mirror-reflectivity.

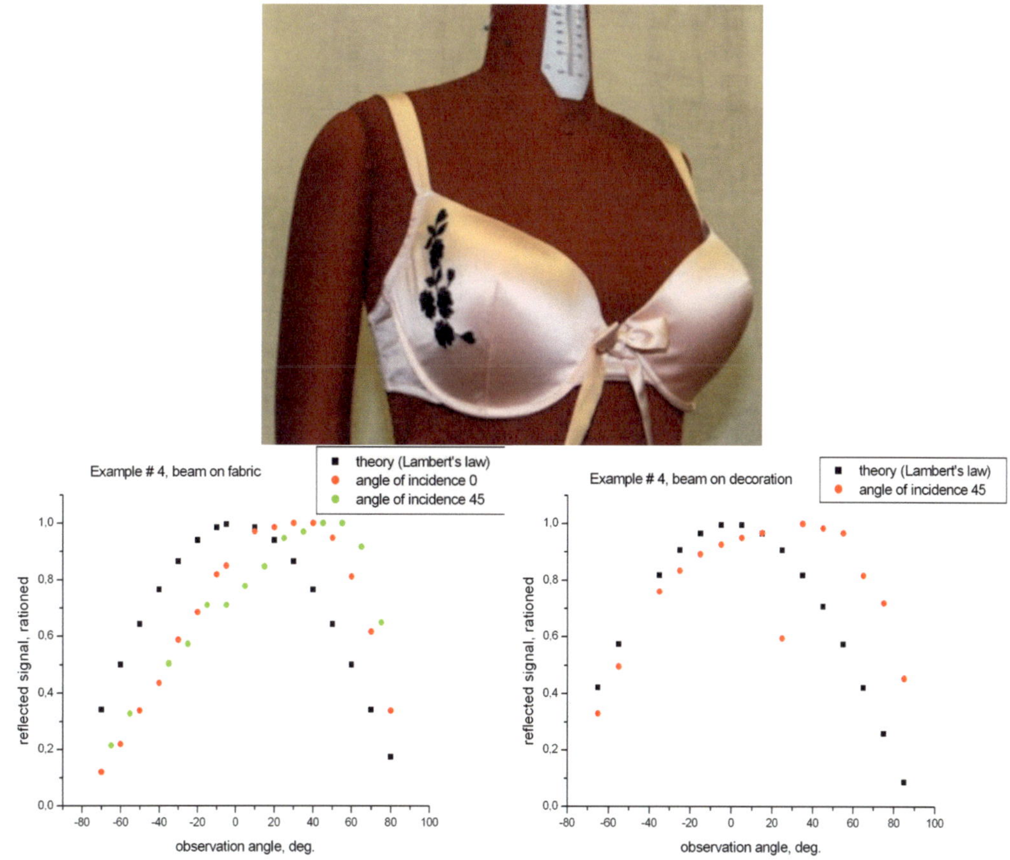

Fig. 7. An example of the results of the reflectivity study experiment: If the beam falls on a decorative element deviations from the diffuse division can be observed, this can be due to the brightness of the fabric. In this case there are significant changes in the division and a fall of the signal almost to the zero level has been observed (40 degree angle).

As a result of the research it can be concluded that smooth, but not bright underwear, without any decorative elements, has to be chosen for scanning. Underwear with decorative elements that can reflect or break the ray of light - crystals, glass particles, and pearls - should be used under no circumstances.

An analysis of the oscillations of the human body in rest state has been performed and the significance of these oscillations for 3D anthropometrical measurements have been studied (Fig.8.).

The experiment has been performed for three different postures of a person: back view, side view and front view. Since the front and back view analysis did not show any differences, the result of the analysis has been reflected for the side view and front view only. Photographing has been performed in two cycles.

In the first cycle differences in the posture have been evaluated photographing the person in one and the same posture every three seconds, for each posture. Afterwards the changes in the posture were analysed. The analysis of the front view and back view postures show little change in the posture. A person can oscillate in the range from 3 to 12 mm.

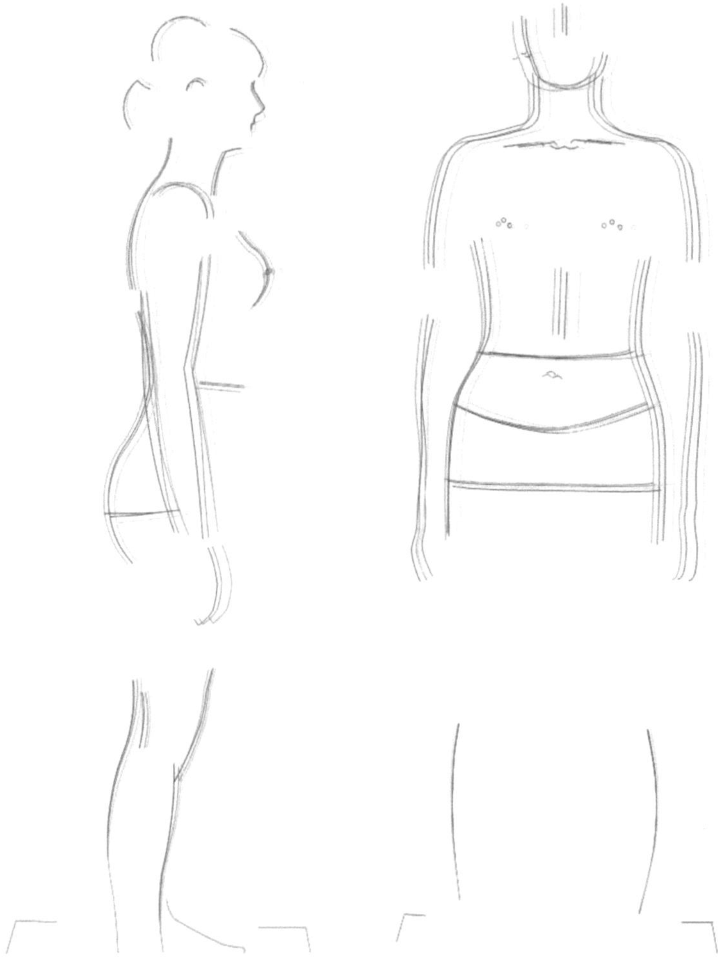

(a) (b)

Fig. 8. Change of the posture (analysis of five sequential positions): a) side view, b) front view

The side view oscillations are greater – those can vary in the range from 9 to 21 millimetres. Such a difference can be explained by the fact that ankles are more likely to move back and forth than sideways. The results of the analysis show that the volume of oscillations increases the higher the person is from the ground. In this case not only oscillations, but small changes in the positioning of the body and posture have been observed.

In the second photo analysis cycle posture changes were evaluated sequentially stepping off the platform and changing the position of the feet and the body by 90° as it is in scanning devices with change of posture. The range of the oscillations of the front and back views is from 10 to 40 millimetres, in its turn the side view oscillation range is from 11 to 51 millimetres while the feet and the ankles remain in a fixed position. Such oscillations are characterized not only by the change of posture, but also by the change of the stand and corpus position (EN ISO 15536-1; EN ISO 15536-2). The changes can affect the scanning process causing inaccuracies in the data (Gomes, 2009; Hsueh, 1997; Luhmann, 2006).

3D scanning has several advantages comparing to manual measurements - it is fast, sequential, and has a higher precision level. Using 3D scanning, no professional knowledge is needed to acquire the measurements - most of the systems generate the measures of the human body self-dependently (EN ISO 20685; EN ISO 7250). What makes 3D scanning so attractive is the fact that is a non-contact method, but it also has disadvantages - most of the systems cannot determine hidden areas (armpits, chin, etc.), as well as vague scanning contours. The latter one is mainly affected by the oscillations of the body in time. Therefore the scanning time should be shortened as much as possible.

6. Virtual environment and virtual reality

Clothing purchasing via catalogues, e-commerce, made to measure, etc. - all these innovations are evidence of manner how people likes to shop (Protopsaltou, 2002; Sayem, 2009). So the research and development of garment CAD/CAM systems are related to this preference - general tendency is to make 3D system for garment creation and virtual usage before real production. That is why we can assert for pretty sure - it will be possible to obtain, purchase, try on to our virtual avatar, checking ease and designing properties to self-chosen or self-designed garment in e-system.

One of the most telling examples of e-commerce is a system called Fits.me (with the same Internet address) created in Estonia. Fits.me is a virtual fitting room for online clothing retailers. It has brought together competences from diverse fields ranging from apparel design and anthropometrics to IT, robotics and engineering. The system allows evaluating the external looks of a model. The user can visualize a sketch of a human with the selected garment. 4 shirt models with different fittings form men and 1 model for women. At present the system works better for the male auditory, nevertheless the developers have promised to improve the system very soon.

There are several attempts to create virtual fashion show, a model in motion, a virtual twin and to try to fit the fashion garments for demonstration purposes, as well as the chosen garment on an Internet store, and at present there are already systems with the option to create movement imitating models of a person. For instance the 3D designing system 3D MAX Studio, Maya and other similar systems, have created templates to materialize the model. These systems are not connected to a direct usage in the garment production industry, nevertheless the result, although very simplified, is very similar to a virtual fashion show.

The creation of a virtual image of a person can be performed in two ways - a digitalized pattern created by an artist, a real scanned human body. By creating the human body manually it can seem lifeless and unreal, especially the facial trail, but the scanned image reflects the human proportions more realistic. Nevertheless the implementation of a virtual twin has to be performed following mathematical calculations, with the help of dynamic anthropometry and the use of appropriate computer software. To reflect the movements of a human body, a realistic reproduction of the operation of its muscles, joints and bonds is necessary. It can turn out to be very difficult if using a scanned human body reproduction one of the scanning imperfections appears - the hidden regions. Besides, the special pose of the human body necessary for scanning changes the external characteristics of the body and makes it inadequate for the natural posture. Human Solutions GmbH, one of the world's leading laser scanner producers, solves this problem by scanning people in a free, stately, unconstrained posture, detaching the extremities form each other and from the torso with the help of calculations afterwards. This method can have drawbacks in cases when due to the specific weight of the soft tissues the extremities of the person not only fit close to each other and the torso but are so close that they misshape each other.

The creation of such a realistic reproduction of the human body allows developing services available in the e-environment. For instance in the spring of 2011 the company Human Solutions (Germany) presented a virtual mirror that reflects the scanned virtual twin of a person which can be used to fit the chosen garment and evaluate the set. Although there are different e-commerce catalogues available in the computer environment, this type of fitting is a novelty and is expected to be a great success since the bothersome and exhausting garment fitting process is excluded. Ditto Vidya Human Solutions in cooperation with Assyst 3D have developed an innovative 3D system, that not only allows virtual "sewing", fitting and evaluation of a garment, but also define the technological placement of seam ease allowances, the pocket spread and even evaluate the functionality of button snap.

7. Conclusions

There is high level of pattern making systems. Modern computer aided designing software provides the possibility to avoid small operations and manual work, to raise precision, productivity and organize information flow. The usage of garment designing systems excludes the time consuming manual preparation of patterns, creation of layouts and relocation of written information. The computer systems are meant for the execution of every single process and the integration of all processes into one joint flow, for the organization of logistics and the mobility of work tasks. Computer systems allow making two dimensional as well as three dimensional product illustrations and visualizations. It is possible to create computer aided garment constructions, as well as gradations, and create a virtual first pattern of the model - such computer aided operations significantly decrease the time consumption and cost necessary to design a product. The costs of the product itself can be calculated with the help of the product management systems following the development parameters, the layout of patterns, textile expenditure, model complexity and specification, as well as previous experience of the company stored in a data base.

Although computer systems significantly facilitate the development of a product, the knowledge and skill of the user are still very important. One of the most important garment creation stages is constructing. Constructing is the reproduction of a spatial model (clothing) on a plane (construction); this transformation has to be reflexive when joining the parts of the construction a garment is originated. The creation of the drafts of the construction is the most complicated and responsible stage of garment designing, because a non-existent complicated spatial shape product surface layout has to be created (drawn). One of the most topical problems in garment designing has always been the search of garment designing methods scientifically reasoned, precise and as little as possible time and labour consuming. Several factors depend on a precise development of garment surface layout - material expenditure, garment set quality, labour intensity level, the aesthetical and hygienic characteristics of the finished product.

The specialists in the different fields are interested in reproducing of human figure in a virtual environment: designers, what uses information of ergonomics (engineering, interior design), animation creators, and also medicine and apparel designers. There is a chain of problems in the production of clothes which is related to the features of the figure of a customer to get maximally conformable clothes. It is very important to have exact human body measurements without significant mistakes for garment construction. The traditional mass production ever decreases the volumes of series, the production becomes more elastic and the choice of goods expands; the wear time decreases. Along with the serial production, individual production becomes more and more popular. The current economic situation shifts the search for labour more and more to the East, but the creation of individually oriented products could make it possible to maintain working places and production units in Europe. People will be willing to pay more for this type of clothing and receive it in a possibly short term. Thereby the promotion of individualized production is affected by social and economic aspects.

The research of scientists regarding the improvement and development of 3D garment designing is directed into different directions:

The development of mass customization process schemes;

The development of a virtual twin;

The study of coherence and definition of projection ease allowances;

The improvement of fabric visualization means.

The garment production companies mostly support the development of the company and the introduction of CAD/CAM systems, since these ensure a higher product quality, higher productivity, humanization of the working process, a more elastic production process and process control. Nevertheless the distribution and introduction of computerized systems in companies of all levels (small and large) can be a problem because of the system costs as well as the incompetence of the employees.

8. References

3D Ouest Ltd. [Live]. - Korux human body laser scanning technology. - www.3douest.com. - France.

3D-Shape GmbH [Live]. - Body and Face Scan Stripes projection technology. - www.3d-shape.com. - Germany.

4D Culture Inc. [Live]. - 4D Culture 3D human body laser scanning system. - www.4Dculture.com. - South Korea.

AceApparel CAD/CAM [Live] // Clothing designing. – the company was established 2001 by Mo Deok Won. - www.pattern-cad.com.

Assol CAD/CAM [Live] // Clothing designing. - Centre of Applied Computer Technologies ASSOL; Moscow Institute of Physics and Technology, Dr. Gennadij Andreev. - www.assol.mipt.ru.

Assyst CAD/CAM [Live] // Clothing designing. - Assyst-bullmer. - www.assyst-intl.com.

Audaces CAD/CAM [Live] // Clothing designing. - fashion technology. - www.audaces.com.

Beazley Alison & Bond Terry Computer-aided pattern design & product development [Book]. - UK: Blackwell Publishing, 2003. - p. 220. - ISBN 1-4051-0283-7.

Bernina [Live] // Clothing designing. - OptiTex/Siemens#3: FIT Technology Bernina MyLabel. - www.berninamylabel.com.

Bodymetrics Ltd. [Live]. - 3D body data analysis software. - www.bodymetrics.com. - UK.

Buxton Bernard Dekker Laura, Douros Ioannis, Vassilev Tsvetomir Reconstruction and Interpretation of 3D Whole Body Surface Images [Report]. - Gower Street London : Department of Computer Science University College London, 2006. - WC1E 6BT United Kingdom.

CAD Modelling Ergonomics S.r.l. [Live]. - Antrophometrics dummies by silhouette extracting technology. - www.cadmodelling.it.

Comtense CAD/CAM [Live] // Clothing designing. - © Комтенс. - www.comtense.ru.

Cyberware Inc. [Live]. - Cyberware whole body 3D laser scanner technology. - www.cyberware.com. - USA.

Dāboliņa I., Blūms J. and Viļumsone A. Lāzera stara plūsmas atstarošanas izpēte veļas materiālos/ A study of the laser beam reflections on underwear materials [Magazine] // RTU scientific articles. - Riga: Riga Technical University, 2008. – part 9: Material Science 3. - p. 62-70 - ISSN 1691-3132-2008-3132.

Dāboliņa Inga and Viļumsone Ausma Trīsdimensiju antropometriskā modelēšana/ Three dimensional anthropometrical modelling [Article] // RTU scientific articles, 2007. - Part 9: Material Science, Vol. 2, p. 103-110. - ISSN 1691-3132-2007-2.

D'Apuzzo Nicola Feasibility study: Full Body Scanning, Virtual-Try-On, Face Scanning, Virtual-Make-Over with application in apparel. [Report]. - Zürich, Switzerland: Hometrica Consulting, 2008.

D'Apuzzo Nicola Recent Advances in 3D Full Body Scanning With Applications to Fashion and Apparel [Article] // Optical 3-D Measurement Techniques IX. - Vienna, Austria: 2009. - p. 10.

D'Apuzzo Nicola Surface Measurement and Tracking of Human Body Parts from Multi Station Video Sequences [Report]: Doctoral thesis. - Zurich: Swiss Federal Institute of Technology Zurich, 2003. - p. 148. - ISSN 0252-93355; ISBN 3-906467-44-9.

Dekker L., Douros I., Buxton B. F., Treleaven P. Building Symbolic Information for 3D Human Body Modelling from Range Data [Article] // Proceedings of the Second International Conference on 3-D Digital Imaging and Modelling. - Ottawa, Canada: [no title], October, 1999 - IEEE Computer Society, p. 388 - 397.

Devroye L., Mucke E. P. and Binhai Zhu A Note on Point Location in Delaunay Triangulations of Random Points [Magazine] // Algorithmica (22) - Springer-Verlag New York Inc, 1998. - p. 477 – 482.

Digimask Ltd [Live], Face modelling software hybrid technology from images., www.digimask.com.

DOI Generating unified model for dressed virtual humans [Report]. -: Visual Comput, 2005, p. 522 - 531. - DOI 10.1007/s00371-005-0339-6.

EN ISO 15536-1 Ergonomika. Datormanekeni un ķermeņa maketi. 1.daļa: Vispārīgās prasības./Ergonomics-Computer manikins and body templates - Part 1: General requirements. [Report]. - Brussels: CEN - European Committee for Standardization, 2005. - ISO 15536-1:2005.

EN ISO 15536-2 Ergonomika. Datormanekeni un ķermeņa maketi. 2.daļa: Kompjūtermanekenu sistēmu funkciju verifikācija un izmēru validācija./Ergonomics-Computer manikins and body templates - Part2: Verification of functions and validation of dimensions for computer manikin sist. [Report]. - Brussels : CEN - European Committee for Standardization, 2007. - ISO 15536-2:2007.

EN ISO 20685 3D skenēšanas metodoloģijas starptautiski saderīgām antropometrisko datu bāzēm/ 3D scanning methodologies for internationally compatible anthropometric databases [Report]. - Brussels: CEN - European Committee for Standardization, 2005. - ISO 20685:2005.

EN ISO 7250 Cilvēka ķermeņa pamatizmēri tehniskiem projektiem/ Basic human body measurements for technological design [Report]. - Brussels: CEN - European Committee for Standardization, 1997.

Fan J., Yu W., Hunter L. Clothing appearance and fit: Science and technology [Book]. - Cambridge, England: Woodhead Publishing Limited, 2004. - p. 240. - ISBN 0-8493-2594-3.

FashionCad CAD/CAM [Live] // Clothing designing. - Cad Cam Solutions Australia Pty. Ltd. - www.fashioncad.net.

FitMe.Com Inc. [Live]. - Size Genie 3D software. - www.fitme.com. - USA.

Gemini CAD/CAM [Live] // Clothing designing. - Contact person for distributors: Mr. Traian LUCA. - www.geminicad.com.

Gerber CAD/CAM [Live] // Clothing designing, founder - Joseph Gerber. - www.gerbertechnology.com.

GFai Gesellschaft zur Forderung angewandter Informatik e.V. [Live]. - Full body scanner hybrid technology stripes projection and silhouette extraction. - www.gfai.de.

Gomes Abel J.P., Voiculescu, I., Jorge, J., Wyvill, B., Galbraith, C. Implicit Curves and Surfaces: Mathematics, Data Structures and Algorithms [Book]. - [no publ. ind.] : Springer-Verlag London Limited, 2009. - p. 351. - ISBN 978-1-84882-405-8; DOI 10.1007/978-1-84882-406-5.

Grafis CAD/CAM [Live] // Clothing designing. - Partner authorised to represent: Dr. Kerstin Friedrich, Responsible for the content of this site: Volker Friedrich. – June 2009. - www.grafis.de.

Hamamatsu Photonics K.K. [Live]. - Hamamatsu bodyline full body laser scanning. - http://www.hamamatsu.com.

Hamano Engineering Co. Ltd. [Live]. - Hamano laser scanning technology. - www.voxelan.co.jp.

Hannelore Eberle, Hermann Hermeling, Hornberger Marianne, et.al. Clothing Technology [Book] / red. Roland Kilgus. - Wuppertal, Germany: Verlag Europa-Lehrmittel, 1999, 2nd English Edition, p. 256. - ISBN 3-8085-6222-6.

Hsueh Wen-Jean & Antonsson Erik K. Automatic high-resolution optoelectronic photogrammetric 3D surface geometry acquisition system [Article] // Machine Vision and Applications. : Springer Verlag Group, 1997, 10:98 – 113, p. 98 - 113.

Human Solutions GmbH [Live]. - 3D human body measurement software. - www.human-solutions.com. - Germany.

Hwang Su-Jeong Three dimensional body scanning systems with potential for use in the apparel industry [Article]. - Raleigh, 2001. - p. 63.

InSpeck Inc. [Live]. - 3D Capturor human body stripes projection scanning, www.inspeck.com, Canada.

Intellifit Corporation [Live]. - Cilvēka ķermeņa skenēšana ar elektromagnētisko viļņu metodi/ Scanning the human body with the electromagnetic wave method, www.corp.intellifit.com.

InvenTex CAD/CAM [Live] // Clothing designing, developed & manufactured by SEMACO company, 2009, www.inventex.eu.

ISPRS International Society for Photogrammetry and Remote Sensing [Live], 2009 – January 23, 2010, www.isprs.org.

Istook Cynthia L. Hwang Su-Jeong 3D body scanning systems with application to the apparel industry [Article] // Journal of Fashion Marketing and Management.: Henry Stewart Publications 1361-2026, 2001, Vol. II, p. 120 - 132.

Jindex CAD [Live] // Apģērbu projektēšana/ Clothing designing, Hong Kong Jindex Stock Co. Limted, www.jindex.net.

Kang Tae Jin and Kim Sung Min Optimized garment pattern generation based on three-dimensional anthropometric measurement [Magazine] // International Journal of Clothing Science and Technology. - 0955-6222: MCB University Press Ltd, 2000 - 4, Vol. 12, p. 240 -254. - ISSN: 0955-6222.

Koblakova E.B., Ivleva G.S. and Romanov V.E. Garment construction within CAD systems. [Book] Moscow 1988 – Vol. 4. p. 464. - ISBN 5-7088-0239-1.

Lectra CAD/CAM [Live] // Apģērbu projektēšana/ Clothing designing. - Publishing Director: Daniel HARARI. - 2009. - www.lectra.com.

Lectra Ltd. Kaledo Style or Kaledo Collection? [Report]. - France : Lectra Ltd., June 2009. - p. 7. - MS PowerPoint presentation.

Leko CAD/CAM [Live] // Apģērbu projektēšana/ Clothing designing. - Vilar Soft. - www.latelye.ru.

Luhmann T, Robson S and S. Kyle, I., Harley Close Range Photogrammetry. Principles, Methods and Applications. [Book]. - Scotland, UK: Whittles Publishing, 2006. - p. 510. - ISBN 1-870325-50-8.

OptiTex CAD/CAM [Live] // Apģērbu projektēšana, imitācija/ Clothing designing and imitation. - President and CEO - Ran Machtinger. - www.optitex.com.

PadSystem CAD/CAM [Live] // Apģērbu projektēšana, imitācija/ Clothing designing and imitation. - PAD System International Limited. - www.padsystem.com.

Pavlovskaya V. CAD „Comtense" usage for garment development. [Magazine] Kurer Moscow: , March 2009. - 4. - p. 9 - 10.

Protopsaltou D., Luible C., Arevalo M., Magnenat-Thalmann N. A body and garment creation method for an Internet based virtual fitting room [Report]. – Proceedings of the 2002 International Conference on Computer Graphics, pp. 105-122, 2002

Razdomahins Nikolajs, Viļumsone Ausma and Dāboliņa Inga CAD OF THE CLOTHING INDUSTRY [Article] // RTU Scientific article corpus. - Riga: 2007. – Textile and Clothing Technology – part 9: Material Science, Vol. 2. - p. 111 - 116.

Razdomakhin N.N. 3D CAD for fashion industry. [Book]. - St. Petersburg: STAPRIM, 2006. - p. 134.

Razdomakhin N.N. et.al. Womens apparel design in 3D CAD STAPRIM for made to measure dressmaking and production. [Report]. – St. Petersburg: p. 133, 2003.

RichPeace CAD/CAM [Live] // Apģērbu projektēšana/ Clothing desinging. - Richpeace Group Co., Limited. - www.richpeace.com.

Rupp Martin & Kirchdörfer Elfriede Possibilities and capabilities of 3D-body-scanning systems for the purpose of risk assessment [Report]. - Germany : Bekleidungsphysiologisches Institut Hohenstein, Department of Clothing Technology, 2005. - p. 23. - HETRA RfP C1.6 Human Health Projects - Consumer Exposure.

Sanyo Electric Co. ltd [Live]. - Hibrīdsistēma 3D skenēšanai izmantojot silueta nolasīšanu un kodētas gaismas projekciju/ Hybrid System for 3D Scanning Using Silhouette Readings and Coded Light Projection. - www.sanyo.co.jp; www.pierimo.net.

Sayem Abu Sadat Muhammad 3D Design of Garments [Report]. - UK: University of Manchester, Department of Textiles, 2009. - Submitted to IMB Innovation Award 2009.

Scharrenbroich Christine Mehr Brust, Mehr Taille, Mehr Hüfte [Article] // FRANKFURTER ALLGEMEINE ZEITUNG. - 2009. Part 9, Vol. 93.

Siegmund Jana et.al. Development of parametric virtual dummies; 3D patterning of corsetry [Magazine] // Textile Network. - Dresden: apparel, 2007, 7 - 8. - TU Dresden.

Simmons Karla, Istook Cynthia L. & Devarajan Priya Female Figure Identification Technique (FFIT) for Apparel Part1: Describing Female Shapes [Article] // Journal of Textile and Apparel Technology and Management. – 2004, 4. Vol. I. p. 16.

Singular Inversions FaceGen [Live]. - Face modeller software hybrid image technology. - www.facegen.com.

Staprim CAD/CAM [Live] // Apģērbu projektēšana/ Clothing Designing. - founder&developer Раздомахин Н.Н. - www.staprim.com.

Sungmin Kim and Chang Kyu Park Basic garment pattern generation using geometric modelling method [Magazine]. - South Korea: Emerald Group Publishing Limited, 2007. - Vol. 19. No.1. p. 7 - 17. - DOI 10.1108/09556220710717017.

Szabó Orsolya Nagy & Tamás Péter SYLVIE® 3d System Using For Skirt And Trousers Constructions [Report]. - Biela,Italy : Autex 2008, 2008. p. 7.

TanyaGeo CAD/CAM [Live] // Apģērbu projektēšana/ Clothing designing. - Tanya Geometrik Pvt. Ltd. - www.tanyageo.com.

Telmat Industries [Live]. - Symcad full body scanner stripes projection technology. - www.telmat.com, www.symcad.com. - France.

Vanags Valdis Fotogrammetrija/ Photogrammetry [Book]. -: LR Valsts zemes dienests, 2003. - p. 275. - ISBN10: 9984950891; ISBN13: 9789984950891 .

Viļumsone Ausma Adaptējamas automatizētas apģērbu konstruēšanas sistēmas struktūras un algoritmu izstrāde/ Development of a structure and algorithms of an adaptable computer aided apparel designing system [Report] : Doctoral thesis/ Engineering sciences, Textile Technologies and Machines. - Riga: RTU, 1993. p. 129. - Nr.000198748.

Viļumsone Ausma and Dāboliņa Inga The Estimation and Approbation of 3D Garment Designing and Photo Measurement Method [Article] // 4th INTERNATIONAL TEXTILE, CLOTHING & DESIGN CONFERENCE - Magic World of Textiles. - [no publ. ind.] : Faculty of Textile Technology, University of Zagreb, Zagreb, Croatia, October 2008 - Book of proceedings of the 4rd INTERNATIONAL TEXTILE, CLOTHING & DESIGN CONFERENCE – Magic World of Textiles. - p. 676 - 681.

Viļumsone Ausma and Dāboliņa Inga The Possibilities of Garment 3D Designing [Conference] // XI International Izmir Textile and Apparel Symposium. - Izmir: Ege University Textile Engineering Department, Year 2007. - p. 161 - 170. - Proceedings.

VisImage Systems Inc. [Live]. - Human body measurement silhouette extraction technology. - www.vis.ca.

Vitronic Stein Bildverarbeitungssysteme GmbH [Live] // Vitus laser scanning technology. - http://www.vitronic.de/. - Germany.

Wen Z., Li M., Li Y., Guo Y. and Wang K. Delaunay triangulation with partial least squares projection to latent structures: a model for G-protein coupled receptors classification and fast structure recognition [Magazine] // Amino Acids (2007) 32. - 2007. - DOI 10.1007/s00726-.

Wicks and Wilson Limited [Live]. - Wicks and Wilson human body scanning stripes projection technology. - www.wwl.co.uk. - England.

WildGinger CAD/CAM [Live] // Apģērbu projektēšana/ Clothing designing. - President - Dr. Lisa Shanley. - www.wildginger.com.

Winsborough Stuart An Insight into the Design, Manufacture and Practical Use of a 3D Body Scanning System [Report]. - England : Wicks and Wilson Limited, 2006. – p. 11.

Winsborough Stuart Towards Photo-realistic 3D Image Capture [Report]. - England: Wicks and Wilson Limited, 2001. - Scanning 2001 – TriForm, p. 18.

Xu B. et.al. Three-dimensional body scanning system for apparel mass-customization [Magazine]. -: The University of Texas at Austin Department of Human Ecology Optic Engineering, 2002. - 41(7). - p. 1475 - 1479.

XX Production online GmbH [Live]. - Hardware and software solutions for body scanning hybrid technology laser spot and 5 manual measurements. - www.xxpo.de; www.bodyscanningcrm.com.

Yan He and Fiorito Susan S. CAD/CAM diffusion and infusion in the US apparel industry [Magazine] // Journal of Fashion Marketing and Management. - USA: Emerald Group Publishing Limited 1361-2026, 2007. - 2: Vol. 11. - p. 238 - 245. DOI 10.1108/13612020710751400.

Youngsook Cho, Okada, Naoko; Park, Hyejun; Takatera, Masayuki; Inui, Shigeru; Shimizu, Yoshio. An interactive body model for individual pattern making [Article] // Emerald International Journal of Clothing Science and Technology. - 2005 – II, Vol. 17. - p. 91 - 99.

4

Human Visual Field and Navigational Strategies

J. Antonio Aznar-Casanova[1,2], Nelson Torro-Alves[3] and José A. da Silva[4]
[1]*Faculty of Psychology, University of Barcelona,*
[2]*Institute for Brain, Cognition and Behaviour (IR3C),*
[3]*Universidade Federal da Paraíba, João Pessoa,*
[4]*Universidade de São Paulo, Ribeirão Preto,*
[1,2]*Spain*
[3,4]*Brazil*

1. Introduction

Spatial navigation is an important cognitive ability which has contributed to the survival of animal species by allowing them to locate sources of the food, water and shelter (Epstein, 2008). In order to navigate, animals and humans use environmental landmarks as references to calculate their own position and the location of targets in the environment. In such cases, landmarks are used to estimate distances and directions of objects and targets (for a review of landmark navigation in vertebrates see Rozhok, 2008).

In a classic study, Morris (1981) demonstrated that rats could locate an object that they were unable to see, hear or touch by using spatial landmarks. In the test situation, rats learned to escape from the water by swimming to an invisible platform located under the water line. Subsequent tests done without the platform corroborated those findings. Further research using a virtual version of the Morris water maze showed that humans use landmarks in a similar way to locate a hidden goal (Astur, et al., 1998). Similarly, Chamizo et al. (2003) and Artigas et al. (2005) used virtual reality environments in order to study spatial navigation characteristics in humans.

Two experimental procedures have been commonly used to study human and animal spatial navigation based on landmarks. After a training period in which individuals learn to navigate to locate a target, the experimenter changes the experimental setting by 1) increasing the distance between landmarks (Tinbergen, 1972) or 2) removing one or more landmarks from the environment (Collett, et al., 1986).

Collett et al. (1986) studied spatial navigation in gerbils by training them to find hidden food in an arena. As shown in Figure 1A, food was located between two identical landmarks. After learning acquisition, trials were done without food. When tested in the presence of only one landmark (removing procedure), the gerbils searched for food on the left and right sides of the landmark, maintaining the corresponding distance and direction from it (Figure 1B). In a second test, the distance between landmarks was increased (expanding procedure) and the gerbils searched for food in two different locations but also maintained distance and direction with regard to the landmarks (Figure 1C). Collet et al. (1986) concluded that gerbils calculated the distance and direction of the food by using each landmark independently. In this case, search behaviour could be explained by a vectorial summation model in which gerbils use the learned vectors (between the goal and the landmarks) to calculate the direction and distance of the food. The vectors are added up and the resulting vector converges on a certain part of the space that corresponds to the location of the food.

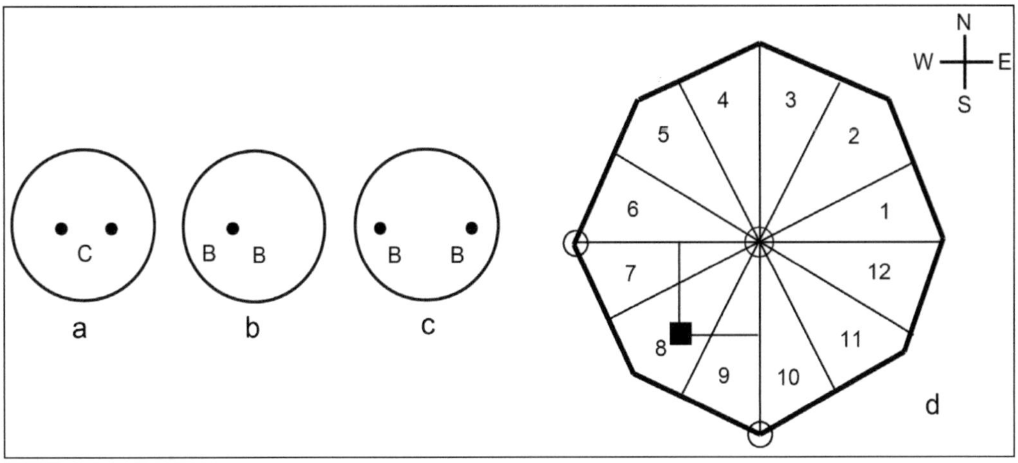

Fig. 1. Layout of the arena (left panel) and the virtual pool (right panel). In the left panel, landmarks are represented by black dots. The letter "a" shows the experimental setting in the training trials, "b" represents the situation in which one of the landmarks was removed, and "c" shows the condition in which the landmarks were separated. Capital letters "C" and "B" respectively represent the food and the regions where the animals search for the food during the test. The virtual pool used in this experiment is shown in the right panel ("d"). A black square represents the platform and the two empty circles represent the landmarks. The virtual pool was divided into 12 sectors. The central region of the pool was defined as the 0th sector.

Subsequent research, however, led to different results. Cheng (1988, 1989) trained pigeons in the presence of two landmarks. After acquisition, the pigeons were tested with the landmarks being moved further away and it was verified that they search for the food in midline between the new positions of the landmarks. Cheng assumed that pigeons navigate using an average vector that indicates the position of the food with regard to the animal.

MacDonald et al. (2004) applied the procedure of separating landmarks in a study with marmoset monkeys, children and adult humans. They concluded that a "middle rule" strategy is the common navigational strategy used by adults. However, children and primates used a different strategy, preferring to search near the landmarks. From these results, authors suggested that "among vertebrates, adult humans appear to be outliers" MacDonald et al. (2004) suggest that two strategies can be adopted by the participants in a virtual reality environment: a) encoding the goal location by means of its spatial relation with regard to the landmarks (configural strategy); and b) encoding a vector from each landmark to the goal (elemental strategy). Only the configural strategy elicits the use of the "middle rule", i.e. navigating using the resulting vector as a reference.

In this study we use a particular virtual reality environment to investigate spatial navigation in human adults in two viewing conditions. In the first, participants could simultaneously see both landmarks of the virtual environment which inform about the location of the goal (simultaneous vision). In the second, participants could see only one landmark at a time (sequential vision). Basically, conditions differed with regard to the amplitude of the visual fields, which might influence the strategy adopted by the participant to navigate in the virtual space and locate the goal. When people have visual access to both landmarks, they can use all relevant information to navigate. However, when people see only one landmark at a time, they need to integrate the partial viewings of the environment in order to reconstruct the visual space. Consequently, simultaneous and sequential vision tasks involve different cognitive demands.

In order to investigate the spatial learning in those visual conditions we used a virtual reality model of the Morris water maze (Morris, 1981) adapted for a human task (see Chamizo, et al., 2003 and Artigas, et al., 2005). Participants were trained to locate a hidden platform in the presence of two landmarks. In Experiment 1 one of the landmarks was removed (removing procedure), and in Experiment 2 the distance between landmarks was increased (increasing procedure). In both experiments participants were tested in simultaneous and sequential vision conditions. After the training period, the platform was removed and the time spent in each sector of the platform was registered.

We expected that the simultaneous vision of the two landmarks would promote a configural strategy so that participants would spend more time searching for the platform in the area between the landmarks ("middle rule"). The successive viewing task, on the other hand, would promote the use of an elemental strategy in which participants would spend more time searching in the adjacent regions, i.e. applying the "connecting cues rule" (from landmark to landmark). The results of these two experiments converge in the same direction, suggesting that different navigational strategies depend on visual conditions.

2. Experiment 1

2.1 Method

2.1.1 Participants

Forty-seven students of psychology at the University of Barcelona ranging in age from 22 to 24 years old took part in the experiment. Twenty-four participants were assigned to Group 1 (simultaneous vision) and performed the location task using a visual field of 90°, which allowed both landmarks to be viewed simultaneously. Twenty-three students were assigned to Group 2 (sequential vision) and performed the task using a visual field of 30°, which allowed only one landmark at a time to be viewed. The study was approved by the institutional ethical committee of the University of Barcelona in accordance with the ethical standards laid down in the 1964 Declaration of Helsinki and students received course credits to take part in the experiment.

2.1.2 Materials and apparatus

The experiment was conducted in a room containing four individual soundproofed compartments equipped with a PC computer (Pentium IV 2.4 GHz) connected to a 15" monitor. Headphones were used to present sound in the experimental task. The computers were equipped with an ATI Radeon 9200 Graphics Card, which allows graphics acceleration and high resolution. Experiments were programmed in C++/Open GL, using a software interface for 3D graphics, with hardware developed by Silicon Graphics. The program controlled the virtual environment and the auditory information (background sound and positive and negative feedback) and registered the time taken to reach the platform. The positive feedback consisted of a brief three-second song ("That's all folks") and the negative auditory feedback consisted of an unpleasant melody (the sound of mournful bells). The auditory background sound was slightly unpleasant in order to generate some distress in the students and reproduce the conditions of an escape task. Participants used the keyboard arrow keys ("up", "down", "left" and "right") to navigate in the virtual environment.

The virtual space was an octagonal swimming pool (radius = 100 units) situated in the middle of the virtual space and surrounded by a pale blue surface (sky). Objects were placed hanging from an invisible ceiling. A circular platform (radius = 8 units) could be placed in the pool below the surface of the water (i.e. an invisible platform). Two spheres (pink and green) were used as landmarks (diameter = 20 units). The pool was divided into 12 sectors of 30°. The platform was placed in sector 8, perpendicular to the landmark (Figure 1d). The participants started the experiment in the centre of the pool (0th sector).

2.1.3 Procedure

Participants were tested in groups of four individuals and received the following instructions: "In this experiment you will be swimming for a long time in a circular pool from which you want to escape. You are very tired and you will only rest if you find the floating platform. You will see the platform only in the first trial. In the following trials, the platform will be hidden

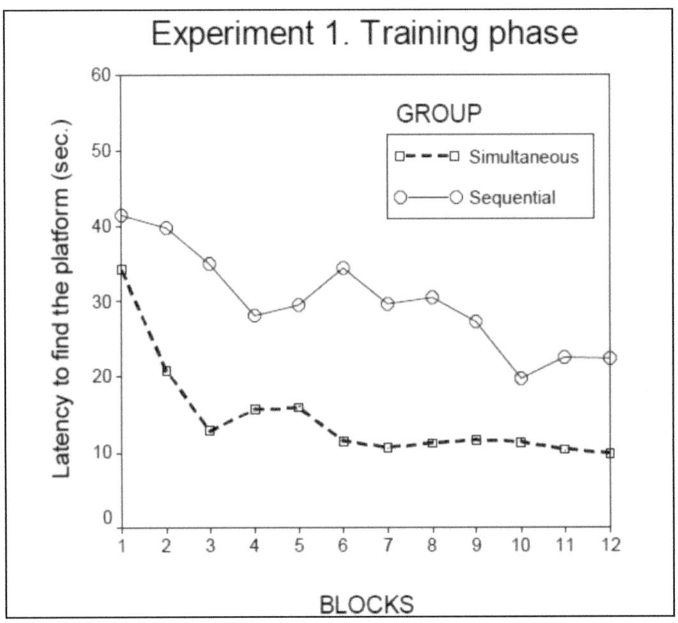

Fig. 2. Mean escape latencies of the groups of participants with simultaneous and sequential vision of the landmarks.

but located in the same position with regard to the other objects. Occasionally only one object will be presented. Your goal in the task consists of reaching the platform."

After the training period, participants find themselves in the middle of the pool (0th sector) facing a different direction each time (NE, SE, SW or NW). In the "escape trials" the platform was hidden and in the "final test trial" the platform was absent. Landmarks consisted of the two similar spheres of different colors, with an angular separation of 90º. Participants performed 24 trials with an inter-trial interval of 10 sec. Participants had 60 s to find the platform. When they reached the goal a positive feedback was presented (song "That's all folks"). Otherwise, if they could not find the platform, a mournful sound was presented.

After acquisition, test trials were done. Half of the participants performed the search task with only one landmark. The other half did the task with both landmarks being presented in the virtual pool. A measure of interest was the time spent in the relevant sector of the pool (8th sector) which contained the platform. Participants had 60 s to search, but only the first 20 s were included in data analysis. The time spent in the different sectors of the pool was taken as a dependent variable.

3. Results and discussion

An analysis of variance of escape latencies, with "groups" (simultaneous and sequential vision) and "blocks of trials" as factors, revealed a main effect for "groups" [$F(1,45) = 23.27$, $p < .001$] and "blocks of trials" [$F(11,495) = 13.99$; $p < .001$], and a statistically significant interaction between "groups" and "blocks of trials" [$F(11,495) = 2.28$ $p < .014$]. Figure 2 shows the mean escape latencies during acquisition. Although participants improved their performance in the course of the experiment, the group with simultaneous vision reached an asymptotic level after three blocks of trials. The group with sequential vision took more blocks to reach an asymptotic level. These data suggest that simultaneous access to both landmarks improves spatial navigation.

An additional analysis of variance was conducted with "groups" (simultaneous and sequential vision), and "types of test" (two landmarks or one landmark) as between factors, and "sectors" of the pool as a within factor. Figure 3A shows the time spent in sectors 5 to 11 for each group in the test trial with one landmark. Figure 3B shows the time spent in the test trial with the two landmarks.

This analysis showed a significant main effect of the variables "types of test" [$F(1,43) = 7.46$, $p < .009$] and sectors [$F(6,258)=16.17$, $p < .001$]. Data analysis also showed statistically significant interactions between "sectors" and "types of test" [$F(6,258)=2.19$, $p < .04$] and "sectors" and "groups" [$F(6,258)=10.53$, $p < .001$], and a second order interaction between "sectors", "groups" and "types of test" [$F(6,258)=2.58$, $p < .02$].

Post hoc tests indicated that the type of test (one or two landmarks) did not affect the time spent in sectors 7, 8 and 9 in the simultaneous ($p < .128$) and sequential ($p < .082$) viewing conditions. Results also showed that, in both types of test, participants with simultaneous vision spent more time in the relevant sector (8th) ($p < .007$). For the group with sequential vision, no differences were found between types of test (one or two landmarks) with regard to the time spent in the 8th sector.

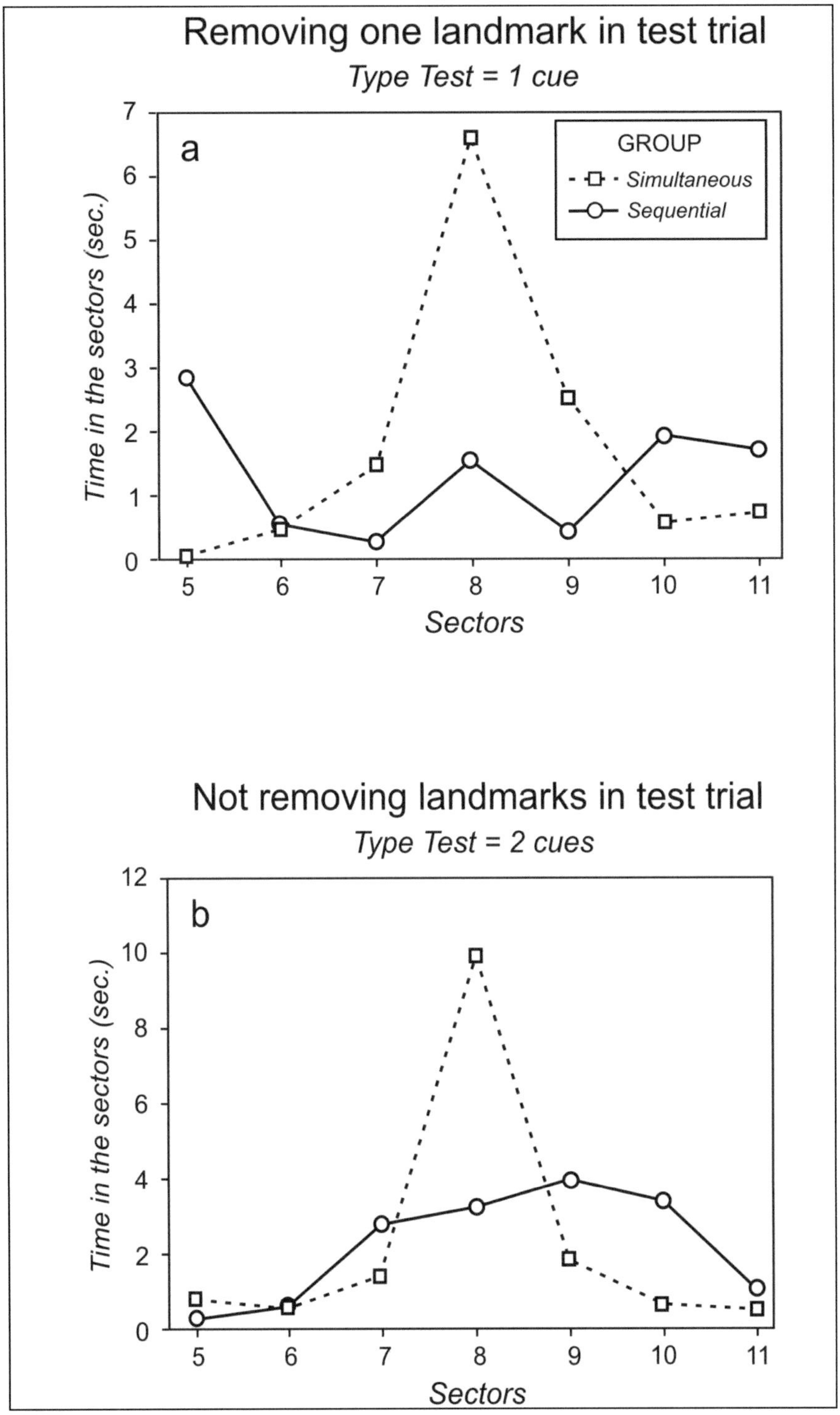
Removing one landmark in test trial
Type Test = 1 cue
a
GROUP
Simultaneous
Sequential
Time in the sectors (sec.)
0
1
2
3
4
5
6
7
5
6
7
8
9
10
11
Sectors
Not removing landmarks in test trial
Type Test = 2 cues
b
Time in the sectors (sec.)
0
2
4
6
8
10
12
5
6
7
8
9
10
11
Sectors

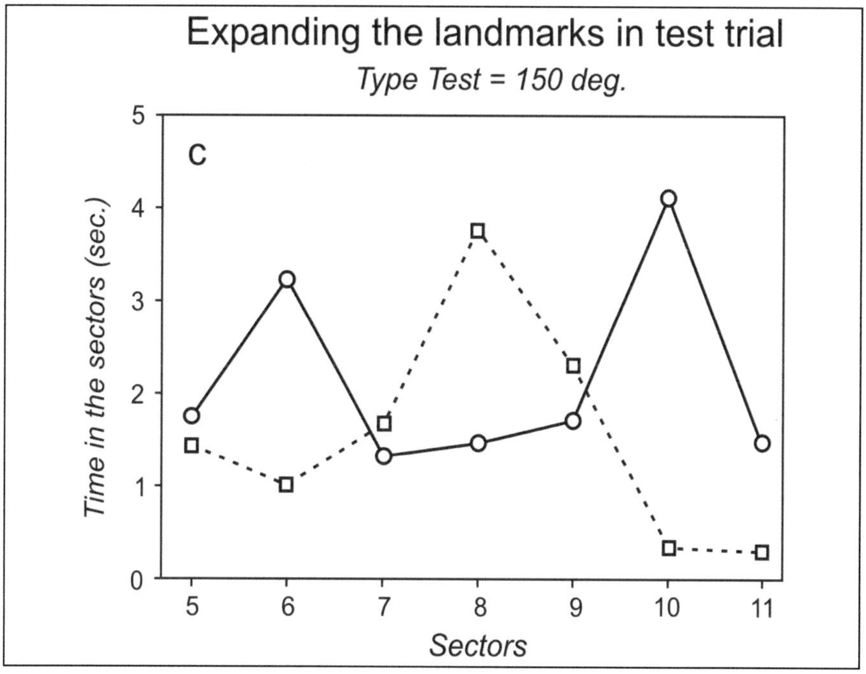

Fig. 3. Mean time spent in seven important sectors of the pool for the two groups with simultaneous and sequential vision of the landmarks. Panel "a" presents the results of Experiment 1, in which a landmark was removed during the test trial. Panel "b" represents the situation in which the test trial was identical to the training trial. Panel "c" corresponds to the results of Experiment 2, in which the distance between the landmarks was increased in the test trial.

Finally, *post hoc* tests revealed that in the simultaneous vision group for one landmark, participants differed only in the time spent between the 7th and 8th sectors [$t(11)= 2.82$; $p < .017$]. However, in the case of the same group with two landmarks, *post hoc* tests indicated differences between the 7th and 8th sectors [$t(11)= 5.01$; $p < .001$] and between the 8th and 9th sectors [$t(11)= 4.51$; $p < .001$]. With regard to the sequential vision group, no differences for the time spent in sectors 7, 8 and 9 were found.

Since no difference between escape and test trial was found, we considered it would be interesting to analyze the time spent at the starting point position as a function of the visual conditions. An ANOVA with "groups" (simultaneous and sequential vision) and "types of test" (one or two landmarks) as factors were conducted, using the time spent in the 0th sector (starting-point) as the dependent variable. Results revealed that only the factor "types of test" was significant [$F(1,43)=7.33$; $p< .010$]. Both groups spent more time at the starting point during the trial test (Figure 4).

In summary, a comparison of the viewing conditions, as we can see in Figure 3, clearly demonstrates that participants make use of two different strategies depending on whether they can see both landmarks simultaneously or just one at a time. In the test with one or two landmarks, the group with simultaneous vision spent more time looking for the goal in the 8th sector, while the subjects of the group with sequential vision spent their time in a different way, exploring the 8th but also the adjacent 7th and 9th sectors. As we predicted, participants of the sequential vision group seem to use an elemental strategy, applying the "connecting cues" rule (from landmark to landmark). In Experiment 2, we investigated the effect of the increasing procedure on the navigation strategies adopted in the task.

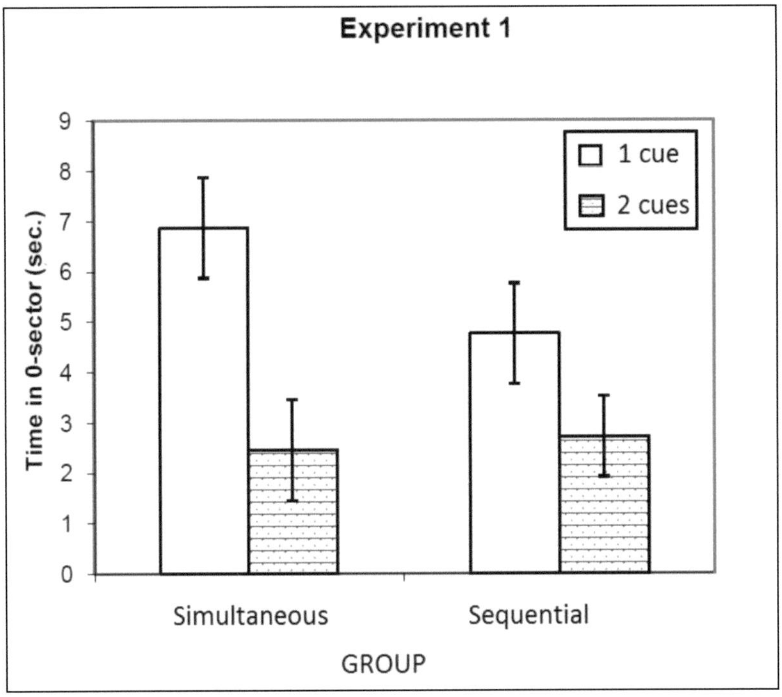

Fig. 4. Mean time spent in the 0th sector (starting point) for each group (simultaneous and sequential vision) as a function of the type of test trial (with one or two landmarks).

4. Experiment 2

In this experiment we tested human spatial navigation in a virtual environment by increasing the angular separation between the landmarks (expanding procedure). This procedure was important for analyzing whether navigational strategy depends on the kind of manipulation done in the test trial. As in the previous experiment, during the training trial the angular separation between the landmarks was kept constant (90º), while the visual field was manipulated: 1) Group 1 = 90º (simultaneous vision); Group 2 = 30º (sequential vision). In the test trial, half of the participants were submitted to the condition in which the distance between the landmarks was the same as in the training trials. For the other half we applied the expanding procedure, changing the angular separation between the landmarks from 90º to 150º. In the latter condition, we considered that if participants distributed the search time in sectors 7, 8 and 9, it would suggest that they had adopted a navigational strategy "from landmark to landmark". On the other hand, if participants spent more time in the 8th sector (platform) in comparison to the 7th and 9th sectors, it would suggest that they had adopted the "middle rule" strategy (following an egocentric vector from the starting point to the platform).

4.1 Method

4.1.1 Participants

Sixty-nine students of psychology at the University of Barcelona ranging in age from 22 to 24 years old were randomly assigned to two groups, differing with regard to the visual field condition. Thirty-three students took part in Group 1 and had visual access to both landmarks during the session (90º of visual field - simultaneous vision). Thirty-six students took part in Group 2 and had visual access to only one landmark at a time (30º of visual field - sequential vision). Volunteers were naive about the hypothesis of the experiment and received course credits to take part in the research. The experiment was conducted in the same room as the previous session.

4.1.2 Procedure

Experiment 2 was identical to Experiment 1 except for the use of the "expanding landmarks" procedure. In the test trial, half of the participants were submitted to the condition in which the distance between the landmarks was identical to the training trial (90º). For the other half of the participants, the expanding procedure was applied and the angular separation increased (150º). As in Experiment 1, we considered only the first 20 s of searching in the test trial for data analysis.

5. Results and discussion

An analysis of variance with "groups" (simultaneous and sequential vision) and "blocks of trials" (1-12) as factors revealed a statistically significant main effect of "groups" [$F(1, 68) = 16.077$, $p < .001$] and "blocks of trials" [$F(11, 748) = 23.071$, $p < .001$], as well as an interaction between "groups" and "blocks of trials" [$F(11, 748) = 2.544$, $p < .004$]. Although participants improved their performance in the course of the blocks, Group 1 (simultaneous vision) speeded up the latency time in finding the platform in comparison to Group 2 (sequential vision). Similarly to the previous experiment, analysis indicated that participants with simultaneous vision learned more quickly than participants with sequential vision (Fig. 5).

Afterwards a second analysis of variance was conducted with "groups" (simultaneous and sequential vision) and "types of test" [expanded landmarks (150º) and non-expanded landmarks (90º)] as between factors, and "sectors" of the pool as a within factor. This analysis showed no main effects for "groups" [$F(1,66)=2.60$, $p < .15$] or "types of test" [$F(1,66)=0.56$, $p < .45$]. We found a statistically significant effect for "sectors" [$F(6,396)= 14.15$, $p < .001$] and first order interactions between "sectors" and "types of test" [$F(6,396)=7.09$, $p < .001$] and "sectors" and "groups" [$F(6,396)=12.17$, $p < .001$]. A second order interaction between "sectors", "groups" and "types of test" [$F(6,396)=3.06$; $p<.006$] was significant. Figure 3 shows the time spent in the relevant sectors (5-11th) in the test trial with non-expanded landmarks (Fig.3b) and expanded landmarks (Fig.3c) .

In order to analyze the second order interaction ("groups" by "types of test" by "sectors") we conducted *post hoc* tests. For non-expanded landmarks (90º) we found differences between simultaneous and sequential groups in the 8th [$t(22)= 4.07$; $p < .001$] and 10th sectors [$t(22)= 3.12$; $p < .005$]. This implies that participants with simultaneous vision spent more search time in the 8th sector than the sequential vision group. Participants in the group with sequential vision spent more time in the 10th sector in comparison to the simultaneous group.

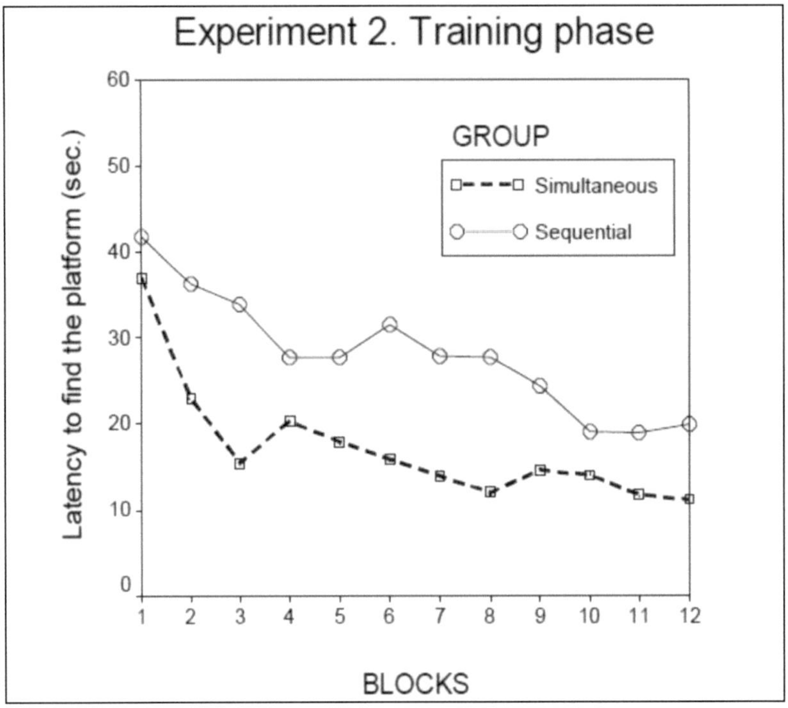

Fig. 5. Mean escape latencies of the two groups with simultaneous and sequential vision in Experiment 2.

In the expanded landmarks condition (150º) we found differences between simultaneous and sequential vision for the 6th [t(44)= 3.26; p < .002], 8th [t(44)= 2.21; p < .033] and 10th sectors [t(44)= 4.89; p < .001]. These data revealed that participants with simultaneous vision spent more time in the relevant sector (8th), suggesting that they adopted a strategy of advancing directly to the goal. However, participants with sequential vision and submitted to the "expanding procedure" spent more time in the 6th and 10th sectors, located adjacent to the landmarks. These results suggest that participants used a strategy of navigating from one landmark to another ("connecting cues" strategy).

As regards the participants in the group with simultaneous vision submitted to non-expanded landmarks, we verified that they spent more time in the 8th sector compared to the 6th, 7th, 9th and 10th sectors [t(11)= 4.51; p < .001]. Likewise, in the expanding procedure, participants spent more time in the 8th sector in comparison to the 6th and 10th sectors [t(21)= 2.91; p < .008]. A further analysis in the simultaneous group, comparing the two types of test (90º vs. 150º), only showed differences for the 8th sector [t(32)= 3.49; p < .001].

Our data showed that participants with simultaneous vision spent more time in the relevant sector (8th) than in the sectors adjacent to the landmarks. For the condition in which the distance between the landmarks was expanded, we could attribute the non-significant difference between the 7th, 8th and 9th sectors to a decrease in accuracy in finding the resulting vector that leads to the goal (platform).

For the group with sequential vision submitted to non-expanded landmarks, we found significant differences only between the 8th and 6th sectors [$t(11)= 2.66$; $p < .022$]. However, for the participants submitted to the expanding procedure (150º), the time spent in the 8th sector differed from that spent in sectors 6 and 10 [$t(23)= 2.20$; $p < .038$]. Additionally, we found that the time spent in the 6th sector differed from that spent in the 7th [$t(23)= 2.41$; $p < .024$] and that the time in the 10th sector differed from that in the 7th and 9th sectors [$t_{min}(23)= 2.62$; $p < .015$]. This showed that participants in the group with sequential vision predominantly searched for the platform in the 6th and 10th sectors rather than in the relevant sector (8th). A final analysis in the sequential group, comparing two types of test trials (90º vs. 150º), showed that only the time spent in the 6th sector differed [$t(34)= 3.19$; $p < .003$]. Generally speaking, these data indicate that participants with sequential vision submitted to non-expanded landmarks spent approximately the same time in the relevant (8th) and adjacent (7th and 9th) sectors. However, the group of participants with sequential vision submitted to the expanded landmarks (150º) spent more time in the sectors adjacent to the landmarks (6th and 10th) than in the relevant sector (8th). This pattern of results differs from that found in the group with simultaneous vision, suggesting the use of two navigational strategies. Analogously to Experiment 1, we predict that participants with sequential vision use an elemental strategy.

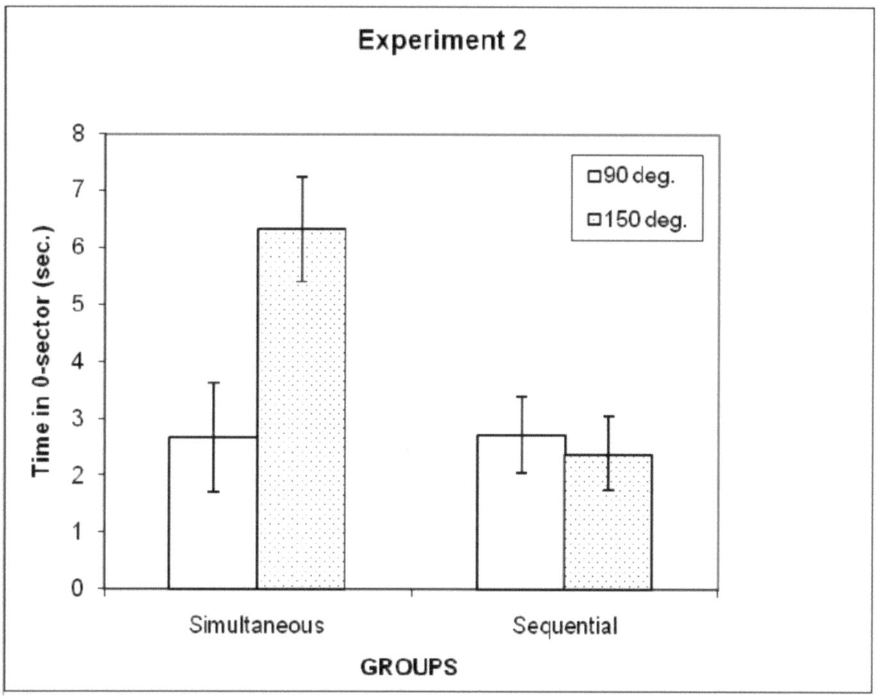

Fig. 6. Mean time spent in the 0th sector (starting point) for each group (simultaneous and sequential vision) as a function of the type of test trial (expanded and non-expanded landmarks).

Finally, an analysis of the variance with "groups" (simultaneous vs. sequential vision) and "types of test" (expanded vs. non-expanded landmarks) as factors was conducted. The time in the 0th sector (starting point) was taken as the dependent variable. Results revealed a statistically significant effect of "groups" [$F(1,66)= 5.63$; $p < .021$] and "types of test" [$F(1,66)= 4.106$; $p < .047$] as well as an interaction between them [$F(1,66)= 5.879$; $p < .018$].

A *post hoc* analysis of the interaction indicated that, only for the group with simultaneous vision, the distance between the landmarks affected the time spent at the starting point (Figure 6). In such cases, participants submitted to expanded landmarks (150°) spent more time (mean = 6.32 s) compared to those submitted to non-expanded landmarks (90°) (mean = 2.50 s). We can consider two possible explanations for these results. On the one hand, the change *per se* in the distance between landmarks promoted a decrease in the generalization of the response, and on the other, when the landmarks are further apart, the time to define the correct vector and direction increases.

6. General discussion

In this study we investigated the influences of simultaneous and sequential vision on human spatial navigation by using two classic procedures adapted from animal research. A virtual model of the Morris water maze (Morris, 1981) was used in the task, in which participants had to locate a hidden underwater platform in the pool. Experiments were designed in order to analyze in test trials the effect of the removal of one of the landmarks (Experiment 1) and the influence of increasing the distance between them (Experiment 2). The time spent by the participants in each sector of the pool was registered and taken as a dependent variable in data analysis.

In Experiment 1 we verify that participants with simultaneous vision spent more time in the relevant sector (8th) in comparison to other sectors of the pool. However, participants with sequential vision spent approximately the same time in the relevant and adjacent sectors. These results indicate that simultaneous vision compared to sequential vision improves spatial navigation in a virtual environment.

Similarly, in Experiment 2 participants with simultaneous vision also spent more time in the relevant sector (8th) compared to the other sectors in both conditions (expanded and non-expanded landmarks). But when participants with sequential vision were submitted to the condition of expanded landmarks they spent more time in the 10th and 6th in comparison to the 7th, 8th and 9th sectors. For the case in which participants with sequential vision were submitted to non-expanded landmarks (90o), they spent more time in the relevant (8th) and adjacent (7th and 9th) sectors.

As a whole, these results indicate that participants use different strategies depending on the visual condition. Participants submitted to simultaneous vision tended to navigate directly to the relevant sector (8th), indicating that they used a "middle rule" strategy based on a configural learning. However, participants with sequential vision submitted to the procedure of the removal of one landmark (Experiment 1) spent more time in the three sectors between the two landmarks (7th, 8th and 9th), suggesting that they navigate from one landmark to another based on an elemental learning. The latter finding is reinforced by the observation that when the distance between the landmarks was increased, participants with sequential vision spent more time in the sectors near the landmarks (6th and 10th). This pattern of results reveals that participants adopted two different strategies. The "middle rule" strategy takes into account the egocentric direction to determine the correct bisector between the starting point and the landmarks, while the "landmark to landmark" strategy takes into account the exocentric direction.

In the context of visual control of the action, Goodale and Humphrey (2001) state that perceptual tasks differ from motor tasks as a consequence of information processing in two independent neural pathways: the ventral (related to perception, e.g. object recognition) and the dorsal (related to directed action, e.g. blind walking). Dissociation between perception and action can be found in many studies (Goodale & Milner, 1992; Loomis et al., 1992; Smeets & Brenner, 1995; Philbeck et al., 1997; Fukusima et al., 1997; Kelly, Loomis & Beal, 2004; Kudoh, 2005). However, there is also evidence against this dissociation, with many papers trying to reconcile the pathways (Kugler & Turvey, 1987; Goodale & Humphrey, 2001, Norman, 2002). In this study, results might sustain the hypothesis of the dissociation between perception and action, with the "middle rule" being related to a perceptual strategy, while the navigation from "landmark to landmark" implies an action strategy.

We verified that the expanding landmarks test helped to clarify the strategies adopted by the participants with sequential vision. According to Sutherland & Rudy (1989), if the responses of the participants were based on an elemental learning, they should present a good performance in the test with two landmarks, but a worse performance in the test with one landmark. However, if the responses of the participants are based on configural learning, they should present a good performance in both types of test (removal and expanding procedure). If we apply those criteria to the data, we conclude that the group with sequential vision adopted an elemental strategy, whereas the group submitted to simultaneous vision adopted a configural one. However, we should note that these authors made this assertion in the context of discriminatory learning and it has not been applied to a spatial task until now.

These results differ from those obtained by MacDonald et al. (2004), who pointed out that human adults use a "middle rule" strategy, but that children and other primates do not. Our results suggest that only participants with simultaneous vision used a "middle rule" strategy, while participants with sequential vision employed a strategy of advancing from one landmark to another. In other words, navigation with simultaneous vision follows an egocentric vector directed to the middle of the landmarks, while sequential vision follows an exocentric vector that connects landmark to landmark.

The simultaneous visual access of the participants to the relevant information enables them to integrate the spatial relation easier and promotes a configural encoding which, in turn, allows the use of "middle rule" strategy. The visual access to only one landmark at a time makes the learning of global spatial relations difficult but promotes the elemental relationship between landmarks, enabling participants to apply the "connecting landmarks rule". However, more research is necessary in order to conclude whether these results could be attributed to general rules in spatial navigation or to the extensive training in the sequential condition.

7. Conclusion

In this work we have demonstrated that the amplitude of the visual field can affect the type of navigational strategy used by humans in a virtual environment. This study shows that simultaneous access to spatial cues in the training period improves the finding of routes and pathways which can be relevant when one of the landmarks is missing or when the distance between the landmarks is increased. Therefore, our study also emphasizes the importance of the amplitude of the visual field in the exploration of a virtual environment. Indeed, the area covered by the visual field may facilitate or hinder the integration of available information that is scattered in the environment. The results of this study can provide guidelines to the development of virtual environments more realistic and compatible with natural conditions of visual stimulation.

8. Acknowledgment

This research was supported by a grant from the Spanish Ministerio de Ciencia y Tecnologia (Refs No. PSI2009-11062 /PSIC). We are very grateful to Antonio Alvarez-Artigas and Victoria Diez-Chamizo for your very valuable help in these experiments.

9. References

Astur, R. S., Ortiz, M. L., & Sutherland, R. J. (1998). A characterization of performance by men and women in a virtual Morris water task: a large and reliable sex difference. Behavioural Brain Research, 93(1-2), 185-190.

Chamizo, V. D., Aznar-Casanova, J.A., & Artigas, A.A. (2003). Human overshadowing in a virtual pool: Simple guidance is a good competitor against locale learning. Learning and Motivation, 34, 262–281.

Artigas, A. A., Aznar-Casanova, J. A., & Chamizo, V. D. (2005). Effects of absolute proximity and generalization gradient in humans when manipulating the spatial location of landmarks. International Journal of Comparative Psychology, 18, 225-239.

Cheng, K. (1988). Some psychophysics of the pigeon's use of landmarks. Journal of Comparative Physiology A, 162, 815-826.

Cheng, K. (1989). The vector sum model of pigeon landmark use. Journal of Experimental Psychology: Animal Behavior Processes, 15, 366-375.

Collett, T. S., Cartwright, B. A., & Smith, B. A. (1986). Landmark Learning and Visuospatial Memories in Gerbils. Journal of Comparative Physiology A - Sensory Neural and Behavioral Physiology, 158 (6), 835-851, 1986.

Epstein, R. A. (2008). Parahippocampal and retrosplenial contributions to human spatial navigation. Trends in Cognitive Science, 12(10), 388-396.

Fukusima, S.S., Loomis, J. M., & Da Silva, J. A. (1997). Visual perception of egocentric distance as assessed by triangulation. Journal of Experimental Psychology: Human Perception and performance, 23(1), 86-100.

Gazzaniga, M. S., Ivry, R., & Mangun, G. R. (2002). Cognitive Neuroscience: The Biology of the Mind. W.W. Norton, 2nd Edition.

Goodale, M. L., & Humphrey, G. K. (2001). Separate visual system for action and perception. In E. B. Goldstein, Blackwell Handbook of Perception, (p. 311-343). Oxford: Blackwell.

Goodale, M. A. & Milner, A. D. (1992). Separate visual pathways for perception and action. Trends in Neurosciences, 15 (1), 20-25.

Kelly, J. V., Loomis, J. M. & Beal, A. C. (2004). Judgments of exocentric direction in large-scale space. Perception, 33, 44-45.

Kudoh, N. (2005). Dissociation between visual perception of allocentric distance and visually directed walking of its extent. Perception, 34, 1399-1416.

Kugler, P. N., & Turvey, M. T. (1987). Information, Natural law, and the self-assembly of rhythmic movement. Hillsdale: Erlbaum.

Loomis, J. M. & Knapp, J. M. (2003). Visual perception egocentric distance in real and virtual environments. In L. J. Hettinger & M. W. Haas (Eds.), Virtual adaptive environments (pp. 21-46). Mahwah: LEA.

Loomis, J. M., Da Silva, J. A., Fujita, N., & Fukusima, S.S. (1992). Visual space perception and visually directed action. Journal of Experimental Psychology: Human Perception and Performance, 18(4), 906-921.

MacDonald, S. E., Spetch, M. L., Kelly, D. M., & Cheng, K. (2004). Strategies in landmark use by children, adults, and marmoset monkeys. Learning and Motivation, 35 (4), 322-347.

Morris, R. G. M. (1981). Spatial localization does require the presence of local cues. Learning and Motivation, 12, 239-260.

Newcombe, N. S. & Huttenlocher, J. (2000). Making space: The development of spatial representation and reasoning. MIT Press.

Norman, J. (2002). Two visual system and two theories of perception: attempt to reconcile the constructivist and ecological approaches. Behavioral and Brains Sciences, 25 (1), 73-144.

Philbeck, J. W., Loomis, J. M., & Beall, A. C. (1997). Visually perceived location is an invariant in the control of action. Perception & Psychophysics, 59, 601-612.

Rozhok, A. (2008). Orientation and navigation in vertebrates. Berlin: Springer-Verlag.

Smeets, J. B. J., & Brenner, E. (1995). Perception and action are based on the same visual information: distinction between position and velocity. Journal of Experimental Psychology: Human Perception and Performance, 21, 19-23.

Stewart, C. A., & Morris, R. G. M. (1993). The watermaze. In Ed. Saghal "Behavioural Neuroscience. A Practical Approach. Volume I". IRL Press at Oxford University press, Oxford, New York, Tokyo, pp107-122.

Sutherland, R. J., & Rudy, J. W. (1989). Configural association theory: The role of the hippocampal formation in learning, memory, and amnesia. Psychobiology, 17, 2, 129-144.

Tinbergen (1972). The animal in its world: explorations of an ethologist, 1932-1972. Harvard University Press.

Turano, K. A., Yu, D., Hao, L., & Hicks, J. C. (2005). Optic flow and egocentric-direction strategies in walking: Central vs peripheral visual field. Vision Research, 45, 3117-3132.

Wu, B., Ooi T. L., & He Z. J. (2004). Perceiving distance accurately by a directional process of integrating ground information. Nature, 428 (6978),73-77.

5

Virtual Worlds as an Extended Classroom

Ana Loureiro, Ana Santos and Teresa Bettencourt
CIDTFF/University of Aveiro & Polytechnic Institute of Santarém, Polytechnic Institute of Viseu, & CIDTFF/University of Aveiro
Portugal

1. Introduction

There is a growing trend in education and training towards the use of online and distance learning courses. This delivery format provides flexibility and accessibility; it is also viewed as a way to provide education in a more effective way to a broader community. Online courses are comfortable, they are built under the missive of "anyone, anywhere, anytime". Everyone can participate from home or workplace.

Online courses can be developed in a variety of ways, for example, using a LMS (Learning Management System), a LCM (Learning Content System), or a Web 2.0 tool (or some mixture). These options, however, show limitations in terms of communication and interaction levels that can be achieved between students. Most learning systems are asynchronous and don't allow an effective real-time interaction, collaboration and cooperation. Whilst they typically have synchronous chats and whiteboards, these capabilities are often sterile and don't stimulate the appropriate interactions that enhance learning. A rich interaction does not necessarily involve just verbal exchange since there is an huge learning value to be gained from interacting with the learning content in a more visual and practical way. For instance, imagine the learning benefits from collaborating on a 3D construction jointly and in real-time? Imagine watching the impact of soil erosion, or building and walking inside an heart model or a car engine? All this is possible in a 3D immersive virtual world. Students can engage at a distance building content in real-time, collaboratively and interactively. On the net there can be found an array of virtual worlds, however we have chosen Second Life® (SL®) to show how teaching and learning can be enhanced through the use of this platform. Second Life® is immersive, enabling users to interact, communicate and collaborate as if in the real world. SL® is a model of the real world, it shows an accurate physics simulation and it includes a meteorological and gravitational system; as such, anything can be modelled and simulated. Each user in the environment is represented by an avatar with all the features of a human being and avatars can manipulate the environment. Scientific experiments can be held in a very safe and controlled environment, and can be directly conducted by the scientist in charge. Scientific fields such as architecture, history, medicine, biology, sociology, programming, languages learning among many others can all be tested and researched through this virtual world.

2. Virtual worlds

There is some debate related with the definition of a virtual world. One thing that can be said is that a virtual world is not itself a game (Austin & Boulder, 2007), besides inside of the platform who wants can play games. According to Schroeder (2008) virtual worlds are persistent virtual environments in which people experience others as being there with them - and where they can interact with them. The keyword is immersion. In a virtual world people can have immersive experiences. A virtual world can also be described as multi-user, collaborative or shared virtual environment. Those environments or systems allow users to experience other participants as being present in the same space, they can interact with each other; this creates the feeling of being there together (Schroeder, 2008). This definition is focused on sensory experience. In a virtual world "Interaction with the world takes place in real time. When you do something in the world, you can expect feedback almost immediately. The world is shared. The world is (at least some degree) persistent" (Bartle, 2004), so there is an interaction between users despite not being physically in the same space (Wankel & Kingsley, 2009), stimulating immersive learning.

American National Standards (2007) defines a virtual world as a simulated environment that appears to have the characteristics of some other environment, and in which participants perceive themselves as interactive parts.

For Bell (2008), a virtual world is a synchronous, persistent network of people, represented by avatars and facilitated by computers.

PCMag's encyclopedia defines virtual world as a "3D computer environment in which users are represented on screen as themselves or as made-up characters and interact in real time with other users. Massively multiuser online games (MMOGs) and worlds such as Second Life are examples" (PCMag, 2011).

Here is a list of some of the best known virtual worlds: ActiveWorlds, Blue Mars, IMVU, MOOVE, World of Warcraft, OpenSim and Second Life®. Most part of these platforms were created with a social and entertainment purpose. Most of users use them to meet people, chat and socialize with others remotely. But their potentialities are not limited to the social level.

Virtual worlds already have an impact in real world society, particularly at business, art and education levels. For instance, as PCMag notes, "there are countless Second Life cultures and subcultures organized around arts, sports, games and other areas. Groups can be formed that simulate mini-companies and mini-communities. Even real companies, such as Coca-Cola and Adidas, participate in Second Life as a marketing venue. Numerous universities, including Harvard, Princeton and Vassar, offer online classes. Religious organizations hold meetings and starting with the Maldives and Sweden, countries have created virtual embassies. People find partners, have virtual sex and even get married in Second Life. In other words, Second Life is the *virtual real world*" (PCMag, 2011).

Talking about "real" and "virtual" in this context had led to the need to clarify the meaning of "virtual", recognizing the importance and the impact that preconceptions have in any learning or teaching or training process. Usually "virtual" is easily related to something that does not exist, that does not occupy space or consumes time, like if it belonged to another dimension that a person cannot reach because it is not tangible (Bettencourt, 2010). This is a conception of "virtual" as an antagonism of "real" that can represent an obstacle to understand and preview the educational potentialities of the virtual worlds. One must be aware that, in virtual worlds, when the avatar - the person is, for instance, talking with another avatar - person, those persons are really talking with each other, consuming time, discussing ideas, sharing knowledge, thinking, socializing. They are using a virtual medium to do something very real. The "virtual" has a real expression. The "virtual" must be seen and understood more like an extension of real life, than something that is antagonist to the real life. Like Bettencourt (2010) we agree that this conception is the first condition to ensure all the educational potentialities of virtual worlds.

Those potentialities are also related with another concept that arises from the immersive character of virtual worlds and from the fact that virtual worlds were not created with educational reasons in mind: the natural context of the environment where learning and teaching experiences occur (Bettencourt, 2010). This concept is not only quite different from formal, or nonformal or informal learning environments but as well is independent from them. Formal and nonformal or informal learning can be characterized by who has the control of the educational objectives or competences to achieve or to develop (Cross, 2007). In a natural context, like virtual worlds, the learning process is individual and occurs because the learner wants to no matter where he/she is, the person learns by his/her own pace, not necessarily within the context of a school, or any educational entity, in an autonomous way. Skills learned or competences developed tend to be transferable giving a whole dimension of the learning process.

As well as the learning process is individual it also depends on the socialization of the person. More the socialization more the person will learn. Within the concept of natural context that we are explaining the apprenticeships are embedded in a community of sharing (Bettencourt, 2010). This idea is inspired in the communities of practice from Lave and Wenger (1991) who, already in those years, explained the importance of sharing between newcomers and old-timers. They wrote: "*We place more emphasis on connecting issues of sociocultural transformation with changing relations between newcomers and old-timers in the context of a changing shared practice*" (pp. 49). The "changing shared practice" assumes an enormous actuality nowadays. In the natural context that we were explaining, the learning processes are focused in communities of sharing, where avatars - persons learn one with another. These communities are nonhierarchical and any individual contribution will enrich the whole community without any kind of value judgments.

Taking into account our experience, literature review and the research that is being developed, we believe the virtual world that offers better features and more potentialities for educational use is Second Life®. This platform is the best known, more populated and integrates several and important features of usability.

We define Second Life® as a free to use 3D multi-user virtual world, immersive, imagined, designed, built and created by its users (residents or avatars). It is considered a playground for our imagination, a limitless platform - design, build, code, perform and collaborate, expanding the boundaries of creativity. It is a real life simulator (Loureiro & Bettencourt, 2010).

3. Exploring virtual worlds - Learning and teaching strategies

For the most part, virtual worlds were not designed for educational use. As already mentioned, the purposes are related with social and entertainment areas although many of the features available in these platforms can be explored in educational contexts. In the specific case of Second Life® the simulations, emulation and role-playing features have been widely explored and with good results.

The immersive nature of SL® allows walk through contents and information - students can learn by living or experiencing. With a 3D representation of 'self' – the avatar - learning can be done in the 1st person. Features like communication, cooperation, collaboration, interaction and information sharing are in real time. Students can learn by doing and they can more easily engage with content (Loureiro, Wood & Bettencourt, 2010). SL® is also a major social network and a wide community of practice (Wenger, 1998). SL® is not a game but it offers the attractiveness of 3D gaming and therefore the sensation of learning by playing (Loureiro, Wood & Bettencourt, 2010). As Lim (2009) suggested there are six learning styles that can be applied within SL®:

- Learning by exploring: students can learn by visiting and explore buildings, landscapes, communities that are simulated and modelled.
- Learning by collaborating: students can work in teams, collaboratively and in real-time on common projects or on problem-solving tasks, discussions can also be made in group and collaboratively.
- Learning by being: students can immerse in role-playing and performance activities, they can also explore the self and experiment different identities through avatar customization and by creating different characters.
- Learning by building: students can with no restrictions build any kind of objects or environments and experiencing in real-time the results.
- Learning by championing: students can get involved into activities and causes related and with an impact in real-life (such as cancer campaign, earthquake victims support).
- Learning by expressing: students can show and present their in-world activities to out-side world audience, by authoring blogs, machinimas, papers, posters or by participating in conferences and meetings.

By exploring those potentialities, virtual classrooms can emerge and learning can be enhanced.

One particularly interesting feature of version 2.0 of SL® viewer is the possibility of adding shared media to an object. This means anyone can add web-based media content to the surface of any object and place it in-world or attach it to an avatar. For instance, it is possible to be inside SL®, running, adding and modifying contents in an external web site and the audience in-world can watch in real-time. These tasks can be made collaboratively.

Another interesting feature, especially for those who use Moodle as a LMS is the possibility of connecting and integrating it into SL® - through Sloodle (Simulation Linked Object Oriented Dynamic Learning Environment). The use of LMS in e-learning has limitations as the students only have to deal with specific activities (Yasar & Adiguzel, 2010) but Sloodle provides a variety of tools for supporting learning contexts in immersive virtual worlds, providing experiences and opportunities for students to collaborate, cooperate and interact with the objects. By connecting Moodle and SL® it is possible, for instance, to have the same chat session running in real-time on both platforms – students can chose in which one to be or connect at both. Chat logs are also saved in the Moodle database. A tool, called Web-intercom, "is really useful to enhance the communication between learners who are involved in the activities within both SL® and Moodle" (Yasar & Adiguzel, 2010) and it is important to students as "an aide-memoir and to help them reflect later on their experiences in the virtual world" (Livingstone, Kemp & Edgar, 2008). Another feature of Sloodle is that SL® and Moodle accounts can be linked. This feature provides a better management of students' progress, allowing teacher to track students by their avatar names (Yasar & Adiguzel, 2010). It is possible to set quizzes - QuizChair - where students "attempt a standard Moodle multiple-choice quiz inside SL, with the answers being stored on Moodle" (Kem, Livingstone & Bloomfield, 2009) (in Yasar & Adiguzel, 2010). Students can create 3D objects and deliver their assignment using drop-box tool and teachers can review their work and provide feedback in Moodle (Livingstone, Kemp & Edgar, 2008). It also has the Presenter tool with the possibility of showing slides and/or webpages, where students can share their work in virtual space or for the teacher in class. An advantage of using Presenter is that you don't need to spend money (linden dollars - SL® currency) on uploading images (Yasar & Adiguzel, 2010). For those who like to have a more close control over participants it is also possible to set (via a Sloodle toolbar) a function to collect a list of avatars or Moodle users connected at a certain time/date.

As a simulation or modeling tool, SL® has several uses. Many examples of buildings and cities (some of them already missing in the real world) have been built and now can be visited in SL®. The Sistine Chapel has been modelled in great detail; the aim of this recreation was to explore the use of virtual reality in the context of learning about art and architecture, allowing students experience the context, scale and social aspects of the original monument (Taylor, 2007). Another example is the reconstruction of ancient Rome or the city of Lisbon pre-earthquake 1755[1]. The potential is not limited to art, history or anthropology. An example in the field of physical science is related with the simplicity of how we can model molecules and observe their interactions when exposed to physical variables such as temperature. Also in the field of medicine, some experiments in training students are being conducted covering biology and doctor/patient role-play. SL® is also a great tool for language learning, with the possibility of direct contact with native speakers, allowing the development of language skills at a writing and speech level. And because there are full and reliable constructions of real world scenarios, direct contact with the culture of a country or community is a reality that is easily reachable by every classroom with an Internet connection. Generally speaking we can say that the use of 3D immersive virtual worlds in education have an important part to play since they allow multiple learning styles and they can be used in any subject of the curriculum. It allows students to acquire and develop formal competences and also to develop social and collaborative skills.

In § 4 we will describe some studies that are being carried out in Second Life® by the authors of the paper.

4. Virtual worlds as an extended classroom - Benefits

In the following sub-sections, two examples of constructivist learning will illustrate the advantages of both distance and face-to-face education working closely together. It will be shown how they can be effective as a teaching and learning strategy.

---

1 http://lisbon-pre-1755-earthquake.org

Today's students have grown up surrounded by digital society, to them traditional teaching is poorly stimulating, for their are used to utilize simultaneously diverse types of media. Currently there is several gadgets that allow access to Internet and consequently access to wireless network, so more users are connected and be able to interact with others. This reality of being connect to the network called "always on", leads to the creation of communication strategies that suits both "digital natives" and "digital immigrants" (Prensky, 2001). It's a way of communicate where users spend more time browsing and posting than in e-mail - a clear shift for social websites / social networks. There is a clear change in users behaviours, and consequently in the way how students act. For nowadays' students learning does not necessary mean being sit in rows at school. Learning is at the distance of a click, for those digitally savvy. Although, to actually retain knowledge there´s the need of acquire digital skills and have digital literacy, to be able to do better research, select information, reflect, collaborate, produce, share and achieve knowledge.

Learning in a digital and connected age does not depend on "individual knowledge acquisition, storage, and retrieval; rather, it relies on the connected learning that occurs through interaction with various sources of knowledge (including the Internet and learning management systems) and participation in communities of common interest, social networks and group tasks." (Siemens, 2004). Students need to acquire certain skills and competences specific of a digital and connected society in order to "effectively benefit from e-government, e-learning and e-health services, and participate actively in the knowledge society as co-creators, and not simply consumers, as highlighted by the European e-skills strategy" (McCormack, 2010, pp 27). Besides e-skills and e-literacy competences, soft skills are also a demand. Many of the mentioned skills and competences can be practiced and enhanced in social, collaborative and virtual environments. Individuals have access to communities of practice (Wenger, 1998), virtual worlds with role-play and simulations, social networks and a wide range of web 2.0 tools. The fact of having access to different online tools demands a shift in students' profile and competences.

4.1 The use of Second Life® and online tools as an extended classroom

We set a study in Second Life®[2] to gain experience of the use of virtual worlds and social web tools (namely Facebook[3] and Diigo[4]) in learning contexts, in order to bridge the gap between students and teacher contact. We seek to understand how effective a virtual world, allied with online tools, is as a proxy for face-to-face interaction.

4.1.1 Methodology

This specific case study emerged from the need of observe some of the variables (cf Fig. 1) already identified (Bettencourt, 2009) and that are related with:

- persons and their motivations - engaging and compelling factors - to register and attend virtual worlds
- relationships that are established between avatars and persons - in-world relationships that evolve into out-world relationships

[2] http://secondlife.com/
[3] http://www.facebook.com
[4] http://www.diigo.com

- social integration in Second Life® and sense of community belonging - as an allusion to Wenger's (1998) concept of community of practice

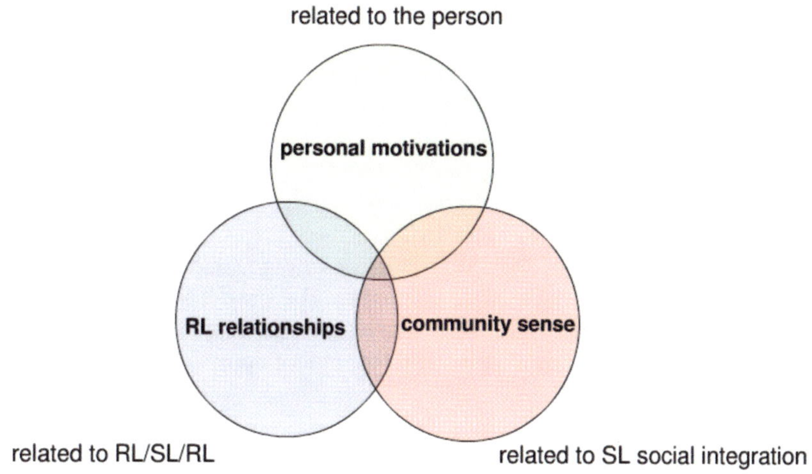

Fig. 1. Identified variables (Bettencourt, 2009)

The study components are connected with (i) construction and knowledge sharing, (ii) interpersonal relationships and (iii) 3D immersive virtual worlds combined with web 2.0 tools. We seek to understand if there are best practices orchestrating learning in collaborative, immersive virtual worlds and web 2.0 tools, and if they will enhance blended learning through knowledge sharing and socialization. The premise is that socialization is a key factor for collaborative learning. We perceive collaborative learning as a situation where two or more persons learn, or try to learn, something together (Dillenbourg, 1999).

The study goals are to:

- identify the variables that might influence knowledge sharing
- contribute for richer learning contexts through the use of online tools (Diigo, Facebook) and virtual worlds (Second Life®)
- provide tutorial support to night class through a virtual world
- encourage collaboration 'out of hours' by providing means for students and teacher to interact
- learn what advantages we can find in an online tutorial implemented using an immersive virtual world
- understand how and which students engage with an immersive 3D world and how effective it is as a proxy for face-to-face interaction
- understand how well online tools and virtual worlds promote knowledge sharing and enhance socialization in order to contribute for classroom cohesion
- provide some insights for better online teaching strategies

The participants in this study are Portuguese higher education students from a school of education. Students belong to two different groups, undergraduate regular day classes and mature night classes (ages > 23 years old). They follow exactly the same syllabus in an identical curriculum. This is a non probabilistic sample for a qualitative study having an inductive and exploratory nature. The researcher, which is also the teacher, has a dual role in the study and it is a participant-observer. The data has being collected by direct observation and through electronic records; additionally questionnaires were designed to survey students for feedback.

The teacher meets each class, in a common physical space (traditional classroom), once a week. The teacher also has some hours of contact out of the classroom (support hours). These support hours suit the regular students very well but don't meet the mature students' needs since they are part time. A night class student typically has a full-time job and studies in the evenings and at weekends. The challenge for the teacher is to provide a way for students collaborate on coursework, in a tutorial context, making use of the support hours in a creative way. The main goal of the study is to encourage collaboration 'out of hours' by providing means for students and teacher to interact. The project is intended to evaluate the effectiveness of blended learning as a tool to achieve the teaching goals. Here we see blended learning as a "learning that combines online and face to face approaches" (Heinze & Procter,

Fig. 2. Learning orchestration

2004). In Fig. 2 we present an image showing how learning was orchestrated in the extended classroom in order to enhance knowledge sharing and socialization among students.

4.1.2 Findings and reflections

The study is ongoing but has already demonstrated early gains. The level and quality of participation has improved alongside increased collaboration and interaction amongst students.

First we found that the initial set up cost of starting SL® in terms of time spending was high. The students had no prior experience with the virtual world so the first tutorial session became a focus for fixing 'new user' issues. The SL® environment has a steep learning curve: how to move, how to communicate and interact, how to customize. Predominantly this was navigating the world and helping with avatar appearance. However we felt that this was time well spent as rapid integration into the virtual world is an important prerequisite to collaboration and for the survival in the virtual world. Two in-world sessions were devoted to students' acquisition of basic skills (approx. 6 hours). A number of students engaged in-world beyond tutorial hours. In future sessions it was easy to see those who had spent more time learning - avatar appearance is one indicator.

As referred a Questionnaire was used to get students feedback on their expectations and learning experiences in tutorial sessions and extended classroom. Respondents included 34 undergraduates (day and night classes) taking the same course via face-to-face and online instruction. The Questionnaire is under analyses.

With the data already collected, through observation sessions and online records, and analyzed, some preliminary findings can be outlined:

- tutorial sessions were considered as a success for the mature night class
- students didn't use the support hours available at school (physical space)
- night students shared more information at Diigo
- day students created a Facebook page for a more direct communication
- night students elected email as primary way for communication
- students posted more information than teacher, particularly night students
- the quality of shared information was high (relevant) - development of search competences
- posts were moderated (by teacher and students) - stimulating development of critical analysis and reflection skills
- students prefer in-world sessions out of official school islands – *i.e* informal places not perceived as an extension to the 'bricks and mortar' university
- night (mature) students appear more independent as learners
- night students have less time and more desire to learn in the most effective way
- night students are more motivated since they have stronger reasons to study in their spare time
- virtual spaces support the work patterns of mature students in particular

We can summarize saying that the contrast of behavior between day and night students is a function of maturity; level of independence as learners and intrinsic motivation. The motivation aspect needs further and deeper evaluation - where free will is involved. In that way we may say that an online tutorial established in a virtual world might suit better the mature students and this might be a way to help them to keep in touch with the teacher and to maintain class cohesion.

4.2 The use of Second Life® as a virtual simulated newsroom

In the information age, marked mostly by technological advances in communications, there's an urgent need to create courses with high-quality interactive interfaces with emphasis on student interactions with content, tutors and peers. However, technological resources are not enough to ensure those interactions in a successful way. There's also a necessity to break paradigms and change traditional teaching and learning environments. It is time to learn how to be aware of the future as learning now comes from multiple sources and acquired knowledge is never enough.

The simplicity offered by modern technological development is changing online interaction possibilities by making available to teachers and students safe interfaces, interactive and efficient communication.

Online environments put together various interfaces that allow greater interaction strategies. These tools are classified into synchronous and asynchronous. Synchronous interfaces are communication spaces that require the participation of students and teachers in scheduled events with specific times, such as chats, video conferences or conference calls. According to literature these tools have benefits such as: motivation, interaction and feedback in real-time collaborative environment.

As for asynchronous interfaces they do not depend on time or place meetings. Examples of these platforms can be pointed out discussion forums, email, blogs, wikis, etc.. Some asynchronous tools benefits are time management flexibility (allowing anytime and anywhere access) as well as time to reflect and contextualize the information and discuss ideas.

These interfaces have been shown to be extremely important for the teacher who, from that information, can better follow student learning process. Based on an innovative suggestion for collaborative learning, teachers and students can help each other in adapting to this new methodology. The intervention, the exchange of information, the collective knowledge building between students and teachers is of vital importance.

Learning through this methodology moves from an individual perspective to group learning. It puts aside the overrated assessment of independent work and rather focuses on collaboration. As so, this interface strategy for technology education is focused on solving planned activities that may require participation, cooperation, interaction and collaboration. These teaching strategies must address the student predisposition to learn and expand experience skills.

It is also important to understand that in order to develop new teaching approaches and methodologies teachers need to work on their own continuous training as well as some basic pedagogical skills. According to Market (2009) it is essential to always do a good educational process planning; to find new ways to introduce topics for discussion; to provide some minimum necessary resources for students to organize the construction of their own knowledge; to successfully deal with previously established schedule to meet the students; to provide a continuous learning atmosphere; to maintain constant interaction with participants throughout the course; and to gain insight on the technical and educational resources it uses.

The changes performed by digital technologies in education have brought a great deal of impact on teachers and students. Both teachers and students need to be prepared to act in this new educational format. As so in spite of using new interaction, cooperation and collaboration strategies, participation and intervention success for a course of this scope will depend on the postures adopted by those involved, and especially their willingness to take full advantage of the course.

The most appropriate and traditional learning and knowledge building environment is, of course, the school. However, historically, school has been proven to be a traditional and conservative stage so that new technologies arrival created somewhat resistance to the regular use of these digital media. Adopting new teaching and learning techniques is a challenge that inevitably will cause a change in the lives of both students and teachers. Naturally the experience says that any change requires an adjustment phase but it is always necessary in the construction of new knowledge.

The new forms of teaching and learning are opening a new paradigm in education. Considering these changes, this study main purpose is to identify in what extent a virtual simulated newsroom in Second Life® could influence the practical knowhow of the journalism students.

As students are increasingly asking for more flexible educational experiences (being able to take classes on a computer from home or work) researchers have been asked to investigate whether teaching an online class is a benefit or an obstacle to the educational experience for students. The course selected for this study provided a great opportunity to explore the value of online teaching methods.

This new teaching and learning way take full advantage of the fact that virtual worlds present a combination of a video game interface with social connections and this mean there was a great improvement of the students' practical skills as they had the chance to face real problems as if they were working on real life.

The investigation took under consideration some of the latest studies concerning e-learning and b-learning strategies and mostly learning strategies through Second Life®.

As previously said the teaching/learning experience selected for this case study provided a good opportunity to evaluate some different online teaching/learning methods. As the main study focus was about practical behaviours, this popular virtual 3D platform showed to be a very handy tool to develop and at some extent evaluate a few of the Journalism course procedures. Using a new environment the study tried to evaluate the use of a 3D platform - like Second Life® - for teaching and learning on higher education as well as evaluate the use of a 3D virtual simulation on a journalism course.

A group of the 3rd year undergraduate students participated on online classes and traditional classes in a b-learning environment. All the students involved took pre and post surveys and underwent direct observation.

The results showed that, despite many technological handicaps, students had a better performance concerning best newsroom practices, the results also indicated that online students learned just as much as in a face to face situation and also that students enjoyed the teaching and learning experience better than the traditional way.

4.2.1 Methodology

In similar studies the main variable that could influence more the results relates to the sampling. For this investigation we have to add the technological skills of each individual as well as Internet access off campus for each student involved.

Having this pointed out as the first major study concern we have to access the following research questions:

RQ1: Is there a significant enhancement of journalism students' practical skills using a virtual simulation of a real newsroom?

RQ2: In what extent these virtual environments provide better basic journalism proficiency like news gathering, writing and reporting skills?

RQ3: What are the students' expectations prior and after using a new online teaching and learning methodology?

The main focus of the procedure was to virtually create a newsroom where students and teacher could gather together and decide the agenda.

The group met periodically foreseeing the problems and discussed collaboratively ways to solve those issues as so all together prepared news gathering strategies on a collectively manner.

Those meetings provided that the teacher could closely accompanying the students work progress, since getting in touch with the sources, getting interviews, news gathering, organizing information, and reporting.

In-world meetings aimed as well to support students and in real classes the group usually discussed problems they had faced and new strategies for success stories.

As a motivation goal all the students were told that they had to publish their stories on a real e-zine.

The teacher was seen as an editor-in-chief and communication in world was basically made by voice.

In short:

- Online classes were mostly concerned with reporting teams for the real e-zine
- In world meetings were also focused on the best approach choice for the articles
- All the news gathering, source interviews and report were prepared collaboratively
- Course key words: skills, work, preparation, support, feedback

Before online sessions started all students got used to Second Life® platform as - except for one - all of them had no experience with this virtual 3d platform.

Online teaching methods were developed over four in-world 60 minute sessions and these sessions had each been themed to focus on specific aspects of the journalism curriculum content.

Prior to each online session there was 30 minutes real life class mainly for technological preparation and to discuss solutions for the issues students had been facing.

Newsroom meetings took 60 minutes but students had to return back in world whenever they needed in order to get the interviews and the news gathering done as they were depending on sources agendas.

After each four in-world 60 minute sessions there was a 90 minute session of real life class.

These real life sessions were used to support the news gathering and to improve writing and reporting skills. So all the writing work was made during these face-to-face sessions and after being reviewed by the editor/teacher the articles were published on a real life e-zine.

For this investigation there was a class once a week for 180 minutes. The same instructor taught all the sessions during October 2009.

4.2.1.1 Survey

Pre/post test survey design was used to get students feedback for expectations and attitudes toward learning experiences in traditional face-to-face and online journalism courses

Respondents included 53 undergraduates taking the journalism course via face-to-face and online instruction.

The survey was used as a guide and it was taken by the students prior and after the online teaching period.

The test conducted answers on four sections:

- Demographics: questions querying students about gender and age.
- Computer literacy: to assess technology skills and confidence using those skills. At the same time students were invited to rate their internet access off campus.
- Attitudes: students had to rate their expectations and feelings towards the course.
- Perceived knowledge: students were asked to rate the course content as well as teaching procedures.

4.2.2 Findings and reflections

Under direct observation results suggested that students' experience in a journalism online course showed favourably when combined with traditional face-to-face instruction.

Results also showed that 3D multi-user environments can provide a highly immersive and very rich socially interactive way of enhancing students' skills.

Results also showed a great enhancement concerning foreseeing problems and communications and interaction showed a great improvement.

Students reported significantly better than they did at the beginning. However the course format appeared to have no impact on perceived knowledge gained. This means that the averages were virtually identical for these students and for previous year's students where only a face-to-face class was taken. Nevertheless students showed a lot more interest in the subjects matter.

Also by encouraging student group work the results showed that in combination online and face-to-face instruction can be a very useful way of improving the teaching and learning experience.

Students' expectations prior to online sessions: the survey results showed highly motivated and mainly curious students in spite of their poor Second Life® literacy.

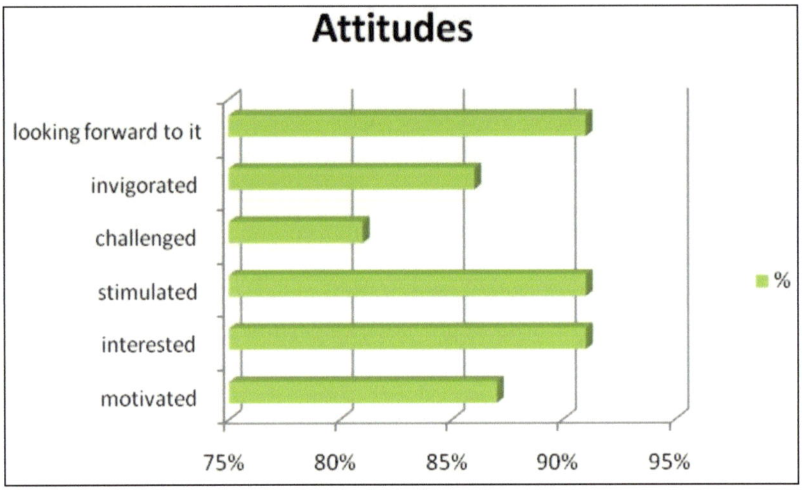

Fig. 3. Students' expectations prior to online sessions

Students' behaviours after online sessions: the survey results showed students felt inspired and find the virtual newsroom useful and very important for better journalism practices

Results showed students:

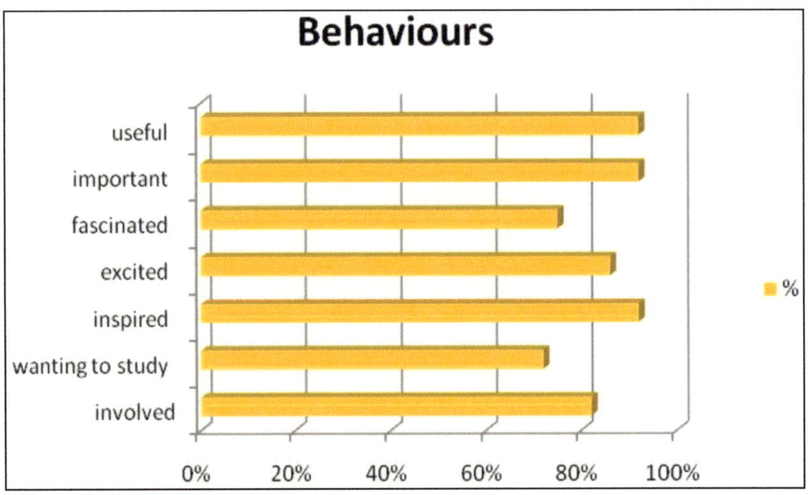

Fig. 4. Students' behaviors after online sessions

Student strategies for the use of Second Life®, such as thinking about creative solutions to problems, planning the use of time among others, point to a better integration of curricular matters seemed to be successful tasks. Also the surveyed group of students seemed to be informed about the advantages and disadvantages of specific skills that these technologies can provide in their learning outcomes.

This has already been pointed out on previous studies from Munguba, Matos and Silva (2003) which confirm that electronic media can help structuring strategies improving awareness, attention and motivation.

The strategy performed in this virtual environment was developed in order to meet the expectations of young people in the classroom and in their academic preparation.

As so students assessed that discussing the strategies according to the new methodology and study time which included topics such as optimization of the time, healthy work and educational skills in identifying and solving problems, promoting analysis and synthesis, proposed a different study, capable of promoting a better reflection and the successful execution of tasks.

These results pointed out the need for schools to reflect on their teaching practices and study strategies improvement. Taking advantage of the use of virtual environments, such as Second Life®, would provide students with metacognition skills, helping them to self-regulate their learning.

These are some of the challenges faced by schools in the future moving towards the implementation of new technologies to overcome and reconcile tradition with participation curriculum contexts that will allow knowledge to make sense.

5. Discussion and conclusions

We see from the different learning experience we studied that the benefits of immersive approaches are significant. 3D virtual worlds can bring immersion and real-time collaboration at a distance. These environments take the distance out of distance learning. Informal and collaborative learning in natural context is the best approach as this is already practiced by students. Virtual worlds seem to make students feel more confident, more open, more participative, more creative, and more responsive. In fact, in the immersive virtual worlds, students seem to attend training sessions because they want to learn (Bettencourt & Abade, 2008). On the other hand the establishment of virtual classrooms allows teachers to better reach and fill students' needs. The virtual classrooms can be set at a time and in a space (virtual) free of restrictions - that can be adapted, allowing a better participation from a larger number of students.

In a 3D immersive virtual world there are no physical barriers or borders. Information flows, people build and share content, relationships are set up, the net of connections extends and knowledge is built. This acquisition is made in a natural way, by participating in a community, by sharing, interact and collaborate, discussing and launching ideas, contents and information, therefore a "learning activity is (...) a conversation undertaken between the learner and the other members of the community" (Downes, 2006). It is a natural process of interaction and reflection with the guidance and correction of expertise or peers. SL® for being immersive neutralizes the sensation of isolation and distance, since actions are taken in 1st person and can be simulated and emulated. The environment, since is built by the users, can be adapted according with needs of a specific teacher, subject or group of students.

Real-time collaboration and cooperation ally to the several connections that can be established from in-world with Learning Management Systems like Moodle or a specific webpage also gives several possibilities for learning contexts. Everything can be built, modeled, emulated and simulated – all education areas can be covered and any subject can be delivered with the help of a 3D immersive virtual world like SL® and online Web 2.0 tools.

Virtual worlds and web 2.0 tools, can bring an amount of benefits for learners (Kreijns, Kirschner & Jochems, 2003; McLoughlin & Lee, 2007) that can be summarized in five clusters:

- Participatory learning - foster participation in creation/editing of content;
- Collaborative learning – collaborative knowledge construction (information shared by individuals can be recombined to create new forms, concepts, ideas, mash-ups and services);
- Autonomous learning - share, communicate, and discover information in communities;
- Communication and interaction capabilities - richer opportunities for networking
- Lifelong learning (join the wisdom of the crowds) - develop digital competences & support lifelong development.

Despite the benefits, some challenges should also be considered. For learners to connect and take benefits they need to be motivated to interact. Social interaction will not automatically occur just because technology allows it. Therefore it shouldn't be taken for granted learners' capabilities and motivation to interact. The borders of the learning environment become diffused, therefore a careful planning and management is mandatory. Virtual worlds and Web 2.0 tools have their own dynamics and are transient environments - moderation becomes a requirement. Students are free to learn according with their own patterns, however a teacher or tutor should be a constant presence to guide and moderate.

Another aspect to consider is the difficulty in designing the new models of teaching and learning (Instructional Design). On the other hand higher level of anxiety are often associated with computer-mediated communication which may limit the degree of social interaction. In order to build group relationships and dynamics, students need to trust each other, feel a sense of belonging, and feel close to each other before they engage in collaboration and sharing - sense of community belonging.

Design and implement an extended classroom through the use of online tools and virtual worlds requires preparation, time and means. We cannot take participation in computer-supported collaborative learning (CSCL) environments for granted, there is the need to ignite and maintain it. Students have to be prompt and reminded about their roles, they should be able to embrace autonomy but teacher needs to provide the right incentives. Interactivity has to be improved (two way connection between distributed students) by organising social interaction, collaboration and shared activities - otherwise it is unlikely to occur or be meaningful. In an extended classroom, teacher also has to foster a sense of community and encourage development of a social presence. It is very important do not replicate traditional classrooms in online environments, it is pointless if what only changes is the place/space (there is no point having students sit in rows listening to lecturers in a virtual world for instance). Employ designs that focus on collaborative, networked communication and interaction which seems to be what students expect nowadays - without losing the informality.

It is crucial to focus more on the actors and their needs rather than the technology (it's all about people after all).

The implementation of online courses - with spaces for communication and synchronous and asynchronous interaction - can be a solution to consider in various circumstances, associated or not with the traditional classroom teaching. The use of virtual worlds allows to expand the capacity of institutions of formal education, while creating the opportunity to serve students outside of their range. The combination and adaptation of different methodologies contribute to the renewal of teaching methods and practices, making them more suited to technological developments of our time.

Web 2.0 and 3.0 are already making changes in the way students learn. It's particularly attractive to younger students who have grown up surrounded by these technologies. To digital society learners traditional teaching is poorly stimulating, for their are used to utilize simultaneously diverse types of media. Education is therefore in need of a change, to be more personalized, reflexive, social connected, involving and permitting instant gratification to embrace both native and digital immigrants (Prensky, 2001).

6. References

ATIS (2007). *ATIS Telecom Glossary 2007* [Online]. Available: http://www.atis.org/glossary/definition.aspx?id=248 [Accessed 18 April 2011]

Au, W. J. (2008). *The Making of Second Life: Notes from the New World.* Collins: Harper Collins.

Austin, T. & Boulder, C. (2007). *The Horizon Report, 2007.* [Online]. Available: http://www.nmc.org/pdf/2007_Horizon_Report.pdf [Accessed 10 July 2010]

Bartle, R. (2004). *Designing Virtual Worlds.* New Riders Publishing.

Bell, M. (2008). Definition and Taxonomy of Virtual Worlds. *Journal of Virtual Worlds Research* [Online]. 1(1). Available: http://jvwresearch.org/page/volume_1_issue_1 [Accessed 18 April 2011]

Bennett, K., & McGee, P. (2005). *Transformative power of the learning objects debate.* Open Learning, 20(1).

Bennett, S. (2005). *Using related cases to support authentic project activities.* In A. Herrington & J.

Bennett, S., Agostinho, S., & Lockyer, L. (2005). *Reusable learning designs in university education.* In T. C. Montgomerie & J. R. Parker (Eds.), Proceedings of the IASTED International Conference on Education and Technology. Anaheim, CA: ACTA Press.

Bettencourt, T. & Abade, A. (2008). Mundos Virtuais de Aprendizagem e de Ensino - uma caracterização inicial. *IE communications, Revista Iberoamericana de Informática Educativa* [Online] Nº 7/8. Available: http://161.67.140.29/iecom/index.php/IECom/issue/view/41/showToc [Accessed 15 September 2010]

Bettencourt, T. (2009). *Teaching & Learning in SL: Figuring Out Some Variables.* [Online]. Available: http://cleobekkers.wordpress.com/2009/01/28/teaching-learning-in-sl-figuring-out-some-variables/ [Accessed 15 September 2010]

Bettencourt, T. (2010). Second Life® - Uma nova forma de expressão de arte. Keynote conference on the *VI Seminário Imagens da Cultura / Cultura das Imagens*. Universidade Aberta e Universidade de Múrcia (Org). Porto: Universidade Portucalense, 2 Julho, Portugal.

Chee, Y. (2001). Virtual reality in education: Rooting learning in experience. In *Proceedings of the International Symposium on Virtual Education 2001*, Busan, South Korea, pp. 43-54. Symposium Organizing Committee, Dongseo University [Online]. Available: http://yamsanchee.home.nie.edu.sg/Publications/2001/ISVE2001Invited.pdf [Accessed 18 April 2011]

Connolly, T., MacArthur, E., Stansfield, M., & McLellan, E. (2005). *A quasi experimental study of three online learning courses in computing*. Computers & Education. Vol. 49 (2).

Cross, J. (2007). *Informal Learning: Rediscovering the Natural Pathways That Inspire Innovation and Performance*. John Wiley and Sons, Inc. Pfeifer.

Current user metrics for Second Life, Retrieved June 2011 from http://community.secondlife.com/t5/Featured-News/Q1-2011-Linden-Dollar-Economy-Metrics-Up-Users-and-Usage/ba-p/856693, Secondlife.com.

Dillenbourg, P. (1999). *Collaborative-learning: Cognitive and Computational Approaches*, Oxford, Elsevier.

Downes, S. (2006). *Learning Networks and Connective Knowledge* [Online]. Available: http://it.coe.uga.edu/itforum/paper92/paper92.html [Accessed 20 March 2010]

Dudeney, G., & Hockly, V. (2007). *How to teach English with Information Technology*. Pearson Education Limited.

Dudeney, G., & Ramsay, H. (2009). *Overcoming the entry barriers to Second Life in higher education*. In C. Wankel & J. Kingsley (Eds.), Higher education in virtual worlds: Teaching and learning in Second Life. Bingley: Emerald Group Publishing Limited.

Hayes, G. (2009a). *ROI 101 & Stickiness of Second Life?*. Retrieved May 2011 from http://www.personalizemedia.com/roi-101-stickiness-of-second-life/

Hayes, G. (2009b). *Some of my 2008 reflections on Virtual Worlds, reflected elsewhere*. Retrieved May 2011 from http://www.personalizemedia.com/some-of-my-2008-reflections-on-virtual-worlds-reflected-elsewhere/

Heinze, A. & Procter, C. (2004). *Reflections on the use of Blended Learning*. [Online]. Available: http://www.ece.salford.ac.uk/proceedings/papers/ah_04.rtf [Accessed 10 July 2010]

Herrington (Eds.) (2006). *Authentic learning environments in higher education*. Hershey, PA: Idea Group Inc.

Kreijns, K., Kirschner, P. & Jochems, W. (2003). *Identifying the pitfalls for social interaction in computer-supported collaborative learning environments: A review of the research.* Computers in Human Behavior, 19(3), 335-353.

Lave, J. & Wenger, E. (1991). *Situated Learning: Legitimate Peripheral Participation*. Cambridge, University Press.

Lim, K. (2009). The six learnings of Second Life. *Journal of Virtual Worlds Research* [Online]. 2(1). Available: https://journals.tdl.org/jvwr/article/view/424/466 [Accessed 18 April 2011]

Livingstone, D; Kemp, Jeremy & Edgar, E. 2008. *From Multi-User Virtual Environment to 3D Virtual Learning Environment, Research in Learning Technology*, 16: 3, 139-150 [Online] Available: http://dx.doi.org/10.1080/09687760802526707 [Accessed 5 April 2011]

Loureiro, A. & Bettencourt, T. (2010). Immersive environments - A Connectivist Approach. In *3rd World Summit on the Knowledge Society (WSKS 2010)*, September 22-24, 2010, Corfu, Greece.

Loureiro, A., Wood, D. & Bettencourt, T. (2010). Online tutorial - meeting students's needs. In *I Encontro Internacional TIC e Educação* (ticEDUCA2010), November 19-20, 2010, Lisbon, Portugal.

Maki, R., Maki, W., Patterson, M., & Whittaker, P. (2000). *Evaluation of a web based introductory psychology course: I. Learning and satisfaction in online versus lecture courses.* Behavior Research Methods, Instruments, and Computers. Vol. 32 (2).

Mattar, J. (2008). *O uso do Second Life como ambiente virtual de aprendizagem.* Retrieved on March 2011 from http://www.educacaoadistancia.blog.br/revista/ucp_joaomattar.pdf

McCormark, A. (2010). *The e-Skills Manifest.* Available http://files.eun.org/eskillsweek/manifesto/e-skills_manifesto.pdf [Accessed 18 April 2011]

McLoughlin, C. & Lee, M. (2007). *Social software and participatory learning: Pedagogical choices with technology affordances in the Web 2.0 era.* In ICT: Providing choices for learners and learning. Proceedings ascilite Singapore 2007. Available: http://www.ascilite.org.au/conferences/singapore07/procs/mcloughlin.pdf [Accessed 18 April 2011]

Mercado, L. (2009). *Integração de mídias nos espaços de aprendizagem.* Em Aberto, v. 22, n. 79, p. 17-44.

Moita, F. (2008). *Second life e estratégias de estudo: interface no aprendizado de universitários brasileiros.* Retrieved on January 2011 from www.anped.org.br

PCMag (2011). *Virtual world Definition from PC Magazine Encyclopedia*[Online]. Available: http://www.pcmag.com/encyclopedia_term/0,2542,t=virtual+world&i=59269,00.asp [Accessed 18 April 2011]

Prensky, M. (2001). *Digital Natives, Digital Immigrants.* Available: http://www.marcprensky.com/writing/Prensky%20-%20Digital%20Natives,%20Digital%20Immigrants%20-%20Part1.pdf [Accessed 18 April 2011]

Rodrigue, C. (2002). *Assessment of an experiment in teaching geography online.* In: http://www.csulb.edu/~rodrigue/cgs02.html.

Schroeder, R. (2008). Defining Virtual Worlds and Virtual Environments. *Journal of Virtual Worlds Research* [Online]. 1(1). Available: http://jvwresearch.org/page/volume_1_issue_1 [Accessed 18 April 2011]

Second Life Education Directory, Retrieved June 2011 from http://wiki.secondlife.com/wiki/Second_Life_Education_Directory, Secondlife.com.

Shelley, D., Swartz, L., & Cole, M. (2006). *A comparative analysis of online and traditional undergraduate business law courses.* In: http://www.actapress.com/PaperInfo.aspx?PaperID=28526&reason=500.

Siemens, G. (2004). *Connectivism: A Learning Theory for the Digital Age.* Available http://www.elearnspace.org/Articles/connectivism.htm [Accessed 18 April 2011]

Silva, E. (2003) *A leitura nos oceanos da internet.* São Paulo: Cortez

Taylor, S. (2007). *Sistine Chapel in Second Life.* [Online]. Available:

http://www.academiccommons.org/commons/showcase/sistine-chapel-in-second-life [Accessed 20 March 2010]

Thomas, R. (2001). *Interactivity and Simulations in e-Learning*. Retrieved on May 2011 from http://www.jelsim.org/resources/whitepaper.pdf

Twigg, C. (2003). *Improving quality and reducing costs: Designs for effective learning*. Change, 35, 2229.

Valente, C., Mattar, J. (2007). *Second Life e Web 2.0 na Educação: o potencial revolucionário das novas tecnologias*. São Paulo: Novatec.

Wankel, C. & Kingsley, J. (2009). *Higher Education in Virtual Worlds: Teaching and Learning in Second Life*. Emerald Group Publishing Limited.

Wenger, E. (1998). *Communities of Practice. Learning, Meaning, and Identity*. Cambridge, Cambridge University Press.

Yasar, O. & Adiguzel, T. (2010). A working successor of learning management systems: SLOODLE. Procedia - Social and Behavioral Sciences Volume 2, Issue 2, 2010, Pages 5682-5685 Innovation and Creativity in Education .[Online]. Available: http://www.sciencedirect.com/science?_ob=ArticleURL&_udi=B9853-5016P5K-166&_user=10&_coverDate=12%2F31%2F2010&_rdoc=1&_fmt=high&_orig=gateway&_origin=gateway&_sort=d&_docanchor=&view=c&_acct=C000050221&_version=1&_urlVersion=0&_userid=10&md5=8e436213aae9fb052dba019f114bf503&searchtype=a

6

3D Multi User Learning Environment Management – An Exploratory Study on Student Engagement with the Learning Environment

Indika Perera, Colin Allison and Alan Miller
School of Computer Science, University of St Andrews
United Kingdom

1. Introduction

3D Multi User Virtual Environments (3D MUVE), or commonly known as 3D virtual worlds, are expanding their application domains from their introduction. These simulated environments with 3D support can be seen as useful applications that facilitate our various needs. Using 3D virtual worlds for supporting learning has shown promising results, introducing a new type of learning platform, known as 3D Multi User Learning Environments (3D MULE). In effect, 3D learning environments based on Multi-User Virtual worlds are a growing feature of UK education (Kirriemuir, 2010). Leading universities are interested in, and have been researching on, applications of this novel technology for their learning needs. 3D MUVE support more intuitive activities for learning complex and advanced concepts. 3D virtual worlds are particularly appropriate for educational use due to their alignment with Kolb's (Kolb, *et al.* 2001) concept of experiential learning, and learning through experimentation as a particular form of exploration (Allison *et al.*, 2008). Interactive 3D virtual environments demonstrate a great educational potential due to their ability to engage learners in the exploration, construction and manipulation of virtual objects, structures and metaphorical representations of ideas (Dalgarno *et al.*, 2009).

In this exploratory study, we investigate the level of student engagement with the 3D MUVE supported learning environment with respect to the system management and administration. 3D virtual worlds are often considered as game environments, associating the entertainment and flexibility factors as intrinsic parameters. A known challenge is associating the pedagogical and formal educational practices with the 3D MUVE supported environments, without affecting the rich and dynamic nature. At the same time, students should not be let for getting overwhelmed by the environment features so that they miss out the intended learning outcomes of the learning task (Perera *et al.*, 2011b). To achieve these crucial goals to facilitate student learning with 3D MUVE, we envisaged a unique approach through management policy considerations.

Our 3D MULE research activities are based on the two prominent 3D MUVE at present, Second Life (SL) (Linden Labs, 2003) and Open Simulator (2007). Second Life and Open Simulator 3D MUVE provide a similar simulated environment for the users except they have two different implementations at the server side. The high degree of compatibility between the two systems has been a major research benefit for our work. Current trends indicate a significant shift of preference towards OpenSim for learning activities, however (Allison, *et al.*, 2011).

This chapter is arranged into the following sections: in section 2 we describe background details along with our experiences on using 3D MUVE for learning; section 3 explains the research problem, including the hypotheses for this study. Section 4 describes the research methodology and the experiment design while the section 5 extensively analyses the research findings validating the hypotheses of the study. The section 6 discusses the contributions of the study, study limitations and the expected future work. Finally, the section 7 gives the conclusions of the research to conclude the chapter.

2. Background and related work

Various studies for enhancing education with 3D MUVE can be found. A recent research on exploring meaningful learning of students in 3D virtual worlds (Keskitalo *et al.*, 2011) shows the importance of developing suitable pedagogies for 3D MUVE learning. Pedagogy to relate 3D presence was introduced by Bronack (*et al.*, 2008), in which avatar engagement with the environment has been considered as an important element for the pedagogy. De Freitas (*et al.*, 2010) has proposed a framework for designing and evaluating learning experience in 3D virtual worlds, considering efficacy and challenges of new learning styles. Burkle and Kinshuk (2009) have elaborated the potential possibilities of using 3D virtual worlds for the needs of 21st century education. These signify the importance of associating 3D MUVE for learning. However, most of the studies on 3D MUVE based learning assume the fact that 3D MUVE implicitly facilitate learning needs. Since 3D MUVE are not designed for educational needs, users have to consider system and environment properties extensively for integrated blended learning experience (Perera *et al.*, 2011a). For managing e-Learning environments, an approach using policy based management on security and usability was introduced by Weippl (2005). We investigate the same with 3D MUVE as the principal research; in this study, we focus on identifying factors for 3D MULE management and their effect on student engagement.

Students' comfortable ability to engage in the learning environment is an essential factor for the virtual world supported education (Burkle & Kinshuk, 2009). This indeed rationalise our research objectives. Furthermore, technology supported learning environments can help to develop specific self-regulatory skills related to successful engagement in learning (Dabbagh and Kitsantas, 2004). 3D MULE can be a valuable learning platform if students can highly engage with the environment while having self-regulatory skills for their learning. In another study, Wang (*et al.*, 2011) has identified that the visual guidance and support help to increase the self-regulation and student engagement in learning activities. 3D MULE not only include rich 3D content objects for visually enabled learning aids, but also provide learners to engage in the environment with immersion.

Our previous work on using 3D MUVE for teaching and learner support include a range of advanced learning constructs to facilitate students. Wireless Island (Sturgeon *et al.*, 2009) aids collaborative learning and exploration of wireless traffic through interactive multimedia and simulations. Wireless Island was used as the experiment environment for this study and further details will be discussed later. The Laconia Acropolis Virtual

Archaeology (LAVA) (Getchell *et al.*, 2010) project allows students to engage in a simulated archaeological excavation, and then explore a recreation of the site. Similar to the Wireless Island another research project, Network Island in OpenSim, developed a learning island to facilitate teaching network routing (McCaffery *et al.*, 2011). Network Island simulates several routing protocol behavior as an interactive method. Students can create their own topologies and examine the routing behavior. As a part of the evaluation of 3D MUVE for serious learning needs a network traffic analysis of 3D MUVE was performed (Oliver *et al.*, 2010) to identify challenges. Second Life and OpenSim were used for teaching Human Computer Interaction (HCI) to undergraduate students, through creative student projects (Perera *et al.*, 2009). Research on integrating 3D MUVE with e-Learning infrastructure with the objective of formulating a blended learning environment with 3D support is conducted (Perera *et al.*, 2010; Perera *et al.*, 2011a) and the results facilitated this research.

Fig. 1. Selected projects based on 3D MULE: Left side - virtual humanitarian disaster training environment, and right side - the Network Island to facilitate teaching and learning on network routing algorithms

3. Research problem and hypotheses

This study is a crucial step of our main research on supporting policy based management of 3D Multi User Learning Environments. In this phase, we are specific to identify the major factors that contribute for successful policy considerations for 3D MULE management. Student behaviour and control through system administration have been widely considered as major aspects for effective learning environment design and management. Based on our previous studies on 3D MUVE use cases and role analysis (Perera *et al.*, 2011a) and the 3D MUVE system function behaviours, we hypothesised these two parameters to be the most influential factors for successful policy considerations for 3D MULE management. As a result, in this study we examine the three factors: student behaviour, system (environment) management and student engagement with the learning environment as the research variables.

Therefore, we first defined the following two research hypotheses to examine the supposed two variables based on our previous observations.

H1 - Student behaviour with self-regulation is a major factor of the successful 3D Multi User Learning Environment management

H2 - Appropriate system environment management is a major factor of the success of 3D Multi User Learning Environment management

For the second objective of this study, we investigated the impact of the above said two variables on the student engagement with the 3D MULE. Importantly, the engagement with the 3D MULE may not necessarily represent the student engagement with the learning, although there can be a positive correlation if the learning tasks are constructively aligned (Biggs, 1996). However, the opposite of the above condition is trivial; if the student engagement with the 3D MULE is low, then their engagement with the learning tasks that depend on 3D MULE, tend to be low as well, for obvious reasons. Nevertheless, since many researchers on 3D MUVE supported learning have indicated, as mentioned above, there are unique advantages of using 3D MUVE for teaching and learner support, which we may not be able to obtain through the other methods. If that is true, then deductively, we can presume that if students do not highly engage with 3D MUVE that host learning task, there is a high tendency on them having less engagement with the learning tasks as well.

Furthermore, as we are expected to formulate policy considerations for 3D MULE management, those policy considerations should not negatively affect the student engagement with the environment. Therefore, to examine the influence on student self-regulation and system environment management on student engagement with 3D MULE, we defined the following two hypotheses for the analysis.

H3 - Students' self-regulatory behaviour has a positive and significant effect on student engagement with 3D Multi User Learning Environments

H4 - System environment management has a positive and significant effect on student engagement with 3D Multi User Learning Environments

4. Research methodology and experiment design

Considering the research objectives and the defined research hypotheses, we have designed an experimental setup as the test environment for the study. Since this research investigates about the student engagement in 3D MULE and the two variables which directly relate with the need of 3D MULE management, we decided to conduct a two part study as the experiment. First, students were allowed to experience the 3D MUVE supported learning environment as a part of their studies. We used Open Simulator for creating the learning island; contrast to Second Life, OpenSim gives us the complete autonomy on deciding the server environment and required configurations and scalability. We also realised that, it would provide sufficiently accurate data for the analysis if we use a student credit bearing course activity, which is conducted using 3D MUVE. It is important that students participate in a real learning session to provide accurate data for our study than following a hypothetical set of instruction, which does not provide them a true motivation as they have with their course learning activities. Moreover, such arrangement helps students to comfortably associate the experience they had when they answer the questionnaire.

With that in mind we considered to associate the study with two course modules that use the same learning aid developed in 3D MUVE. We also decided to increase the accuracy of the experiment data using a broad sample of participants by selecting the two course modules one from the undergraduate curriculum (CS3102 - Data Communications and

Networks) and the other from the postgraduate (taught MSc program) curriculum (CS5021 - Advanced Networks and Distributed Systems). Information about the experiment samples is given in the Table 1.

Experiment setup	Module Associated	SCQF level	Number of students	Brief Description of the Learning Task
1	CS3102 Data communication and Networks	10	31	Interact with the Wireless Island and observe the Wireless traffic simulations with different settings. Able to explain basic conditions and problems related with Wireless communication.
2	CS5021 Advanced Networks and Distributed Systems	11	28	Interact with the Wireless Island and observe the Wireless traffic simulations with different settings. Able to explain basic and advanced scenarios and problems related with Wireless communication

Table 1. Details about the experiment samples and associated course modules

It is important to mention that these two course modules have different learning objectives and tasks while representing different levels in Scottish Credits and Qualification Framework (SCQF) (SCQF, 2007). Therefore, the subject content in each level had dissimilar objectives, and the assessment tasks were slightly diverse, although students used the same learning tool. However, for this study, we are focused on student engagement with the environment and the impact on that from the two aspects, their view of self-regulation and the system management. In that regard, we can conclude that, although students had a different level of the same learning task on the same learning aid, both samples had the same characteristics with respect to our measure. Therefore, the experiment has not been affected by the learning tasks given in the modules; hence can be considered as a single sample consisting of 59 students for the data analysis.

The learning environment, Wireless Island (Sturgeon *et al.*, 2009), is a dedicated region for facilitating learning and teaching wireless communication. It was developed as a research project which provides interactive simulations with various configuration settings for students to explore and learn. It also includes supplementary learning content such as lecture notes, lecture media stream and a museum to depict the history of wireless communication development. Figure 2 shows the island layout (left-side image) with different interactive content and places for student learning. The right-side image of the Figure 2 shows the interactive simulation on teaching *Exposed Node Problem* in wireless communication.

To facilitate small group learning with a less competitive environment interaction, we decided to have 6 students per region. Therefore, five regions were created in the OpenSim environment and loaded the Wireless Island on each. This resulted in an identical learning set up for each student, and students were given their assigned region as their home place to start the learning task. Region information is given in the Table 2 and the corresponding 3D MUVE map, and an island map is shown in the Figure 2. The root island (Learn) remained as an empty island with everyone to access as a sandbox so that students can try their desired content creation and other activities without affecting the learning environment.

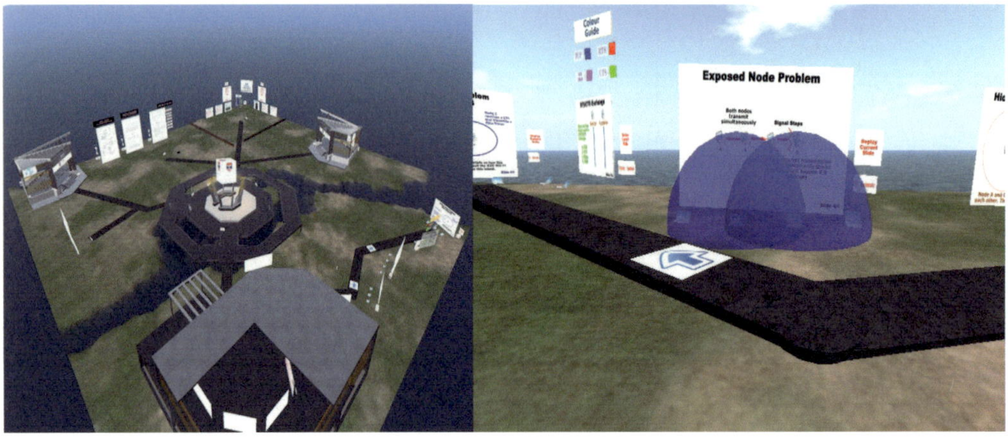

Fig. 2. Wireless Island overview with layout - left side; right side - an interactive learning aid for simulating Exposed Node Problem in Wireless communication

Island Name (Region)	Relative Position Coordinates	Number of Students
Aelous1	X = 1002; Y = 1000	6
Aelous2	X = 1004; Y = 1000	6
Aelous3	X = 1002; Y = 1002	6
Aelous4	X = 1002; Y = 1004	6
Aeluos5	X = 1004; Y = 1002	6/7
Learn (root island)	X = 1000; Y = 1000	-

Table 2. Experiment region information and their relative positions on the Grid

In the Figure 3, a block of square represents an island (256 m x 256 m virtual area), and the islands are distributed as shown in the map, to minimise adjacency problems and to simulate the isolated island look and feel. Tiny green dots indicate the student avatar positions when the image taken.

The second part of the data gathering based on a questionnaire with 15 questions divided into two sections: Avatar Behaviour - 7 questions, and 3D MULE management - 8 questions. Additionally, five open-ended questions were included to help students to express their opinions openly. The 8 questions in the 3D MULE management section had some relevance on the two factors that we are investigating, self-regulation and environment management; however, the questions did not directly represent the variables. We decided to confirm through the statistical analysis, therefore, treated as 8 related questions.

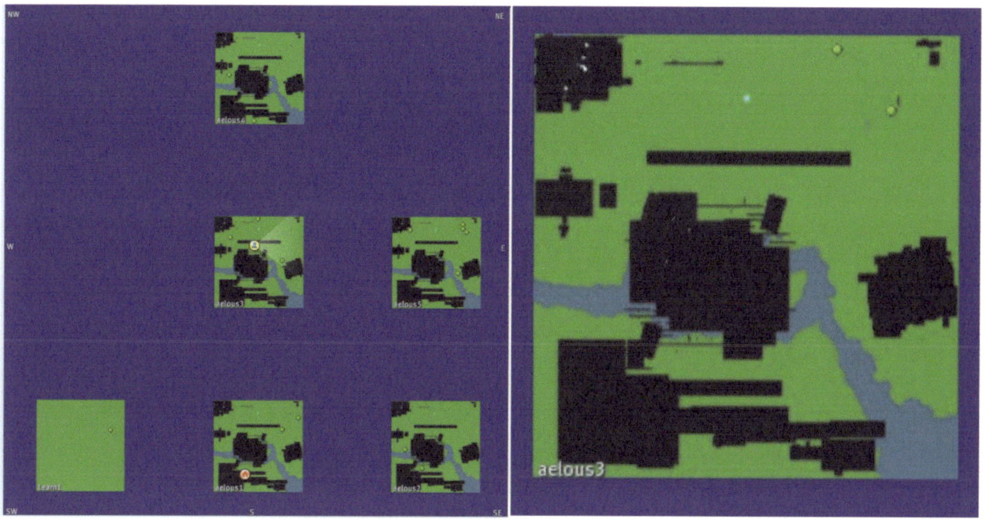

Fig. 3. Map view of the experiment setup (a small square represents an island), right side image - the enlarged map view of the island aelous3

5. Results and analysis

Based on the experiment design described above, our data gathering was conducted during the laboratory sessions by observing the avatar interactions and then at the end of the session through a questionnaire. Let us first discuss the observed student engagements during the laboratory session and then analyse the collected questionnaire data for the hypotheses testing.

5.1 Observations of student behaviours

For the preliminary analysis on observed student activities following scenarios are considered.

Avatar appearance change or outfit creation is an entertaining activity for any 3D MUVE user. However, the ease of creating attractive appearances within a limited time can be one of the critical determinants for student motivation on appearance change. Notably, the OpenSim with Hippo viewer gave an additional step on changing user appearance compared to Second Life. Users first have to create body-part, edit it and then wear to change the shape of the default avatar. Without this step, students could not change the gender of their avatars (default avatar has the view of a female user shown in the top left picture of the Figure 4). However, few students spent more time during their lab session and created more sophisticated shapes, clothes and appearance. Postgraduate students showed relatively less enthusiasm on changing their avatar shape, whereas many undergraduates went to a further step by comparing the avatar appearances with their friends'. In overall, students showed different preferences on spending time for appearance change and their commitments towards complex shape creation. However, we believe that the student commitment for making their avatars look good should not be underestimated as it could take substantial portions of their learning time. Constructive arrangements, such as, pre-sessions for familiarity and entertainment before the actual learning engagement, are therefore, highly encouraged.

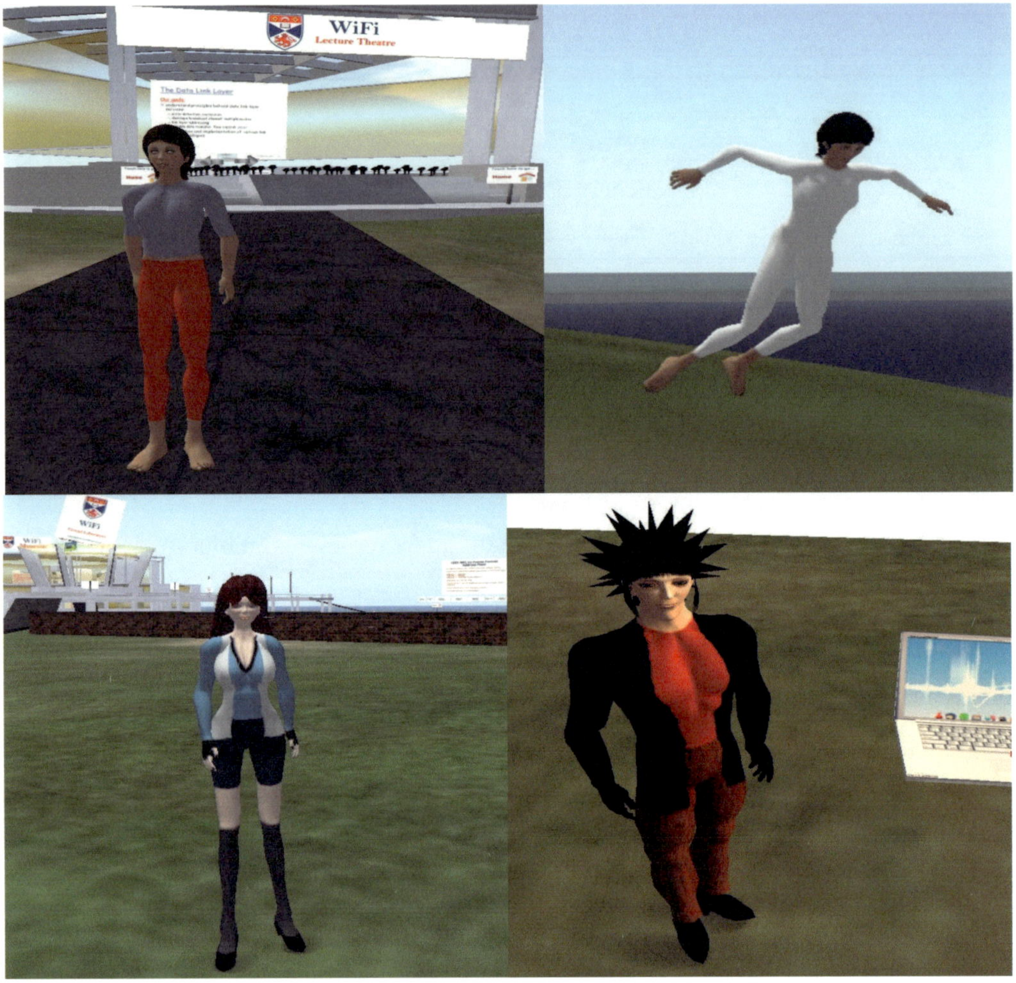

Fig. 4. Varying levels of avatar appearance customisation

Content object creation is one of the fundamental interactivity mechanisms available in 3D MUVE. Second Life and Open Simulator allow its users to create various basic shapes known as prims. Prims can be combined to create complex and compound shapes. The sculptured prims, to represent organic shapes that are difficult to design with basic prims, are also available for advanced content creation. Indeed, allowing students to create these attractive 3D shapes makes them engaged with the environment with passion. As observed, students tried range of constructions as well as editing of the existing objects. Some of these alterations directly affected the learning experience; activities such as wearing the control buttons of the media display, moving and changing the internal arrangement of the lecture theatre, and creating constructs on the simulation area (shown in Figure 5), should have been discouraged through usable policy consideration for a supportive learning. However, in this exploratory study, we wanted to examine such potential actions as empirical evidence to facilitate our future work; hence, students were given unrestricted access to their environments.

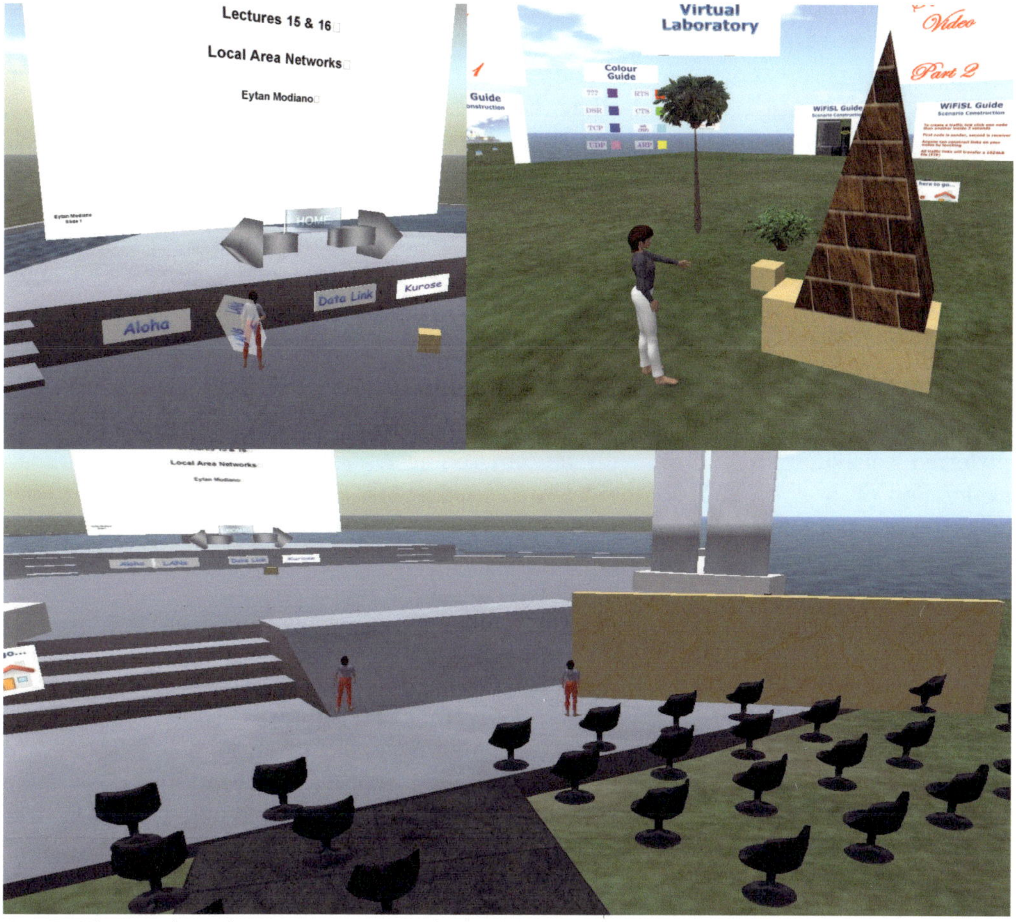

Fig. 5. Observed student engagements through content creation and content alteration

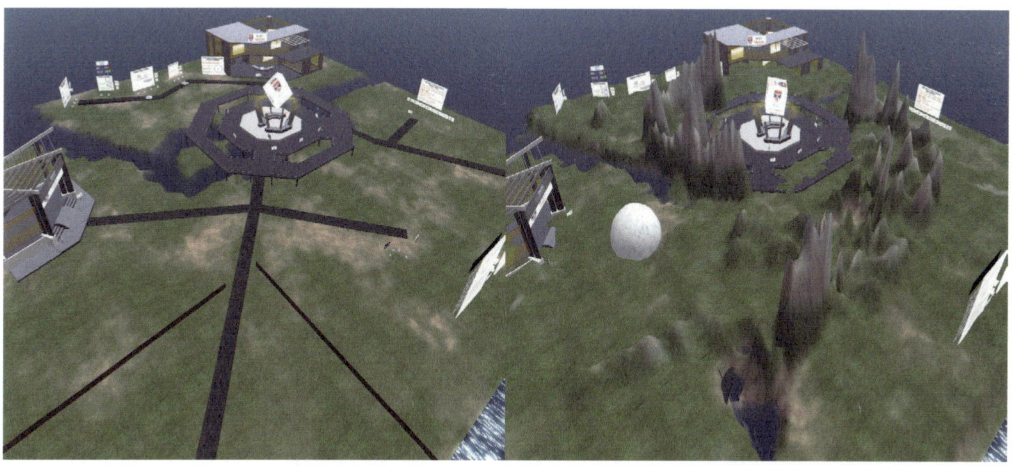

Fig. 6. A terraformed and altered island (right side) compared to its' original layout

The Figure 6 shows a higher degree of student interaction that caused the learning environment to be significantly altered compared to its original layout and appearance. However, this observation was a one-off incident, as majority of students retrained from changing land settings, although they have tried content creation, often. Moreover, compared to the Masters students, the junior honours students showed high interactivity and environment alteration, resulted in a range of user created objects, altered content and changed land terrain. The undergraduates showed more enthusiasm on exploring potential game-like features, and associate their real-world friends for collaborative activities/plays, although such acts were not necessarily related with the Intended Learning Outcomes (ILOs) or Teaching and Learning Activities (TLAs). In contrast, Postgraduate students showed a higher tendency to complete the given tasks, which may have, in certain instances, resulted in less motivation to entertain themselves by exploring the 3D MUVE features.

It is important to note that, in all of these cases, students were allowed to follow their preferred behaviour to interact with the environment as a mean of learning through exploration (Kolb *et al.*, 2001) without any restriction. An assurance was given that their behaviour or environment interactions do not affect their assessments, but the completion of learning tasks.

5.2 Analysis of questionnaire data

We received 32 completed questionnaires (54.28%), which consisted of 20 responses from postgraduate students (71.4%) and 12 responses from undergraduate students (38.7%). A preliminary observation was performed to examine the question characteristics and to validate the designed mappings of variables based on the collected responses. Descriptive statistics and the literal meanings of the questions were considered to understand the user responds and possible classifications. Analytical observations of the question and respond behaviour resulted in preliminary clustering of questions into two major categories, as designed in the questionnaire: User Behaviour and 3D MULE Management, which include questions Q1 to Q7 and Q8 to Q15, respectively, supporting the design rational of the questionnaire.

The seven questions in User Engagement section (Q1 to Q7) indicates a high level of internal consistency among the questions with Cronbach's alpha = 0.802 (>0.7) table7. Furthermore, the intended data collection on user behaviour section was mainly based on student behavioural activities within the environment; therefore, the seven questions were designed to cover seven different student engagement aspects. In that respect, statistical observation of internal consistency validated the combined use of questions to represent the associated variable.

5.2.1 Pre-test for factor analysis

The questionnaire section on 3D MULE management was designed, as explained in the research design, examining two prime variables associating system administration and user self-control by retaining from misconduct. Although, we had this in mind when the questionnaire was designed, we were compelled to analyse the set of questions statistically for an accurate identification of the variables as a method to test the research hypotheses.

Exploratory Factor Analysis tends to provide reliable factor identifications when the sample size is larger. There are many criteria to decide the appropriate sample size; however, many scholars agree that the suitable determination of the ratio between Minimum Sample Size (N) to Number of Variables (p) i.e., *N:p* should be a more reliable practice. Costello and Osborne (2005) concluded, through empirical tests, that high *N:p* provides higher accuracies compared to lower ratios. In our analysis on variable exploration *N:p* is 16:1 suggesting higher reliability in the solution model; hence validating the Factor Analysis outcome with our sample. Previous research (Moose and Azevedo, 2007) have suggested citing Nunnally (1978) that 10:1 is adequate and has performed Factor Analysis (N=49, p=3) validating our sample size and ratio.

Moreover, the Bartlett Test of Sphericity, a strict test on sampling and suitable correlations, was performed to test the appropriateness of data for the Factor Analysis, using PASW [version 18.0] statistical software. The Bartlett Test of Sphericity gave $\chi^2 = 155.257$, $p<.001$ suggesting that the correlation matrix (R-Matrix) of items shows highly significant relationships and can be clustered based on relationships. Furthermore, the Null Hypothesis of R-Matrix being an Identity Matrix can be rejected with significance, indicating high suitability for Factor Analysis.

Finally, Kaiser-Meyer-Olkin (KMO) test was performed to examine the accuracy of using the data sample for the factor analysis. KMO value obtained was 0.714 (>0.7 threshold for goodness) (Field, 2006) validated the data sample for Factor Analysis. Having all the conditions for Factor Analysis met through the pre-test, we performed Factor Analysis using PASW.

5.2.2 Exploratory factor analysis – Hypothesis test

With the positive results for the pre-tests performed to examine the appropriateness of using Exploratory Factor Analysis to confirm the research hypotheses (**H1** and **H2**), we used the Factor Analysis provided in PASW [18.0]. As the standard practice, our factor selection was based on the Principal Component Analysis with factors that have higher Eigenvalues (>1). The PASW output, shown in the Table 3, indicates two factors with Eigenvalues over 1. It is a clear separation of the contributing factors against the weak components, as the 3rd highest Eigenvalue is .648. Moreover, the highest two factors contribute nearly 72% of the total variation of the aspect 3D MULE Management.

For further analysis, we employed Orthogonal Verimax Rotation with Kaizer Normalization and obtained the rotated factor loadings per items as shown in the Table 3. For the suppression of weak loadings we used Stevens (1992) and Field (2006) suggestions for the cut-off for small samples, and used .6 as the limit, considering the exploratory objectives of the analysis. With the rotated loadings, we obtained improved factor loadings for the identified two factors. We also felt that the Orthogonal Verimax Rotation is accurate as the two factors more or less equally contribute (37.13% and 34.74%) to the underlying aspect of consideration.

Component plot in the rotated space is shown in the Figure 7. Furthermore, the Component Transformation Matrix showed symmetry over the diagonal, indicating that our use of Orthogonal Rotation is accurate, and the rotated factor loadings are correct.

Total Variance Explained

Component	Initial Eigenvalues			Extraction Sums of Squared Loadings			Rotation Sums of Squared Loadings		
	Total	% of Variance	Cumulative %	Total	% of Variance	Cumulative %	Total	% of Variance	Cumulative %
1	4.020	50.250	50.250	4.020	50.250	50.250	2.970	37.130	37.130
2	1.730	21.621	71.871	1.730	21.621	71.871	2.779	34.741	71.871
3	.648	8.097	79.967						
4	.538	6.729	86.696						
5	.500	6.249	92.945						
6	.346	4.330	97.275						
7	.168	2.099	99.374						
8	.050	.626	100.000						

Extraction Method: Principal Component Analysis.

Table 3. Factor Analysis Output from PASW (including rotated loadings)

As the rotated factor loadings indicated, questions Q9, Q15, Q10 and Q8 were considered as a one variable and examined for suitable naming. When the objectives of questions were analysed, we identified a common parameter that governs all the four questions. We concluded it as the student behaviour with Self-regulation, and defined the new variable as Self-Regulation. The second factor represents Q11, Q14, Q12 and Q13 questions and we observed a strong contextual meaning on system administration and control as the common parameter. The questions strongly discuss the student preference and impact on the system control, administration and management of the 3D MUVE. Therefore, we defined this variable as Environment Management to cover all the aspects that associate with this factor.

Rotated Component Matrix[a]

	Component	
	1	2
Q9	.937	
Q15	.904	
Q10	.884	
Q8	.607	
Q11		.868
Q14		.818
Q12		.765
Q13		.711

Extraction Method: Principal Component Analysis.
Rotation Method: Varimax with Kaiser Normalization.

a. Rotation converged in 3 iterations.

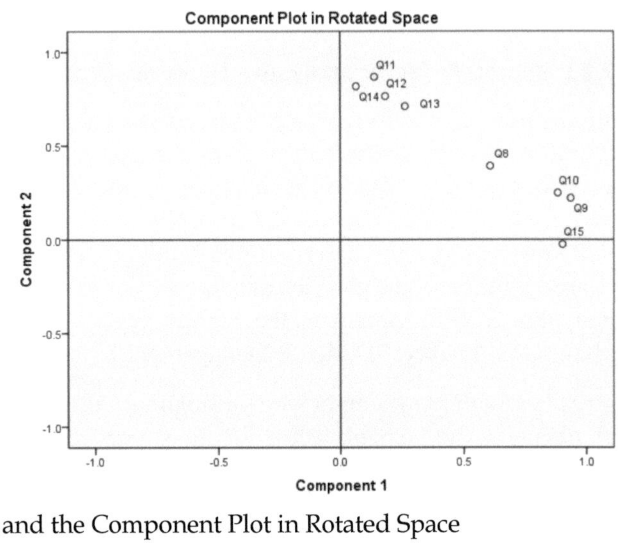

Fig. 7. Rotated Component Matrix and the Component Plot in Rotated Space

The identified two variables explain nearly 72% of the behaviour of the aspect 3D MULE Management. Moreover, there aren't any other strong and significant variable revealed through the factor analysis; therefore, we can conclude that the extracted two variables, Self-Regulation and Environment Management, represent the aspect of 3D MULE Management. Hence, we conclude that the research hypotheses **H1** and **H2** of our study is substantiated based on the exploratory factor analysis.

5.2.3 Variable summary

Including the verified two variables, statistical analyses were performed and obtained the following results that summarises the variable behaviour.

Student engagement

With suitable naming, we examined the questions associated with this variable for descriptive statistics and overall variable behaviour based on the question scores. The table 1 summarises the analysis results

No	Question	Mean	Mode	Std. Dev.	Std. Error
Q1	I changed my appearance as I like to appear	3.09	3	0.466	.082
Q2	I created content objects in the environment	3.69	4	0.471	.083
Q3	I tried to change land or content objects in the learning environment	3.66	4	0.483	.085
Q4	I communicated with others regularly	3.53	4	0.507	.090
Q5	I have followed other avatars collaboratively during my learning	3.44	3	0.504	.089
Q6	I moved to all the places in my island and teleported to other islands	3.81	4	0.397	.070
Q7	My activities in the environment resulted in a high engagement with my learning tasks	3.97	4	0.40	.071

Table 4. Questions on student behaviour and the descriptive statistics

Additionally, the One-Sample Kolmogorov-Smirnov Test for normality indicated the question means are normally distributed [$X \sim N\ (3.598,\ 0.283)$] with significance ($\alpha$=0.997) to retain the hypothesis of normal distribution. This implies that in general, students showed a positive response indicating that there has been a high degree of engaged with the environment.

However, the questions Q1 and Q5 (Q1 in particular) showed averages around 3 corresponding to the answer: "Neither Agree nor Disagree". If we have a closer look at the questions, the Q1 relates the student engagement through the measure on the level of avatar appearance modification. In fact, few students enjoyed by modifying their avatars to represent, either their real identity through physical appearance or having a fantasy look. However, most of the students were comfortable in using the default avatar or with minimum customisation, such as colour change of clothes, and committed their time more on other engagements and learning tasks, which resulted in this lower mean value. The Q5 asks about the student collaboration, specific on following others behaviour or learning steps. Although, we encourage students to collaboratively work with their peers, traditional learning environments are not supportive of collaborative learning unless the students are asked to do so. In this learning activity, the students were given individual task sheets that they should complete, but not specifically asked to collaborate with other students assigned into the same region. Moreover, the majority of the students may have felt that they should not misuse the flexibility given within the 3D MULE, as their individual performances on the tasks are assessed, taking a more self-restrained behaviour on collaborating with others. As a result in both cases (Q1 and Q5) the majority reported scale 3 - "Neither Agree nor Disagree" as their answer (Mode is 3).

The questions Q2, Q3, Q4 and Q6 were based on the remaining avatar actions that associate with the possible major areas of avatar engagement. Content creation, land and content alteration, and avatar communication activities showed reasonably similar average responds agreeing with the asked questions. Additionally, the most of the students confirmed that response (Mode = 4). The question Q6 had the environment exploration aspect within the assigned island and the teleportation to other islands. Almost all the students indicated higher positive average with most of the students agreeing with the statement.

Q7 played the concluding role for the student behaviour question set. It let the students to think about their activities within the 3D MULE and then evaluate his or her learning engagement as a result of the activities performed. This was a crucial question as it directly inspects about the considered aspect of student engagement as a measure of student activity. Student responses showed a high average, indicating that they agree with the question (Mode =4). This strengthened our research hypotheses as a direct measure, while showing a possible relationship between the environment interactions and the learning engagement, which we recommend for further study.

Self-regulation

The One-Sample Kolmogorov-Smirnov Test for normality indicated that the question means are normally distributed [$X \sim N(3.876, 0.378)$] with significance (α=0.516) to retain the hypothesis of normal distribution. This implies that, in general, students have shown a positive response indicating that students agree the self-regulatory practice as an important consideration.

No	Question	Mean	Mode	Std. Dev.	Std. Error
Q8	I think my behaviour affected others' learning	3.31	3	0.592	.104
Q9	The open space and others avatars made me to interact as in a real-world learning session	4.05	4	0.354	.064
Q10	Use of real identities increases the proper behaviour of students	4.02	4	0.309	.056
Q15	Student should responsibly use the learning environment	4.10	4	0.296	.051

Table 5. Questions on student self-regulation and descriptive statistics

The question Q8 tends to be a self-assessing question as students had to think about their behaviour reflectively and critically. This was important to meet the objectives of the question set, as students answer the rest of the questions with a reflective mind associating every little detail that they have experienced or felt during the engagement. In that sense, beyond the literal meaning of the Q8 it helped students to give accurate responses to the rest of the questions as an indirect effect. However, student may have been doubtful about on what degree they consider their behaviour and impact on others' learning; therefore, we observe an average of 3.31 (more towards the respond "*Neither Agree nor Disagree*") while the majority confirming that (mode = 3).

The questions Q9, Q10 and Q15 more or less have recorded nearly same averages (~4 = Agree) while the majority confirms that preference as the Mode is 4 for each question. Q9 was designed associating the privacy concerns of being in an open environment that could be seen by others and with a high probability on simultaneous engagement on same learning activity or content. The association of real-world classroom metaphor reinforces the student comparative observations, resulting in a broader opinion with higher accuracy. Q10 examines the student view on having their real identity (first name and last name) as their avatar username. Avatar anonymity and its impact on student learning has been researched previously on various contexts (Messinger *et al.*, 2008); the majority of students agreed (Mode = 4 and Mean = 4.02) that there is a positive impact of using their real identities on following appropriate behaviour within the environment. The Q15 plays the concluding role for the student's self-regulatory practice with the sense of being a responsible participant in the learning session. Importantly, we did not relate any indirect variable association as the effect of being a responsible student with proper practice; we let the student to self-evaluate the consequences of their practices for the responses. The student responses indicate that majority of the students agreed that students must use the environment responsibly, indicating a positive association of self-regulated interaction as an acceptable practice.

Environment management

The One-Sample Komogorov-Smirnov Test for normality indicated the question means are normally distributed [$X \sim N\ (3.95, 0.175)$] with significance (α=0.796) to retain the hypothesis of normal distribution. This implies that in general student showed a positive response indicating that there has been a high degree of engaged with the environment.

No	Question	Mean	Mode	Std. Dev.	Std. Error
Q11	Land and Content management controls are important for the environment management	3.78	4	0.420	.074
Q12	System control and management practices are important for a reliable learning	3.91	4	0.296	.052
Q13	System management settings should not reduce the 3D MUVE usability	4.19	4	0.592	.105
Q14	Appropriate system security and controls ensure a successful learning experience	3.89	4	0.390	.070

Table 6. Questions on system environment management and descriptive statistics

These four questions associate the system administration and environment control aspect as students perceive. The question Q11 asks about two major 3D MULE system administration function groups for their significance in using as an environment management mechanism. Land and content management related functions are the most significant activities that an avatar can use to affect the existing learning environment. Therefore, it is important to examine the student preference on constraining them from using these features if needed for environment management. As the results indicate, students agreed on this statement. The question Q12 further examines the student view on having a reliable learning experience through system controls and environment management. This statement associates the aspect that the learning environment is trustful. Student responses indicate that they still welcome the controlling measures on the 3D MULE to improve the trust, knowing the importance of the reliability of a learning activity for formal education. The Q13 discusses the associated concern on 3D MULE usability, if the management controls are restrictive and unsupportive for attractive learning engagement. Interestingly, the average feedback was 4.19, the highest value for all the questions, showed the student concern on losing the usability and attractiveness of learning environment. This delivers a very important message to the 3D MULE designers and module administrators, as their environment management policies should always prioritise the usability of the environment. Finally, the question Q14 brings a conclusive statement for the environment management concerns. This, in fact, summarises the student's overall opinion on the use of system environment controls and management practices to ensure successful learning. Students on average agreed to the statement showing their positive attitude for a supportive environment management for their learning facilitation.

5.2.4 Variable analysis

The internal consistency was measured among the question items within the three variables, using Cronbach Alpha. Results, summarised in Table 7, are higher than the recommended thresholds (>0.7 for exploratory studies), indicating higher internal consistency within variable items. As discussed previously, similar to the variable student engagement, the question items that associate Self-Regulation and Environment Management also meet the requirements to be considered collectively to represent the relevant variable.

Variable Name (Factor)	Mean μ	Standard Deviation σ	Cronbach α	Number of Items
Student Engagement	3.598	0.283	.802	7
Self-Regulation	3.876	0.378	.829	4
Environment Management	3.950	0.175	.80	4

Table 7. Summary of the analysis variables and their internal consistency measure

Correlations

			Self_ Regulation	Environment_ Management
Spearman's rho	Self_Regulation	Correlation Coefficient	1.000	.398*
		Sig. (2-tailed)	.	.024
		N	32	32

*. Correlation is significant at the 0.05 level (2-tailed).

Fig. 8. Correlation between the two identified variables self-regulation and environment management

Finally, the Spearman Correlation analysis between the derived variables, Self-Regulation and Environment Management was performed (shown in Figure 8) to examine their relationship. The Spearman Correlation Coefficient (*rho*) was 0.398 indicating a weak positive relationship with significance ($p<0.05$). Furthermore, the weak relationship between the two variables was further indicated as only about 15% of one's variance could be explained by the other. This is important to proceed with our analysis as we have to be certain about the model that we are testing; i.e., the two variables are measuring sufficiently different parameters and the inter-relationship between the two is insignificant to affect the hypothesis test. Therefore, we conclude that, through all these analyses that the two variables Self-Regulation and Environment Management are sufficiently independent as measuring two different aspects, which further proves the Factor analysis and selection of variables to represent the 3D MULE Management aspect.

5.3 Hypothesis testing

To test the research hypotheses **H3** and **H4**, we used regression analysis between the hypotheses variables. Furthermore, this enabled us to examine the variable behaviour and the exact relationships among the dependent and independent variables.

A sample size test was done for the fitness for regression analysis, as the first step. As defined in Cohen (1988) and further elaborated by Field (2006), for the test statistics of *anticipated large effect* (F^2*=0.35*), Number of *predictors* (*n*=2), Probability level of Significance (*a = 0.05*) with the desired *statistical Power level* of (*1-β = 0.8*), the minimum required sample size was 31. Therefore, our sample size *N* = 32 (>*31*) suites well for the analysis and the regression model is reliable.

Variables Entered/Removed[b]

Model	Variables Entered	Variables Removed	Method
1	Environment_ Management, Self_ Regulation[a]	.	Enter

a. All requested variables entered.

b. Dependent Variable: Student_Engagement

Model Summary

Model	R	R Square	Adjusted R Square	Std. Error of the Estimate
1	.871[a]	.759	.743	.15866

a. Predictors: (Constant), Environment_Management, Self_Regulation

ANOVA[b]

Model		Sum of Squares	df	Mean Square	F	Sig.
1	Regression	2.303	2	1.151	45.736	.000[a]
	Residual	.730	29	.025		
	Total	3.033	31			

a. Predictors: (Constant), Environment_Management, Self_Regulation

b. Dependent Variable: Student_Engagement

Fig. 9. Regression analysis output with model test using ANOVA (PASW)

PASW (18.0) linear regression analysis model summary and the model fit (ANOVA) is shown in the Fig.9. R^2 = 0.759, indicates that about 75.9% of the variation in the student engagement is determined by the environment management and student self-regulation with the learning activities in 3D MULE, by means of a combined effect. As the model fit test results in ANOVA shows, the regression model significantly explains the Student

Engagement from the two variables Environment Management and Self-Regulation (*p<0.001*).

The individual relationships of the independent variables Self-Regulation and Environment Management with the dependent variable Student Engagement were obtained through the regression test coefficients, and the summary is mentioned in the Table 8.

Variable	β	**Standard Error**	**t-value**	**Significance**
Self-Regulation	.240	.097	2.482	0.019*
Environment Management	.657	.092	7.312	0.000**

$^{*}p < 0.05$
$^{**}p < 0.01$

Table 8. Regression analysis summary

As the variable relationship with predictor parameters of the model shown in table 6, the model path coefficients are .240 for Self-Regulation, which is significant (*p*<0.05) and .657 for Environment Management with significance (*p<.001*). The resulted research model outcome can be shown as follows (Figure 10).

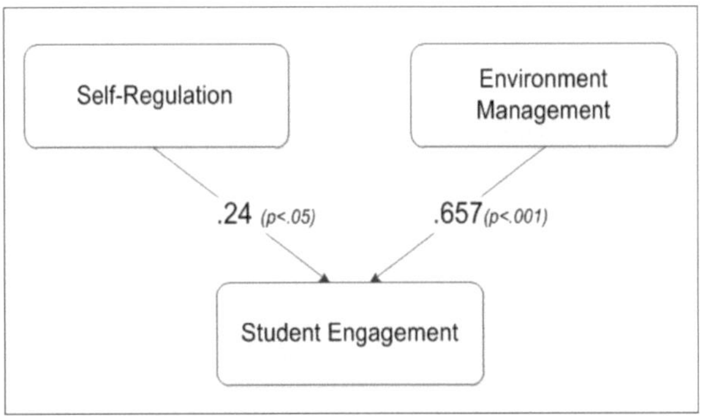

Fig. 10. Hypotheses model summary with path coefficients

Therefore, the research model substantiates our research hypotheses **H3** and **H4**. With reference to **H3**, we can say that the student *Self-Regulation* on learning activities in 3D MULE result in a significant positive effect on the *Student Engagement* with the learning environment and learning tasks. Therefore, we conclude that, for constructive and successful 3D MULE student engagement, we have to consider and promote student self-regulation as a main policy consideration area for 3D MULE management. Thus, we validate our research hypothesis on considering student self-regulation as a prime factor for successful management of 3D MULE and associated learning activities.

Regarding to the hypothesis **H4**, we can say that the *Environment Management* practices, as described previously, result in a significant positive effect on Student Engagement with the 3D MULE and learning tasks. Therefore, we conclude that, for constructive and successful 3D MULE student engagement, we have to identify and implement Environment Management policies as a main policy consideration area for 3D MULE management. Thus, we validate our research hypothesis on considering environment management of 3D MULE as a prime factor for successful management of 3D MULE and associated learning activities.

5.4 Summary of open feedback

The given questionnaire had a section with five open-ended questions, mentioned below, to capture student opinions in general. The most important objective was to identify any concerns or feedback that we cannot capture through the first 15 questions. Therefore, we associated the common parameters such as security and privacy concerns to facilitate the Environment Management policy considerations. We like to mention the fact that not all participants have responded to these questions. However, a wider range of responses was observed with a reasonably good turnout. Few selected student expressions are shown in brackets, for each question.

OFQ1 - Are there any privacy concerns you have regarding the use of 3D Multi User Virtual Environments for learning activities?

This question aims at capturing privacy concerns that the students have or felt while engaging the learning activities. Importantly, this was taken as a measure for both Environment Management and Self-Regulation. Majority of the students felt that their activities are visible to others so the actions were committed consciously knowing that they are in an open environment. It is interesting to see that students felt the immersion at most and felt that their work could be monitored, which is also possible with other information systems as a forensic measure, if they commit misconduct. However, students feeling of being a part of open community may have resulted in shaping their behaviour. However, it is an open research possibility for further study.

[I feel psychologically aware about my progression being observed by others]
[No privacy with my activities]
[It is open, so privacy is a big concern]

OFQ2 - Are there any security challenges on using 3D MUVE for your learning, as an overall opinion?

This question let the students to express their opinions on learning environment security. Importantly, the security enforcement of a learning environment is well researched (Weippl, 2005) and a prominent concern for present technology supported learning solutions (Perera et al., 2011a). With respect to the study, this question had the objective of identifying students' trust on existing 3D MUVE security implementations and policies employed. Moreover, students must have a confidence on the learning environment reliability to engage comfortably with the assessed and serious learning tasks. Overall, students showed their lack of awareness on the security and administrative measures available in 3D MULE. This was an important observation, and we consider it for our future research.

[I believe it is safe and secure]
[There can be, but I'm not so sure, I need to learn more]
[I'm not sure]

OFQ3 - What are the areas of 3D MULE that should be addressed or improved?

This was a general question to see whether students have different thoughts for improving the learning experience with 3D MULE. There were few interesting thoughts expressed, although following two ideas appear to be undoubtedly correct. First, some students expressed their need on having a private space if the learning activities are not designed for collaboration. Secondly, various concerns were raised on familiarising the 3D MUVE. It is a known fact that 3D MUVE have a steep learning curve (OpenSim, 2007). Importantly, some students worried on certain challenges they faced due to the 3D MUVE at the early stages of the learning activity. We also realised the importance of providing necessary user guidance and consider it for future work.

[There should be availability of private space for some activities with data which are secure]
[Students need to be trained before they use the virtual world for assessment and laboratory work]

OFQ4 - If the 3D MULE security enhanced, can it affect the rich features and the usability of the system?

This question helped us to observe the student view on implementing various environment management strategies to enhance the system security. As 3D MUVE are designed mainly for entertainment and gameplay, mapping those use cases for a formal learning engagement can be a challenge and requires additional level of security management (Perera et al, 2010, Perera et al., 2011a). However, there is a growing concern on 3D MUVE control as it can affect the intrinsic characteristics and usability of the environment. Students came up with vibrant answers, both supporting and against. We suggest a contextual approach for deciding the required level of security management for the learning needs.

[Yes, because it might hinder the entire idea of collaborative learning in a virtual environment]
[I don't see an issue of security]
[It can be!]
[May be; but should not implement such measures]

OFQ5 - Any other comment/concern/suggestion about using 3D MUVE for learning

As a final thought, all students who expressed their answers indicated the benefits of using 3D MULE as a teaching and learner support tool. Importantly, their positive comments are highly encouraging and supportive of the future studies on 3D MULE while strengthening our prime objective of facilitating student learning with technology support.

[I believe it should be handled on a wider scale and it is a great tool for interactive and collaborative learning]
[Generally, I like it as an educational methodology]
[It is interesting to use these stuffs]

In general, this open ended feedback showed some of the significant concerns that students have, which we could not relate directly with the questionnaires. As explained in each of these questions, careful analyses on the student answers helped us to associate those with the statistically identified variables. It was observed that the student expressions were scattered on different functional and systems properties of the 3D MUVE when considered in isolation; however, in the general context, we have been able to incorporate those with the identified variables self-regulation and environment management with suitable adaptations for the future steps of this research.

6. Discussion

6.1 Study contributions

We have shown the analysis results of this study previously with reasonable explanations. The first contribution we have is the student engagement observations during the laboratory sessions. We observed varying types of student engagements with the environment. As we have explained previously, this indicates student motivation to perform their preferred tasks comfortably. Essentially, such an interaction would be welcomed by any teacher as we all agree that making students being engaged with the learning tasks is a prime challenge. However, we suggest that teachers and learning activity designers should constructively associate these student-preferred 3D MULE functions for making effective and attractive learning tasks.

With the exploratory factor analysis, we have identified that the aspect of managing the 3D MUVE supported learning environments can be achieved through its components: students' self-regulation and system environment management. In fact, the self-regulatory learning practice is a widely researched and well established practice of learning. Pintrich, (2000) defines self-regulation as "an active, constructive process whereby learners set goals for their learning and then attempt to monitor, regulate, and control their cognition, motivation, and behaviour, guided and constrained by their goals and the learning environment contextual features". Students with better self-regulatory skills tend to be more academically motivated and display better learning (Pintrich, 2003). However, most of the previous studies are based on either traditional learning or e-Learning activities; our study brings a new dimension to the norms of self-regulatory learning. Schunk (2005) has suggested that there is a need for more research aimed at improving students' self-regulatory skills as they are engaged in learning and to examine how learning environment contexts affect the amount and type of self-regulation displayed. In our study, we have specifically identified this challenge and worked to overcome it aiming a general scenario of learning with 3D support. Importantly, previous studies on self-regulatory learning mainly considered student practice that helps them achieving their learning objectives with minimum support or drive from others. When it comes to 3D MULE, students face a new set of challenges and opportunities to explore while they are engaged in learning. Prominently, students have to engage actively with the learning environment and progress through various tasks, in contrast to passive interaction on 2D or traditional learning setup. As we suggest, for success, students should not feel their learning engagement and the environment engagement as two different activities; if we can constructively align the learning objectives, learning tasks and assessment practices with the available 3D MULE functions, we can see a significant success on student learning through self-regulation. Furthermore, such alignment would help students to perceive the environment management controls as a positive construct that enables their preferred learning methods with reliability.

Finally, through the hypothesis testing, we observed that there is a positive influence on student engagement with the learning environment due to the association of self-regulatory and environment management practices. As the obtained values suggest, environment management shows the highest positive impact on increasing the student engagement. This can be mainly due to the students' perception on possible environment and system control mechanisms that relate with their activities. Although, students entertain themselves by various environment engagements such as, content creation, editing land and terraform, and 3D presence with associated actions, they also felt the difficulty of task coordination and unsupportive avatar behaviour during a crucial learning engagement. For example, lecture displays reset whenever an avatar hits the play button, disturbing the other viewers that have been watching. In another instance, if a student's simulation arrangement is too close to another's setup, there can be interferences on communication display spheres. These types of problems can be easily solved if we implement appropriate policy considerations through system environment control.

6.2 Study limitations

Despite all the efforts to make this study accurate as possible, it was affected by the following limitations. Extra efforts and careful analyses were employed to minimise the impact while increasing the accuracy of research models, observed.

Due to the nature of the research objectives, our study sample was limited for a selected set of students. This specialised group of students was chosen, considering their participation in the learning activity designed with 3D MUVE. These students, therefore, have provided their feedback and answers based on their real experiences, which we could validate through the observation of their interaction and the environment changes. In that respect, the mere increase of the sample size from a random student population for the sake of numbers would create a negative influence on the accuracy of results, than having a relatively small, yet accurately representative group of participants. Therefore, we consider the data received as accurate and conclusive though the study had a relatively small sample.

Sample size for the Factor Analysis was another challenge we encountered due to the use of a specialised user group. As we have expressed above, our *N:p* ratio was sufficient to give high reliability on the solution factor model (Costello and Osborne, 2005). Recent studies also suggest that the effect of sample size becomes insignificant if the solution model provides a *stronger* outcome due to the strength of data; in which the strength of data is defined as having 3 or more items that show over 0.7 loadings per factor, and smaller number of factors (MacCallum, *et al.*, 1999). Through a rigorous empirical study on top ranked journal articles that had factor analysis, Lingard and Rowlinson (2005) have proven this observation and recommend a new strategy to validate factor results for smaller sample sizes; higher N:p ratio with stronger data. Our exploratory analysis indicates only 2 factors with each having more than 3 items over .7 loadings. This was suggested in Osborne and Costello (2004) as well. More importantly, irrespective of the sample size impact on the results, the Kaiser-Meyer-Olkin (KMO) and Bartlett Test of Sphericity for the data set showed a very strong and significant ($p<.001$) result, indicating the correctness of Factor Analysis with PCA over the data sample. This further validates the Factor Analysis results and the stronger outcome.

The questions used in the questionnaire were appropriately designed to capture student views, although they have yet to be examined for psychometric measures. Unfortunately, it is a challenge to find a widely accepted standard set of psychometric measures, in particular, for 3D MULE user evaluation and learning activities, as the field of study is still growing. We would welcome the researchers to consider this aspect in their future research.

Another challenge we had was the accurate capturing of the user opinions. Likert scales have been widely used and are the standard mechanism for these research needs. However, users only answer the asked questions or consider the given statements; there can be different opinions with individual users, which we may ignore if we confined the user input to the asked questions. Since this was an exploratory study, we welcomed different aspects that student wish to provide; hence, included a set of open-ended questions to overcome this challenge. Although, we cannot use the student inputs for these questions with the statistical analysis, the comments provided a significant contribution, qualitatively.

6.3 Future work

This research and its findings suggest a number of potential future studies. Some of these can be considered as further extensions of our work. As mentioned above, provision of user guidance on 3D MULE management can be a very valuable future work, since such facility would enable 3D MULE users to experience their learning activities with high confidence and reliability. Moreover, it would reduce the steepness of the 3D MUVE learning curve. This will attract many potential educators to conduct their teaching and learning support activities with 3D MULE. On the other hand, when students and teachers exactly know 3D MULE limitations and suitable functions for their work, they could save a significant amount of their time, which then can be used for achieving productive tasks such as Intended Learning Outcomes (ILOs), instead.

Developing 3D MULE policy consideration based on the research findings will be the most important further extension of this study. The identified two variables, Self-Regulation and Environment Management, sufficiently influence on the user behaviour and their engagement with the learning environment, as the results indicate. Therefore, the required policy consideration for the 3D MULE Management can be designed based on these two variables. Furthermore, as this study reveals, policy considerations based on student self-regulation and environment management may tend to provide effective policy-based practices with high success.

Various views/concerns mentioned by the students associating privacy and collaboration needs with 3D MULE can be considered for future studies that specialise those areas. Various learning aids and tool support with 3D MUVE can be seen in these days expecting the learning benefits. However, we believe that there is a strong need of empirical evidence on student interaction with those learning aids in 3D MULE, which we strongly recommend for further study considering the outcomes of this research.

7. Conclusion

This research has presented several important contributions for the development of 3D Multi User Learning Environments as an effective means of providing engaged student learning. The results and the analysis confirmed that the student self-regulation and system environment management are the two important factors that contribute for the 3D MULE management. Therefore, our research towards developing policy considerations for 3D MULE management will be based on these two factors for its future work. Additionally, we have seen through the analysis that the student self-regulation and the system environment management have positive and significant influence on student engagement with the 3D MUVE. This was an important observation for the researchers who are keen on managing their 3D MUVE supported learning environments. Importantly, this result encourages the policy based management of 3D MULE while enabling those to be considered as successful candidates for formal and serious educational needs.

Our contribution, through research findings and the experiment observations, would help the other researchers by providing empirical evidence on student engagement with 3D

MULE. As the empirical evidence from research on 3D MULE is a growing need, this would open a new research dialogue among researchers who partake in the development of technology supported learning. We are committed to extending this work to enhance the policy based management of 3D MULE and evaluate its impact with a broader perspective. With that we invite frontiers in educational technologies to further research and strategically associate the study outcomes with existing learning infrastructures, in a blended manner.

8. Acknowledgment

This research is supported by the UK Commonwealth Scholarships and the Scottish Informatics and Computer Science Alliance (SICSA). Second Life region rental was supported in part by the University of St Andrews Fund for Innovations in Learning, Teaching and Assessment (FILTA). The Higher Education Academy (HEA) UK supported part of the work on OpenSim. A special thank goes to the INTECH Open for their generous scholarship support to meet the costs associated with the publication of this article.

9. References

Allison, C., Miller, A., Getchell, K., and Sturgeon, T., (2008): Exploratory Learning for Computer Networking, *Advances in Web Based Learning – ICWL*, 331-342,

Allison, C., Miller A., Sturgeon T., Perera I. and McCaffery J., (2011), The Third Dimension in Open Learning, 41st ASEE/IEEE Frontiers in Education, IEEE Press, T2E-1 – T2E-6

Biggs, J. (1996), Enhancing Teaching through Constructive Alignment, *Higher Education*, 32(3), 347-364

Bronack, S., Sanders R., Cheney A., Riedl R., Tashner J., and Matzen N. (2008), Presence Pedagogy: Teaching and Learning in a 3D Virtual Immersive World, *International Journal of Teaching and Learning in Higher Education*, 20(1), 59-69

Burkle, M. and Kinshuk (2009), Learning in Virtual Worlds: The Challenges and Opportunities, *International Conference on Cyber Worlds, CW'09, IEEE*, pp.320-327

Cohen J. (1988), *Statistical Power Analysis for the Behavioural Sciences* (2nd Ed.), Academic Press

Costello, A.B. & Osborne, J.W., (2005), Best practices in exploratory factor analysis: four recommendations for getting the most from your analysis, *Practical Assessment, Research & Evaluation*, 10(7):1-9

Dabbagh, N. and Kitsantas A. (2004), Supporting Self-Regulation in Student-Centred Web-based Learning Environments, *International Journal of e-Learning*, 2(4), 40-47

Dalgarno, B., Bishop, A., Adlong, W. and Bedgood Jr., D., (2009), Effectiveness of a Virtual Laboratory as a preparatory resource for Distance Education chemistry students, *Computers & Education*, 53(3), 863-865,

de Freitas S., Rebolledo-Mendez G., Liarokapis F., Magoulas G., and Poulovassilis A. (2010), Learning as immersive experiences: Using the four-dimensional framework for designing and evaluating immersive learning experiences in a virtual world, *British Journal of Educational Technology*, 41(1), 69-85

Field A., (2006), *Discovering Statistics using SPSS*, 2nd Ed., SAGE, London

Getchell, K., Miller, A., Nicoll, R., Sweetman, R., and Allison, C. (2010), Games Methodologies and Immersive Environments for Virtual Fieldwork, *IEEE Transactions on Learning Technologies*, 3(4), 281-293

Keskitalo, T., Pyykkö, E., & Ruokamo, H. (2011), Exploring the Meaningful Learning of Students in Second Life, *Educational Technology & Society*, 14(1), 16–26

Kirriemuir J., (2010), An autumn 2010 "snapshot" of UK Higher and Further Education developments in Second Life, *Virtual World Watch, Eduserv,*

Kolb, D. A., Boyatzis, R.E. and Mainemelis, C., (2001), Experiential Learning Theory: Previous Research and New Directions, J. Sternberg and L. Zhang, (Eds.): *In Perspectives on Thinking, Learning and Cognitive Styles*, Lawrence Erlbaum, 227

Linden Labs (2003), Second Life, http://www.secondlife.com

Lingard, H.C. and Rowlinson, S. (2005) Sample size in factor analysis: why size matters, pp.1–6, [accessed in] December 2011, [available at] http://rec.hku.hk/steve/MSc/factoranalysisnoteforstudentresourcepage.pdf

MacCallum, R.C., Widaman, K.F., Zhang, S. & Hong, S., (1999), Sample size in factor analysis, *Psychological Methods*, 4, 84-99

McCaffery J., Miller A., and Allison C., (2011), Extending the use of virtual worlds as an educational platform - Network Island: An advanced learning environment for teaching Internet routing algorithms, *3rd CSEDU*, INSTICC, 1

Messinger P., Xin G., Stroulia E., Lyons K., Smirnov K., and Bone M. (2008), On the Relationship between My Avatar and Myself, *Journal of Virtual Worlds Research*, 1(2), 1-17

Moos, D.C., and Azevedo, R. (2007), Self-regulated learning with hypermedia: The role of prior domain knowledge, *Contemporary Educational Psychology*, 33(2):270-298

Nunnally, J.C., (1978), Psychometric Theory (2nd ed.) McGraw Hill, New York

Oliver, I.A., Miller, A.H.D. and Allison, C. (2010), Virtual worlds, real traffic: interaction and adaptation, 1st *ACM SIGMM - MMSys'10*, 306-316

Osborne, J.W. and Costello, A.B., (2004), Sample size and subject to item ratio in principal components analysis, *Practical Assessment, Research & Evaluation*, 9(11)

Perera, I., Allison C., Nicoll, J. R. and T. Sturgeon (2009), Towards Successful 3D Virtual Learning – A Case Study on Teaching Human Computer Interaction, *In Proceedings of 4th ICITST-2009, IEEE*, 159-164

Perera, I., Allison C. and Miller A. (2010), A Use Case Analysis for Learning in 3D MUVE: A Model based on Key e-Learning Activities, *5th ICVL*, Romania, 114-120

Perera, I., Allison, C., McCaffery J., and Miller A. (2011a), Towards Effective Blended Learning with 3D MUVE - An Analysis of Use Case Implementations for 3D MUVE Learning, *3rd Computer Supported Education - CSEDU2011*, INSTICC, 2, 46-55

Perera, I., Allison, C., and Miller A. (2011b), Policy Considerations for Managing 3D Multi User Learning Environments – Achieving Usability and Trust for Learning, *6th ICVL*, 106-112

Pintrich, P. (2000), The role of goal orientation in self-regulated learning. In M. Boekaerts, P. Pintrich, & M. Zeidner (Eds.), *Handbook of self-regulation*, 452–502

Pintrich P. (2003), A motivational science perspective on the role of student motivation in learning and teaching contexts, *Educational Psychology*, 95, 667–686.

Schunk D.H. (2005), Commentary on self-regulation in school contexts, *Learning and Instruction*, 15(2), 173-177

SCQF (2007), Scottish Credit and Qualifications Framework, [available at] http://www.scqf.org.uk/The%20Framework/

Stevens, J.P. (1992), *Applied Multivariate Statistics for the Social Sciences* (2nd Ed.) Hillsdale, NJ: Erlbaum

Sturgeon, T., Allison, C. and Miller, A. (2009), 802.11 wireless experiments in a virtual world, *SIGCSE Bulletin, ACM*, 41(3) 85-89

The Open Simulator Project (2007), Open Simulator, http://www.opensimulator.org/

Wang, M., Peng, J., Cheng, B., Zhou, H., & Liu, J. (2011), Knowledge Visualization for Self-Regulated Learning. *Educational Technology & Society*, 14(3), 28–42.

Weippl, E.R. (2005), *Security in E-Learning*, S. Jajodia, (Eds.) Advances in Information Security, Springer, 16

7

Methodology for the Construction of a Virtual Environment for the Simulation of Critical Processes

Tadeu Augusto de Almeida Silva and Oscar Luiz Monteiro de Farias
Instituto de Radioproteção e Dosimetria(IRD),
Universidade do Estado do Rio de Janeiro(UERJ)
Brasil

1. Introduction

In the so-called real world, any given process occurs simultaneously with a myriad of other processes. All these processes take place on a *continuum* of mass, energy and time *(the world)*. All things in this *continuum* are interlinked in some way. Defining a process as such is in itself already an act of abstraction. One way to study a process is to split it into three entities: the observer, the process itself and the rest of the continuum. The observer usually simplifies a process in his or her attempt to understand it. The observer considers some factors and variables as taking part in the process while ignoring or excluding others. All the variables involved in a given process form a type of microcosm. Using the scientific method, researchers aim to determine laws that govern the interplay among certain entities. To this end, different models and techniques may be used.

A virtual environment is a computer environment. It represents a subset of the real world, where models of real world variables, processes and events are projected onto a three-dimensional space. The creation of a virtual environment is an important tool for simulating certain critical processes, especially those in which human beings or things are likely to suffer irreversible or long term damage. This methodology combines a representation of the three-dimensional space with geographic references, the agent-based models, and an adequate representation of time, and aims to construct virtual environments able to simulate phenomena or processes. The three-dimensional geo-referenced representations of space can either be the spatial representation of traditional geographical information systems (GIS), or the representation adopted by Google Maps™ (Google, 2011). Adding autonomous agents to these spatial representations allows us to simulate events, measure any variable, obtain a possible spatial distribution of people and objects, estimate any environmental impacts, build alternative scenarios and train staff to deal with these critical processes.

2. The architecture of a virtual environment using an agent-based system (ABS) and a geographical information system (GIS)

Simulation is the process of building a model of a real system and conducting experiments with this model, in order to understand the behavior of the system and / or to evaluate how it operates.

Simulations can be used to describe and analyze the behavior of a system, answer questions about it and help to design a system as it exists in the real world. Both real and conceptual systems can be modeled through simulation(Banks, 1998.

Choosing a tool that enables an effective visualization of the results of a simulation is the primary goal in building a virtual environment. Ideally, the architecture of such environments should allow for the presence of sets of concurrently interacting agents which can be monitored.

The implementation of models for elaborate and dynamic systems is a highly complex task since there is no tool that permits to describe, simulate, and analyze the system under study without the need of advanced knowledge of mathematics and programming.

Through the tool of simulation, it is possible to build and explore models that help people gain a deeper understanding of the behaviour of a specific process or system.

The advantages of using simulation include:

- Informed decision-making: a simulation permits implementing a range of scenarios without consuming any resources. This is critical because once a decision to implement a policy is taken in the real world, material and human resources are used, thus generating costs.
- The compression or expansion of time: a simulation can compress or expand the duration of a process or phenomenon, in order to allow a complete and timely analysis of it. One can examine a problem in minutes instead of spending hours observing it while all events unravel.
- In order to fully understand a phenomenon, it is generally necessary to know why, where and when it occurs in the real world. Thanks to simulation, it is possible to get answers by reconstructing a scenario and subsequently carrying out a microscopic analysis. In the real world, it is often very difficult to do this, because it is impossible to observe or control the system completely.
- Problem diagnosis: dynamic phenomena have a high degree of complexity; one advantage of simulation is that it allows us to understand the interactions among the different variables. This helps in the diagnosis of problems and enables researchers to have a better understanding of the process.
- Preparation for change: it is a fact that the future brings changes. Understanding in advance "why" and "how" these changes will take place is very useful in redesigning systems / existing processes and predicting behaviour in accordance with different scenarios.
- Training staff: simulation models are excellent training tools when designed for that purpose. Used as such, staff and teams can come up with solutions and evaluate their mistakes by comparing each proposed scenario.

Some disadvantages of simulation are as follow (Banks, 1998):

- The construction of an effective model is a form of art: it requires special training garnered over time and experience. If two models of the same system are built by two distinct and competent technicians, these may be similar, but they are unlikely to be identical.

- A simulation can be difficult to interpret: when most of the simulation outputs are random variables, the results can be very difficult to analyze.
- Modeling and analysis can be time consuming and expensive.

The goal of the proposed architecture of a virtual environment (VE) is to construct scenarios to analyze the information related to given critical processes (Figure 1).

The models, built to represent different processes, phenomena or systems, are based on the behaviour of objects over time. Eventual movements of people or objects are taken into account, both of which are represented by an agent-based system (ABS). The spatial area will also be incorporated into the model using a geographic information system (GIS).

Typical autonomous agents, in an agent-based system (ABS), have some state variables, which determine their situation in the systems, and some of their behaviour, in the same way as object methods in object-oriented programming. A typical autonomous agent, that represents a person in some process, has the following state variables: i) a personal identity; ii) a position given by a set of coordinates (x, y, z); iii) a direction or angle relating to the true north; iv) a speed. Its behaviour could involve: i) moving to some position; ii) speeding up or slowing down.

The proposed virtual environment (VE) must include an appropriate representation of the space or environment in which these autonomous agents receive sensory inputs and produce outputs in the form of actions. In general, geographic information systems (GIS) use raster or vector structures to represent space in bi-dimensional models. In some cases, a third dimension is represented through the digital elevation models (DEM) of a terrain. A given GIS spatial representation (a shape file, for example) can integrate an agent-based system (ABS) and the structure of a dynamic spatial model, incorporating the dimension of time, in order to simulate a dynamic phenomenon. The GIS spatial representation is the environment in which autonomous agents of these ABS models will operate.

For each specific phenomenon, we are only interested in particular information about the environment. So, considering the geographical space where the phenomenon develops, it is necessary to filter only the aspects of interest to the study. These factors are perceived by the autonomous agents, thus causing their actions. The data is organized in different layers, each layer representing different elements such as: utilities, river and lakes, roads and rails, soil maps, land parcels, etc. It is necessary to select only the elements or layers that are of interest to the study. Objects that are not of interest must be eliminated. An environment full of superfluous objects would unnecessarily complicate the modelling and reduce its effectiveness. So, depending on the problem, it is necessary to considerably simplify the simulation, as has been done in the proposed architecture (De Almeida Silva & Farias, 2009; Farias & Santos, 2005).

In dynamic spatial models, in particular cellular automata models (Lim et al., 2002), it is common to represent space as a cell-based or raster structure (Veldkamp & Fresco, 1996; Verburg et al., 2002; Soares Filho & Cerqueira, 2002; Lim et al., 2002). Time is characterized as an incrementing value of a variable t (each increase corresponding to a simulation cycle). At the start of the simulation (when $t=t_0$), the system will be initialized with all data describing the phenomenon or process under study as seen in the state $t=t_0$. Following this, the simulation as such begins (Figure 2).

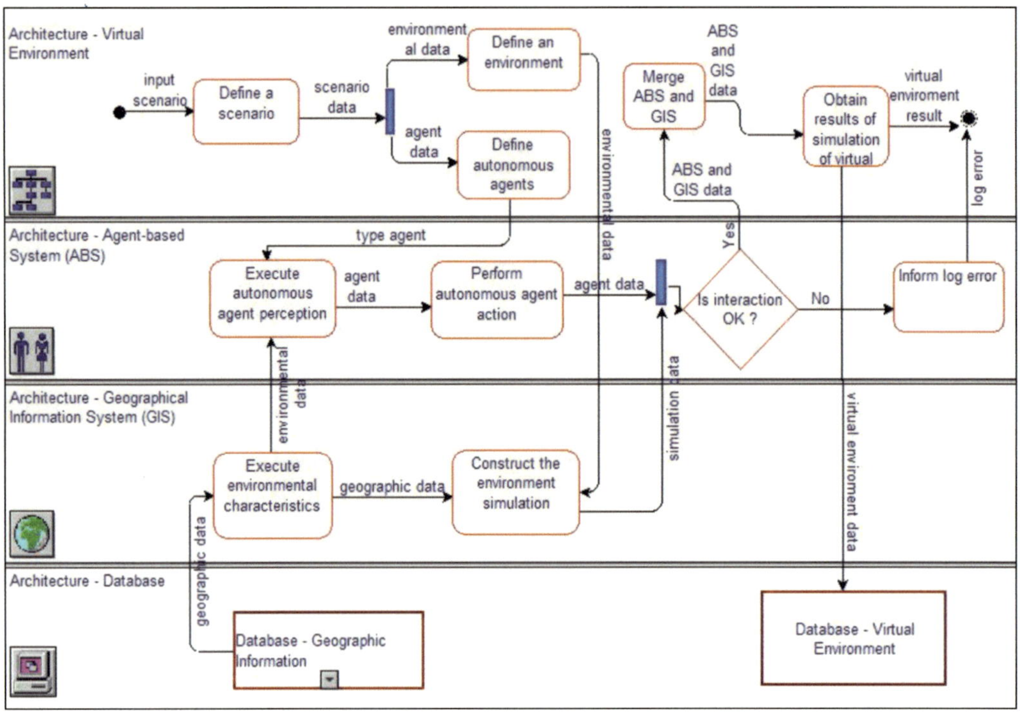

Fig. 1. The architecture of a virtual environment (VE)

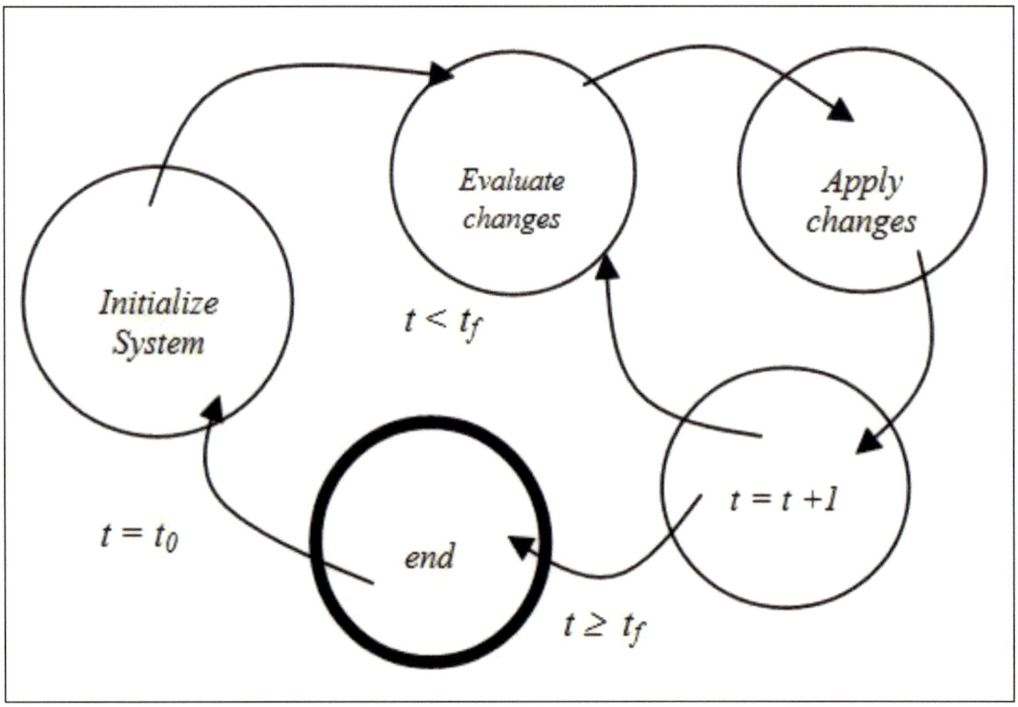

Fig. 2. A common structure of dynamic spatial models.

In the first step, it is possible to analyze, given some inputs and/or a particular configuration of cells, which cells should have their attributes changed. In the second step, certain rules are applied to the cellular automata, in order to alter its structure. In the third step, the *t* variable is incremented; if this *t* variable is less than a pre-determined value t_f - which represents the total time of the simulation - the simulation returns to the first step and the whole cycle repeats itself; otherwise the simulation ends.

This structure of dynamic spatial models can be adapted to a GIS to represent the iterative cycles during which knowledge about the environment is acquired (in other words, sensed and perceived) by the agents who then act correspondingly.

2.1 The characteristics of agent-based systems (ABS)

For thousands of years people have created models to help them understand the world. These models not only help them to better understand the phenomena they study, they also help them to transmit their ideas to other people. Through computational simulation of agent-based systems (ABS), people can better understand the effect of a specific phenomenon in an environment under study, which makes it easier to determine the consequences and risks involved.

The idea of an abstract automaton was developed in the work of Alan Turing on the development machine (Levy, 1992). The cellular automaton was popularized by John Von Neumann and Stanislaw Ulam in 1950 through the development of the tessellation model (Levy, 1992). The idea of connecting and interacting spatial units was developed by Norbert Wiener in his work on cybernetics (1948/1961) (Levy, 1992). Cellular automata were originally used to describe units in a series of networks that interact with and influence each other through messages. These networks have been used to represent a series of phenomena: computing devices, neural networks, the human brain, tissue, cellular and ecological networks, etc. They were popularized in the work of John Horton Conway called The Game of Life (Gardner, 1971), and widely applied in the fields of physics, chemistry, biology and ecology (Wolfram, 2002).

(An entity represents an object that requires an explicit definition.) An entity can be dynamic, meaning it moves through the system, or it can be static and play a complementary role in others' tasks. An entity has specific attributes that distinguish it from others. Like state variables, the attributes defined and used for a particular research interest may not applicable to other investigations.

The word "agent" refers to all beings that possess the capacity to act on its own and others' behalf. Representing humans, agents would be people with more knowledge or a more specialized capability in a determined area, which enables them to help other people accomplish their tasks. For example, a secretary makes decisions and deals with particular situations on behalf of her boss, saving him or her from having to carry out certain tasks, such as scheduling appointments and meetings, etc. (Wooldridge & Jennings, 1995).

Autonomous agents, or agents, are the software equivalent of real world entities such as human beings, animals, viruses, ships, cars, etc. For this reason, there exist several definitions for autonomous agents arising from authors' perspectives on the subject (De Almeida Silva & Farias, 2009; Farias & Santos, 2005). Here is one definition (Wooldridge &

Jennings, 1995): "A system situated within a given environment, which senses that environment through its perception mechanism and acts on that environment and/or on other agents, as time flows, in pursuit of its own agenda, plans or beliefs. Eventually the agent´s perception/action mechanism evolves with time" (Figure 3).

Autonomous agents can be classified according to their amplitude of perception, their capacity to act and the effectiveness of their action. There exist reactive and cognitive agents. Reactive agents merely react—in an opportune way, according to very simple behaviour patterns—to changes in the way they perceive their environment. Cognitive agents are more complex. They not only interact with their environment, but are also capable of remembering previous experiences, learning from these, communicating with one and another, and finally of following a defined goal, strategy or plan.

Multi-agent systems (MAS) are composed of several agents, which, in addition to having the above mentioned characteristics, can interact with one another through communicative mechanisms. In most cases, these autonomous agents can exhibit great variation and display competitive or collaborative behaviour, depending on the context (Wooldridge & Jennings, 1995).

Simulations, using Multi-agent systems (MAS), provide a computational platform in which the dynamic of spatial-temporal systems can be studied. To do this, it is possible to use reactive (simpler) or cognitive (more complex) autonomous agents (Figure 4) (Benenson & Torrens 2004; Wooldridge & Jennings, 1995).

It can also be said that an autonomous agent is a computer system situated in an environment, and that is capable of autonomous action within it, in order to meet its design objectives. For it to be autonomous, the system should be able to act without any direct human (or other agent) intervention, and should have control over its own actions and internal state (Longley & Batty, 2003).

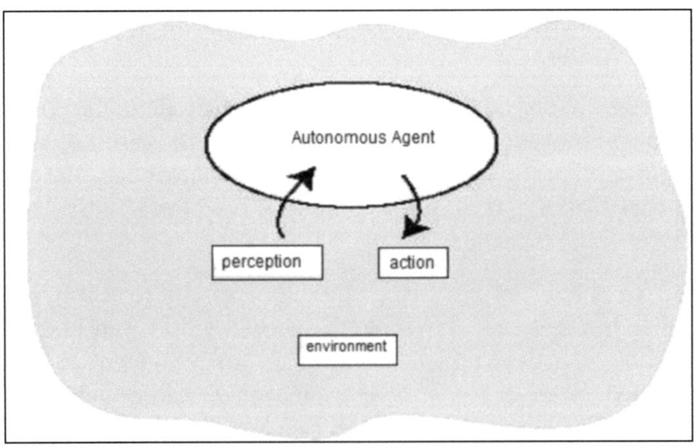

Fig. 3. An Autonomous Agent

An autonomous agent exhibits the following properties:

i. Social ability: agents should be able to interact, as deemed appropriate, with other artificial agents and humans in order to carry out their own problem solving and help others with their activities. This requires agents to follow certain communication mechanisms;

ii. Responsiveness: agents should perceive their environment and respond in a timely fashion to changes which occur within it;

iii. Proactiveness: agents should not simply act in response to their environment; they should be able to exhibit opportunistic, goal-oriented behaviour and take the initiative when appropriate.

In addition to these conditions, a number of other potentially desirable characteristics have been proposed. These include: adaptability - the ability of an agent to modify its behaviour over time in response to changing environmental conditions or an increase in knowledge about its problem solving role; mobility - the ability of an agent to change its physical location to enhance its problem solving; veracity - the assumption that an agent will not knowingly communicate false information; and rationality - the assumption that an agent will act in order to achieve its goals and will not act in such a way as to prevent its goals being achieved without good cause (Maguire et al., 2005).

It is possible to model the behaviour of people in some determined environment through the computational technology of agents, as well as consider other elements that interact with these people using this same technology, observing their behaviour and the consequences of these interactions. An environment can be created where software agents simulate critical process. The agents will have some properties such as: mobility, reactivity and objectivity. People, objects and elements will be also represented by software agents. In this way, it is possible to study, analyse and manage the critical process through agent-based simulation.

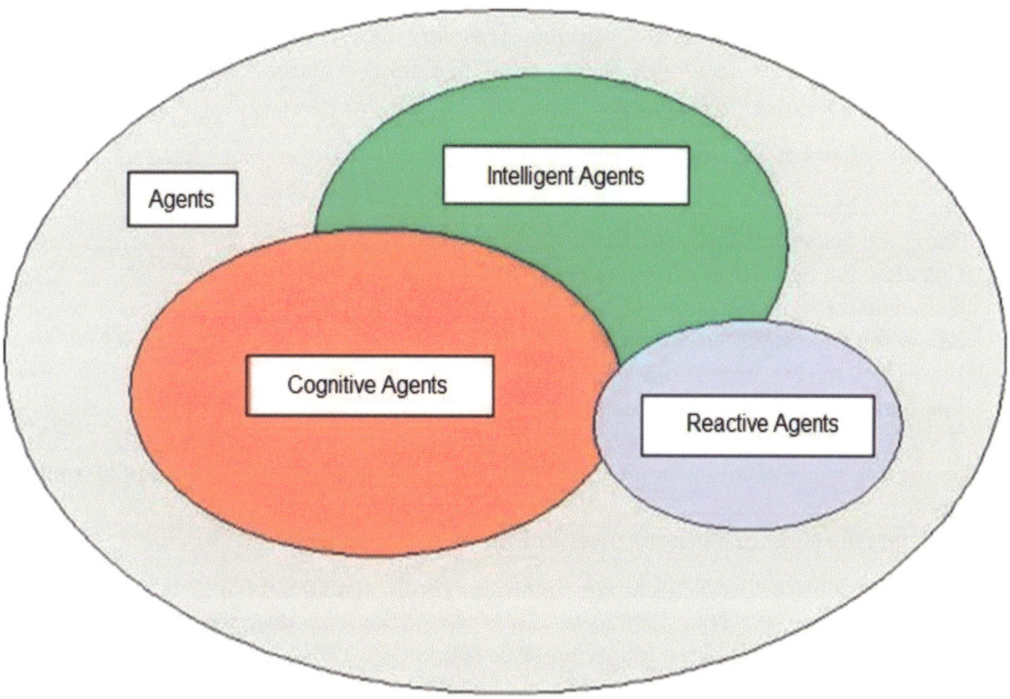

Fig. 4. Types of Agents

2.2 Fundamentals of geographic information systems (GIS)

The record of spatial phenomena through predetermined coding has enabled the creation of a model distribution of natural phenomena and human settlements, which has become very important in thinking about population distribution, environmental analysis, navigation, trading routes and military strategies.

Geographic information systems (GIS) are systems that store, manipulate, analyze and display data that is mapped in a geographic coordinate (or geo-referenced) system. The information is encoded in the GIS through geographic features such as points, lines, and areas or through digital data which stores data as pixels (picture element cells) in a two-dimensional array.

Understanding how to use GIS is not simply understanding how to use of maps, it is necessary to see how a person views the world, what models are used to represent what is observed and what types of coding are used to represent them. The representation of a map in GIS can be regarded as a visual projection of a spatial database at a given time (Burrough, 1998).

The model used in a GIS program consists of a series of entities that are described by their properties and are mapped using a geographic coordinate system. These entities are points, lines and polygons. In order to represent some region of the earth, for example, it is possible to associate these entities to real world object—like rivers, mountains, cities, buildings, etc.—and define theirs attributes, boundaries and location.

The systematic use of GIS enables the building of very huge spatial databases. Data can then be displayed through maps, charts or graphs. Thematic maps compile information related to a specific subject. This facilitates the storage of a large volume of data relevant to a particular phenomenon under study.

The basic functions of GIS are to: (Burrough, 1998):

- Show the location of an entity;
- Show the distance between an entity and a place;
- Calculate the number of occurrences of an entity;
- Calculate the size of an area;
- Allow the crossing of various spatial data;
- Determine the best route from one point to another in a geographic area;
- List the attributes of an entity located a certain points;
- Reclassify or recolor entities that have similar attributes;
- Know the value of an entity at some point and be able to predict its value at another point;
- Simulate the effect of a process over time for a given scenario;

It is necessary to use a specific technique in order to build spatial data models and their data structures used in GIS. This technique allows researchers to describe the geographical phenomenon and consists of the following steps (Burrough, 1998):

i. The construction of the real world model (view of reality);
ii. The construction of the conceptual model (human analog abstraction);

iii. The construction of the spatial model (formalized abstraction without following any convention);
iv. The construction of the data model (that reflects how the data will be stored on the computer);
v. The construction of the physical computer model (How the files are organized on the computer);
vi. The construction of the model defining data manipulation (the rules for data processing);
vii. The construction of the GUI model (the rules and procedures for displaying spatial data);

Geographic information systems (GIS) and its survey methods and software, have been used in different fields. It is possible to use GIS for any activity that requires geo-referenced information (location in geographical space). The potential of remote sensing and GIS facilitates the planning, control and management of large geographical areas.

Compiling geo-referenced data enables temporal and spatial analysis and provides parameters for implementing management programs in certain areas (Figure 5).

In areas where there is a critical process, a geo-referenced map can reveal the extent of the process, existing landforms, roads, cities, and even streets and buildings. These data allow for a detailed analysis of the critical process at hand and its potential impact on an urban area.

GIS works by combining tabular data with spatial data. The structures of the raster (satellite imagery) and vector (point, line and polygon) data types are used to digitally represent spatial objects. The vector structures identify vector space objects by points, lines or polygons (two-dimensional space). This type of identification is combined with the elaboration of a polygon "background", which complements the coverage of the entire plan information. The raster structure (or matrix) uses discrete units (cells) which represent spatial objects in the form of clusters (aggregates of cells). In this way, it is possible to see layers of spatial data and their link with tabulated data (roads, buildings, population, plantations, railways, ports, airports, consumers, buildings, water networks, etc.). Therefore, GIS permits researchers to represent the real world through various aspects of geography, which are separated into thematic layers.

For the GIS technology to be used effectively, it is necessary to define a methodology which represents the geographical area under study and to select the main variables to be analyzed.

- This methodology consists of the following steps:
- Elect the study area (define its limits);
- Define the sources of information;
- Collect data;
- Analyze the data collected;
- Provide geo-referenced data;
- Manage the use of information.

Information systems are widely used by organizations to manage their critical data. Through systems-based database, a large volume of information can be stored in different business areas. The so-called spatial data refer to information in a defined geographical area (latitude, longitude, topography, hydrography, land, cities, population, agricultural production, infrastructure, etc.). These data are managed by geographic information systems (GIS). The GIS provides not only the spatial view of a given area, but also the data about it across time , thus allowing researchers to gain a better understanding and to make more informed decisions. All data are geo-referenced and stored in spatial databases. In this way, GIS makes it possible to register, view, index, standardize and map a large volume of information about an existing geographic area.

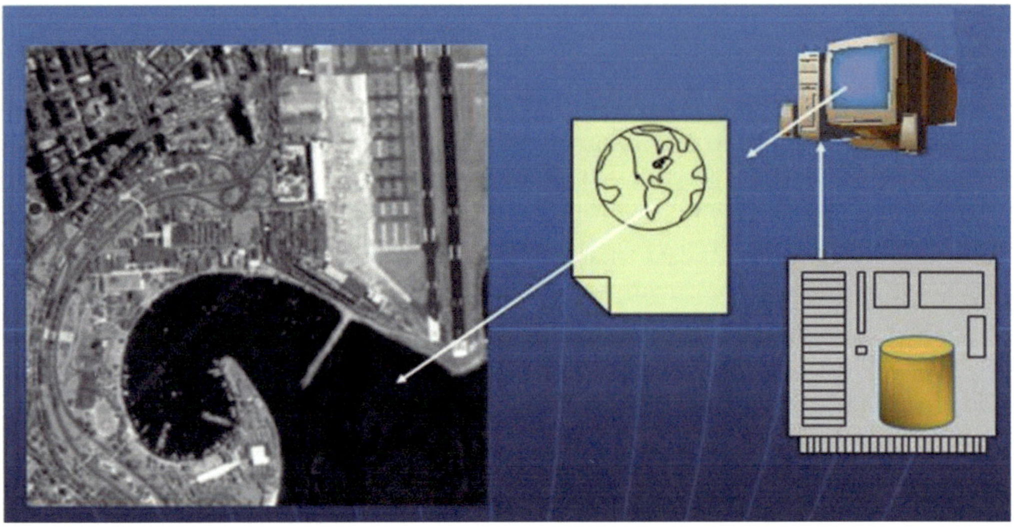

Fig. 5. A geographical information system (GIS)

2.3 Merging an agent-based system (ABS) with a geographic information system (GIS)

When a phenomenon is too complex to be studied analytically, it is necessary to recreate it in an artificial universe in which experiments can be made on a smaller scale and in an environment that simulates the real world but where the parameters can be controlled with greater precision (Drogoul & Ferber, 1994).

Computer models can be used to understand more about how real world systems work. These models allow researchers to predict the behavior of a wide range of real world processes and understand their structure. Computational models reduce the cost and time of conducting actual experiments, which are often impossible to execute in the real world. Simulations can be repeated many times over and are not invasive. The data generated by computer models are easier to analyze than that of real-world systems. (Gimblett, 2002).

A process is deemed critical when it presents complex behaviour over time. Examples of critical processes are population growth, radioactive accidents, chemical accidents, soil erosion, movement of rivers, epidemic diseases, pests, forest fires, slums in urban areas, vehicle traffic in urban areas, climate change and animal migration. These processes provoke critical effects on the population, the surrounding environment and geographical areas, which must be analyzed and mitigated in order to minimize any pre-existing vulnerability (De Almeida Silva & Farias, 2009).

One significant development in the creation of simulation models has been the inclusion of intelligent agents (autonomous agents) in spatial models. This technique enables the simulation of human behaviour in the environment within which a critical process is to be analyzed and facilitates the study of simulation outcomes. (Gimblett, 2002).

The use of GIS allows a more accurate spatial representation of the environment within which autonomous agents will act, thereby representing the elementary processes that exist in the real world. The challenge is to build a simulation that enables the generation of data appropriate to an analysis of the phenomenon under study.

The use of object orientation (OO) represents a new perspective for the integration of geographic information systems (GIS) with agent-based systems (ABS). This technology enables the creation of objects that can represent entities existing in the real world in a simulation environment. The properties (attributes and methods) of these objects entities in an OO design, a modularity capacity, the low complexity of programming code and reusability are characteristics that give great flexibility to modeling the existing elementary processes of complex processes (Gimblett, 2002).

Object orientation is a global trend in terms of programming and development systems. Applied to the area of databases, the concept of OO enables a more accurate definition of models and data structures which better represent the real world. This is especially useful to GIS, since the spatial characteristics of data make it difficult to model using traditional techniques.

The construction of a framework that represents a virtual environment is made possible thanks to the principles of object orientation (OO). The objects built following these principles provide a representation of the real world through software simulation. OO focuses on the object and represents a tool to construct it.

The two fundamental OO concepts are classes and objects. An object is an entity that has attributes) and an identity. A class is comprised of objects that share common properties. OO as applied in GIS is characterized by types of objects, divided into classes, which may have a hierarchical relationship, whereby subclasses inherit the behaviour derived from the main classes (Figure 6). The geographic objects must be represented in a geographic or spatial database. A geographic object is an element that can be geo-referenced and registered into a spatial database. Such databases allow the storing, retrieving and manipulating of spatial data including descriptive attributes that form the basis for the geometric representation of a geographic space (Elmasri & Navathe, 1994).

Objects are programming codes that can represent activities, movements and properties of real world entities (people, animals, cells, insects, chemicals, vehicles, etc.). They have three fundamental characteristics: identity (which distinguishes it from other objects), attributes and methods. A class provides a template for building a collection of objects of the same type. Embedded in an environment, objects are able to simulate a phenomenon through their multiple interactions. The application of a small number of rules and laws to entities (objects) in a given space gives rise to so-called emerging systems, which are able to simulate complex global phenomena, such as vehicle traffic, the growth of cities, etc. These are systems in which the combination of objects and their interaction with the environment reproduce the phenomenon analyzed. The objects contained in these systems are adaptable and act in synergy between one another. The framework built with objects and their combination automata (abstract automaton) lets researchers explore, analyze and predict critical processes in a study.

A greater degree of realism in simulations based on agents can be achieved by integrating the technologies of agent-based systems, geographic information systems and data acquisition via satellite. In other words, the virtual environments in which the agents will act may be two-dimensional (digital maps) or three-dimensional (digital elevation models), which depict reality to a high degree of accuracy, as can be observed through tools like Google Maps™ (Google, 2011; Gimblett, 2002; Longley & Batty, 2003). It is thus possible to achieve a very accurate model environment where agents with their corresponding attributes and behaviours are positioned and interact with each other and the environment, thus simulating dynamic processes or phenomena.

The use of ABS, based on OO and set up through simple rules, should establish standards of behaviour and the fulfillment of tasks in a geo-referenced environment (GIS). The autonomous agents act and react in the geo-referenced environment in which they are immersed.

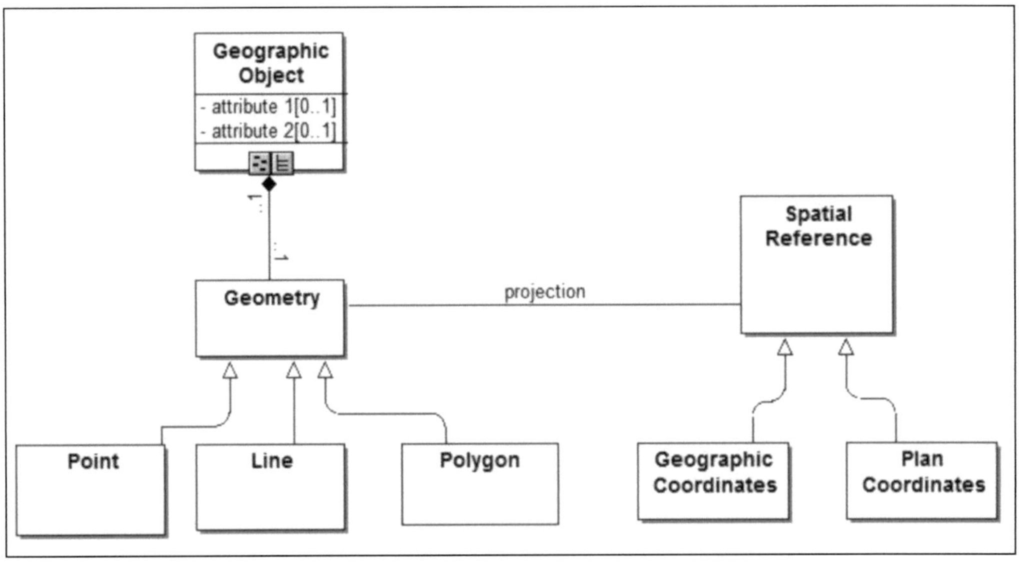

Fig. 6. A class diagram of geographic object orientation

2.4 Methodology for building a virtual environment (VE)

Simulation is the process of building a model of a real system and conducting experiments with this model, in order to understand the behaviour of a complex system and to evaluate strategies for its operation. Simulation, following the proposed methodology, can be used to describe and analyze the behavior of a system, answer questions about it and help to design a better system in the real world (Banks, 1998).

The steps of the proposed methodology are:

i. The construction of a conceptual model representing a phenomenon in the real world;

ii. The planning of the services of the virtual environment system;
iii. The definition of geographic entities, their methods and attributes;
iv. The definition of autonomous agents or entities, their methods and attributes;
v. The definition of activities and their corresponding workflows;
vi. The definition of input and output variables;

The proposed architecture of a virtual environment (VE) requires a spatial framework for modeling a complex system. The main characteristics of the architecture of a VE are the existence of autonomous agents, existing within a geo-referenced environment which simulates the phenomenon or critical process of interest.

The autonomous agents have rules of behaviour and attributes and are capable of positioning themselves in a geographical space. A spatial database system is used to store, retrieve, manipulate and analyze data that are generated by the behaviour of these autonomous agents, through time (years, hours, minutes, and seconds). The main features of the autonomous agents, in this architecture of VE, are their ability to transmit information and to move to another position. They also demonstrate more complex behaviour, such as meeting predetermined goals and storing information. It is also necessary to consider another important feature of the autonomous agents in this architecture: their typology, the environment where they are located and the spatial relationship they have with other agents. It is important to guarantee the process that governs changes in characteristics and that which governs changes in spatial location (De Almeida Silva & Farias, 2009).

The VE architecture is composed of two categories of data: spatial data generated by Google Earth™/Google Maps™ (Google, 2011), which is used as a geographic information system (GIS) and behavioural data generated through autonomous agents. These autonomous agents are built by Repast 3™ (Argonne, 2011; North et al., 2006), a software toolkit that programs the interaction of autonomous agents in a geographic environment. Generated data are stored in a database called MySQL™ (Oracle, 2011; Appleton & Stucker, 2007), which is then used to simulate the critical process.

The proposed VE is based on autonomous agents that act within a predefined geo-referenced environment. They are able to perceive and react to stimuli. There are many software toolkits to build multi-agent simulations such as Repast ™ (Argonne, 2011), Cougar ™, Zeus™, Jack™, Jade™, Swarm™, Star Logo™ and Net Logo™. In the proposed architecture, the Repast™ software was used (Argonne, 2011) for the following reasons (Figure 7):

- It integrates agents with geo-referenced information (GIS);
- Its source code is in Java™, which makes the tool highly portable;
- It is a rapid application development (RAD) tool;
- It allows for the monitoring of both the autonomous agents and the constructed model;
- It uses graphics for the output of results;
- It features a user-friendly graphical interface for the construction of agents;
- It is an open source tool that is constantly evolving;
- It is compatible with three different programming languages/frameworks: Java™ (RepastJ and RepastS), Microsoft.NET™ (Repast.NET), and Python ™ (RepastPy) (Crooks, 2007);

The representation of the area selected (Google Maps™) (Google, 2011) will be the virtual environment in which entities representing objects in the real world will be inserted. The latter are abstractions, called autonomous agents, which represent different types of actors of the real world ranging from living beings endowed with a high degree of intelligence to entities exhibiting basic behaviour. The autonomous agents are able to interact with one another and are modeled as pro-active autonomous objects endowed with a greater or lesser degree of intelligence and which are able to understand the environment in which they are immersed (Wooldrigde, 2002).

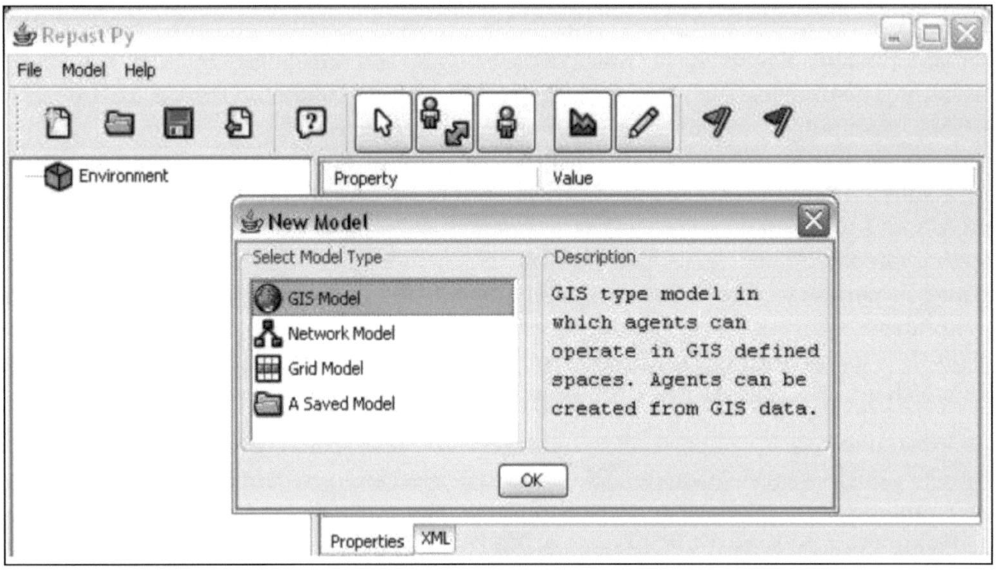

Fig. 7. Simulation tool based on GIS and agents - Repast 3 ™

The architecture of the VE has the ability to organize and display information in a graphical interface whereby the autonomous agents are positioned arbitrarily within a spatial environment and their distribution appears on a geo-referenced map, to be viewed and interpreted (Maguire et al., 2005) (Figure 8). These objects and individuals are modeled by autonomous agents and have the following attributes:

i. object identifier;
ii. the object's position given by its coordinates;
iii. individual identifier;
iv. the individual's position given by its coordinates;

For the construction of this virtual environment, the following tasks were performed (Banks, 1998):

i. Formulation of the problem: define the problem to be studied, including the goal of the solution;
ii. Goal setting and planning of the project: raise questions that should be answered by the simulation and the scenarios to be analyzed. The planning of the project will determine the required time, resources, hardware, software and people ware involved as well as controls and outputs to be generated;

iii. Creation of a conceptual model: build an abstraction of the real world based on mathematical and logical modeling; Data collection: identify the data required for simulation

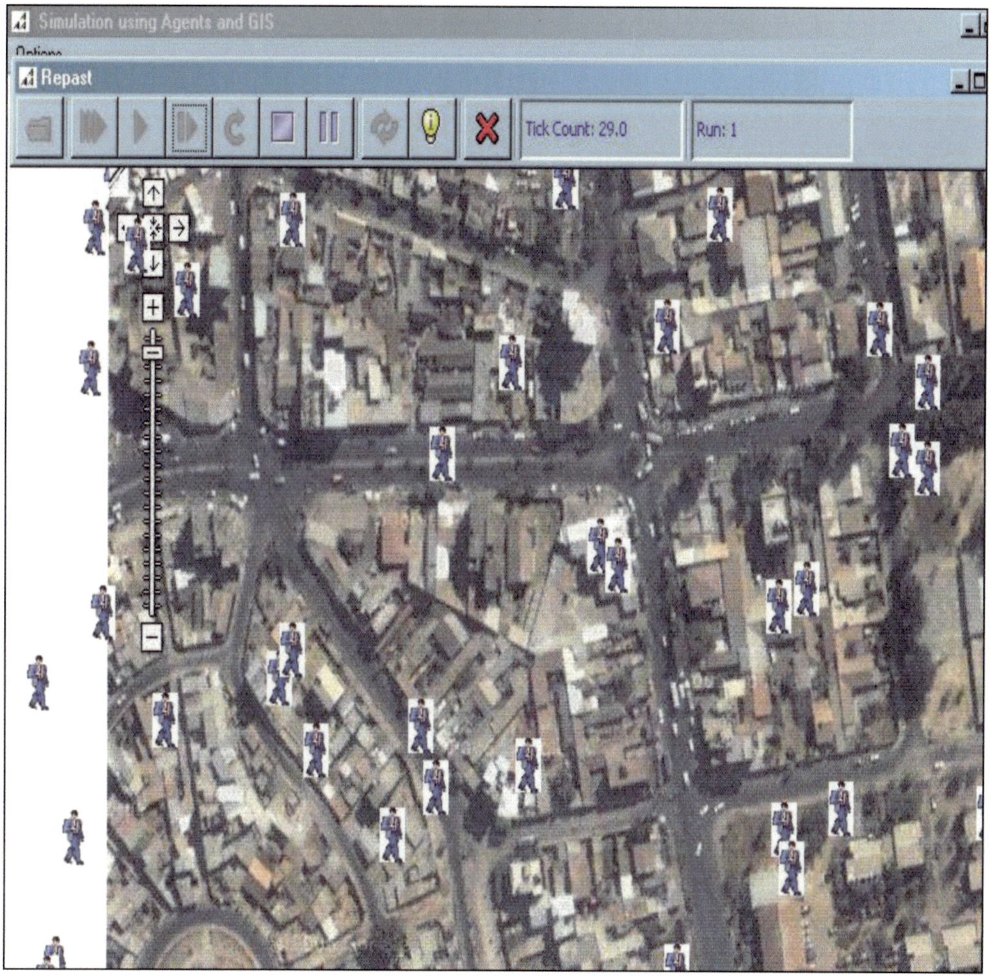

Fig. 8. A virtual environment displaying autonomous agents, Google Maps™ and Repast™

iv. Building the model: create the model using a conceptual tool for simulation;
v. Verification: Check that the implementation of this model has been done correctly;
vi. Test of valididity: verify that the model is a conceptual representation reasonably "accurate" system of the real world;
vii. Simulation of scenarios: define various scenarios and their parameters;
viii. Running and analysis of the scenarios: estimate measures of performance for the scenarios that are being simulated;
ix. Documentation and report generation: provide information about the result of the modeling carried out;
x. Recommendation: determine the actions to be taken to solve the problem that is being analyzed based on the results of the simulation.

For the implementation of this virtual environment, the following steps were performed (Figure 9):

i. Definition of the critical process: choose a type of critical process to study (e.g. population growth, radioactive accidents, chemical accidents, soil erosion, movement of rivers, epidemic diseases, pests, forest fires, slums in urban areas, vehicle traffic in urban areas, climate change and animal migration);
ii. Definition of a scenario: construct a conceptual model representing a phenomenon in the real world;
iii. Planning the services of the virtual environment: define the characteristics of the system necessary to model a phenomenon (procedures, input and output variables of this system);
iv. Construction a physical model of the database: create the structure of the files;
v. Construction of individual autonomous agents whose goals, type, attributes and methods are defined in accordance with the analyzed phenomenon Customization of a Google Maps API: define new features for geographic representation;
vi. Customization of Repast libraries: define the graphics and outputs;

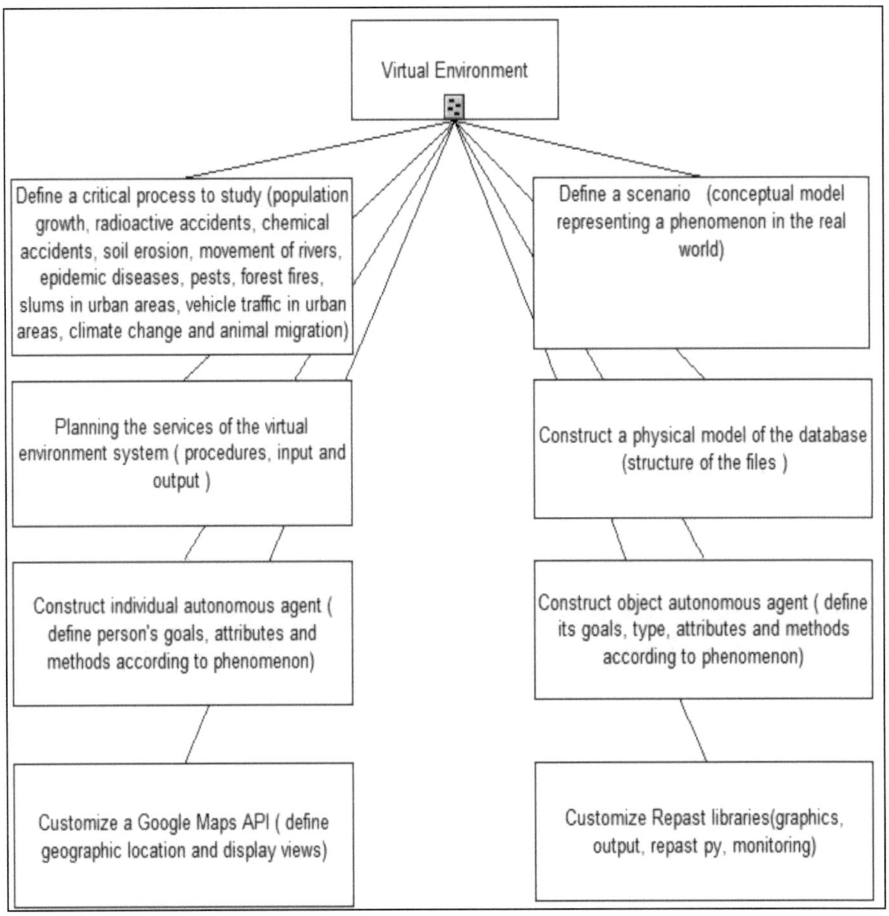

Fig. 9. Methodology for the construction a Virtual Environment (VE).

3. Conclusion

The proposed methodology to construct a virtual environment (VE) for the purpose of simulating a critical process allows us to create a software simulation capable of analyzing a phenomenon that occurs in a specific geographical area. This architecture of a VE explores how systems based on autonomous agents can be effective in simulating complex phenomena. The implemented model that incorporates autonomous agents, existing within a geo-referenced environment and which capable of receiving stimuli as input and of producing actions as output, aims to simulate the dynamics of the phenomenon selected to be studied.

This VE architecture enables researchers to do the following:

i. Construct and analyze scenarios;
ii. Design autonomous agents with goals, behaviours and attributes using Repast™;
iii. Use a powerful and user-friendly GIS: Google Earth™ / Maps™.
iv. Quantify a specific measure;
v. Obtain any spatial distribution of people or objects;
vi. Inform variable inputs and obtain variable outputs;
vii. Storage data output;
viii. Estimate the impact of a critical process;
ix. Define prompt answers;
x. Train personnel to handle the analyzed situation;

Following this methodology, it is possible to integrate both a geo-referenced environment together with agent-based models in order to simulate a critical process present in the real world

4. Acknowledgment

We would like to thank to our families, the Instituto de Radioproteção e Dosimetria (IRD) and Universidade do Estado do Rio de Janeiro(UERJ) for their support throughout the duration our research, which we are grateful for.

5. References

Appleton, Ben; Stucker, Lary (2007). Using PHP/MySQL with Google Maps from http://code.google.com/intl/en/apis/maps/articles/phpsqlajax_v3.html

Argonne, National Laboratory (2011). Recursive Porus Agent Simulation Toolkit from http://repast.sourceforge.net/repast_3/index.html

Banks Jerry, (1998). Handbook of Simulation, Principles, Methodology, Advances, Applications and Practice, Emp Books.

Benenson , Itzhak; Torrens Paul (2004). Geosimulation: Automata-Based Modeling of Urban Phenomena. Wiley.

Burrough, P.A .; McDonnel, R. A. (1998). Principles of Geographical Information Systems, ISBN 0-19-823366-3, Oxford University Press, New York , USA.

Crooks, Andrew T.(2007). The Repast Simulation/Modelling System for Geospatial Simulation, ISSN 1467-1298, Paper 123, Centre for Advanced Spatial Analysis University College London , London, England.

Drogoul, A.; Ferber, J. (1994). Multi-agent Simulation as a Tool for Studying Emergent Processes in Societies. In Simulating Societies. The Computer Simulation of Social Phenomena. edited by N. Gilbert and J. Doran, 127-142. London. UCL Press.

De Almeida Silva, Tadeu Augusto; Farias, O. L. M. (2009). A Virtual Environment for Simulation of Radiological Accidents. Conference on Nuclear Training and Education (CONTE). American Nuclear Society. Florida, USA.

Elmasri, R.; Navathe, S. B. (1994). - Fundamentals of Database Systems, Redwood City: Benjamin. Cummings Publishing Company, Inc.

Farias, O. L. M; Santos N. (2005). Agent-Based Geographical Information System. International Conference on Intelligent Agents, Web Technologies and Internet Commerce - IAWTIC'2005, v. 1. p. 998-1005. , Edited by M. Mohammadian, Vienna.

Gardner, M.(1971).Mathematical games: On cellular automata, self-reproduction, the Garden of Eden, and the game "life". Scientific American 224(2):112-117.

Gimblett, H. Randy (2002). Integrating Geographic Information Systems and Agent-Based Modeling Techniques for Simulating Social and Ecological Processes. Oxford, University Press, USA.

Google (October, 2011). Google Maps Javascript API V3 Tutorial from http://code.google.com/intl/en/apis/maps/documentation/javascript/tutorial.html#Intro

Levy, S. (1992). Artificial Life. The Quest for a New Creation. Penguin.

Lim, K. ; Deadman, P. J.; Moran, E. ; Brondízio, E. ; McCracken, S.(2002).Agent-based simulations of household decision making and land use change near Altamira, Brazil. In Integrating Geographic Information Systems and Agent-Based Modeling: Techniques for Simulating Social and Ecological Processes, ed. R. Gimblett, New York: Oxford University Press, pp. 277–310.

Longley, Paul A.; Batty, Michael (2003). Advanced Spatial Analysis: The Casa Book of GIS., ESRI Press.

Maguire, David; BATTY, Michael; Goodchild, Michael (2005). GIS, Spatial Analysis, and Modeling. ESRI Press.

North, Michael J.; Collier , Nicholson T.; Vos, Jerry R. (2006). Experience Creating Three Implementations of the Repast Agent Modelling Toolkit. ACM Transaction Modelling and Computer, vol. 16, no. 1.

Oracle (2011). MySQL Enterprise Edition Trial from http://www.mysql.com/trials/

Soares Filho, B. S.; Cerqueira, G. C.; (2002). DINAMICA: A new model to simulate and study landscape dynamics. Ecological Modeling.

Winner, N.(1948/1961). Cybernetics, or Control and Communication in the Animal and Machine. Cambridge, MA, MIT Press.

Wolfram, S.(2002). A new kind of science. Wolfram Media, Incorporated.

Wooldridge, M.J. (2002). An Introduction to Multiagent Systems, John Wiley & Sons, London, England.

Wooldridge, M. J., Jennings, N. R. (1995). Agents Theories, Architectures, and Languages: a Survey. Proceedings of ECAI'94 Workshop on Agent Theories, Architectures and Languages, pp.1-22.

Veldkamp A.; Fresco, L. O (1996). CLUE: a conceptual model to study the conversion of land use and its effects. Ecological Modeling 85, pp.253-270.

Verburg, P. H.; Soepboer, W.; Veldkamp, A.; Limpiada, R.; Espaldon, V.; Mastura, S. S. A. (2002). Modeling the spatial dynamics of regional land use: the CLUE-S model. In Environmental Management, Vol. 30, No. 3, pp. 391-405.

8

Immersive Visual Data Mining Based on Super High Definition Image

Tetsuro Ogi[1], Yoshisuke Tateyama[1] and So Sato[2]
[1]*Graduate School of System Design and Management, Keio University*
[2]*System Design and Management Research Institute, Keio University*
Japan

1. Introduction

In recent years, a large amount of data has been generated and recorded in various fields according to the advances of computer simulation, sensor network, and database technologies. However, it is generally difficult to find valuable information or knowledge from the huge data. Therefore, the establishment of a methodology to utilize these data effectively is an important issue. Though data mining is one of the methods to solve such a problem, it is difficult for the user to understand the process of mining data and to evaluate the result intuitively, because the data is processed in the computer (Kantardzie, 2002). On the other hand, the visualization technique can be used effectively to represent the data so that the user can understand it intuitively. This study focuses on the method of visual data mining in which the user performs the data mining by visualizing the data (Wong, 1999) (Keim, 2002).

In the visual data mining, the user can analyze the data interactively with the computer by visualizing the process and the result of the data mining. Then, it is expected that a new information or knowledge can be found by combining the ability of high-speed calculation of the computer with the human's ability such as intuition, common sense and creativity. Particularly, this study aims at improving the effect of visual data mining by enhancing the ability of expressing data and interaction function by using the immersive virtual environment based on super high-definition stereo images. In this system, it is expected that the user can perform accurate and intuitive data mining by using the high resolution stereo images.

This paper discusses the system architecture and the visualization ability of the super high-definition immersive visual data mining environment that was developed in this study, and the effectiveness of this method is evaluated by applying the platform of super high-definition immersive visual data mining to the seismic data analysis.

2. Concept of super high-definition immersive visual data mining

Visual data mining supports the user to analyze a large amount of data and to find new information by combining the abilities of computer and human. The computer has large memory and high speed calculation capability. On the other hand, the human is superior in intuition, commonsense and creativity based on the visual information. By combining the information processes performed by computer and human, a large amount of data could be analyzed effectively to find new information.

In the researches by Wong (Wong, 1999) or Keim et al. (Keim, 2002), data mining is effectively performed in the visualization environment. In these cases, visualization technology is used to transmit the information from the computer to the human and interactive interface technology is used to support the collaboration between human and computer. If the expression abilities of information visualization and the interaction function between human and computer were increased, the performance of visual data mining would be improved based on the improvement of information processing in both human and computer.

As for the increase of the expression ability in the information visualization, super high-definition image would enables the transmission of the detailed information from the computer to the human, and three-dimensional stereo image would be used effectively to represent the relationship among several kinds of data in the three-dimensional space. In the researches by Renambot (Renambot, 2006), high-resolution image is effectively used in the data visualization. And as for the interaction between human and computer, immersive virtual environment would be used to enable the user to operate the visualized data directly and to explore data space as first person experience. Ammoura (Ammoura, 2001), Wegman (Wegman, 2002) and Ferey (Ferey, 2005) discuss the effectiveness of immersive virtual environment in visual data mining.

In this study, super high-definition immersive visual data mining environment was constructed to utilize the effect of advanced visualization and interaction technologies. Figure 1 shows the concept of super high-definition immersive visual data mining that is proposed in this study. In this figure, it is shown that the performance of visual data mining can greatly be improved by increasing the expression ability and the interaction function between computer and human.

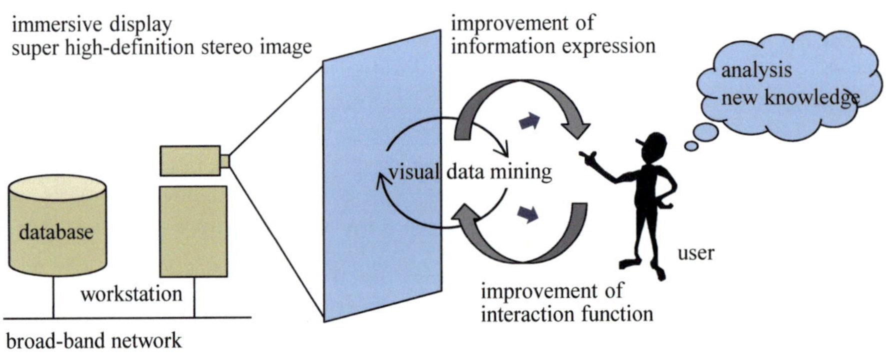

Fig. 1. Concept of super high-definition immersive visual data mining.

3. Immersive visual data mining environment

3.1 4K stereo image

In this study, immersive visual data mining environment using 4K stereo projection system was constructed as shown in figure 2 (Ogi, 2008). 4K means super high resolution image of

4,096 x 2,160 pixels, and its image quality is more than four times of the usual high-definition image. In this system, two stacked projectors (SONY SRX-S110) are used, and the images seen from the right eye and left eye positions of the user are projected. The images output from the projectors are rear projected onto the 180-inch acrylic rear projection screen (Nippura, Blue Ocean Screen) through the polarizing filter. In this condition, 1 pixel in the projected image has approximately 0.97 mm width on the screen. Then, the user can see the high resolution passive stereo image based on the binocular parallax by wearing the polarized 3D glasses. In this system, since two 108-inch LCD monitors are placed at both sides of the 4K screen, various kinds of information can be displayed in the multi-display environment. Figure 3 shows the system configuration of the super high-definition immersive visual data mining environment.

Fig. 2. Super high-definition immersive visual data mining environment.

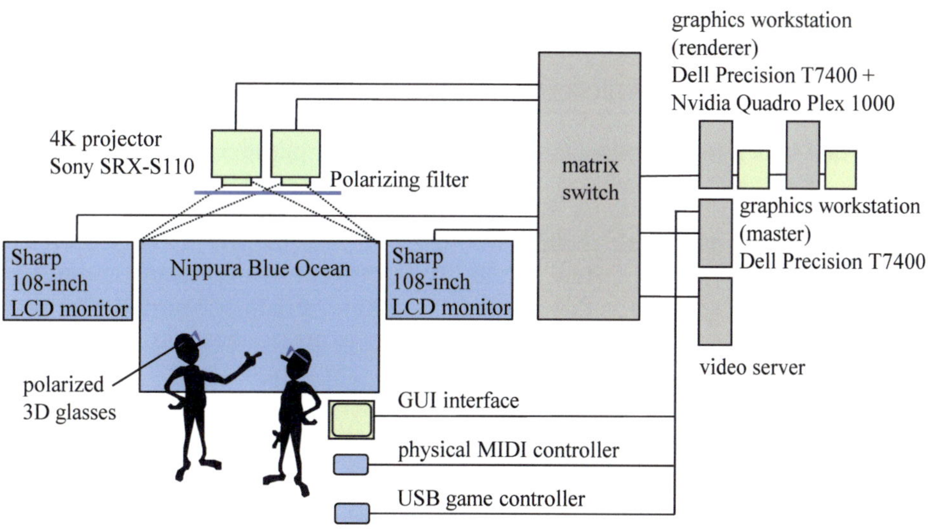

Fig. 3. System configuration of immersive visual data mining environment.

In order to generate and render the 4K stereo image, two high-end graphics workstations (Dell Precision T7400, 2xQuad Core Xeon 3.2GHz) with the graphics engine (NVIDIA Quadro Plex 1000 Model IV) that has a genlock function are used for right eye image and the left eye image, respectively. In this system, interface devices such as a USB game controller and a physical MIDI controller are connected to the graphics workstation. The USB game controller is used to walk through the visualized data space or to change the visualization method. On the other hand, the physical MIDI controller is used to change the visualization parameter minutely. By using these interface devices, the user can perform accurate and intuitive interaction with the visualized data, and the immersive visual data mining using 4K resolution stereo image can be realized.

3.2 Software structure

Figure 4 shows the software structure of the immersive visual data mining environment. As for the software library to develop the visual data mining application in the immersive virtual environment, Open CABIN Library was used (Tateyama, 2008). Open CABIN Library is a software platform to develop the immersive virtual reality application. This library has features of master-renderer programming and plug-in mechanism.

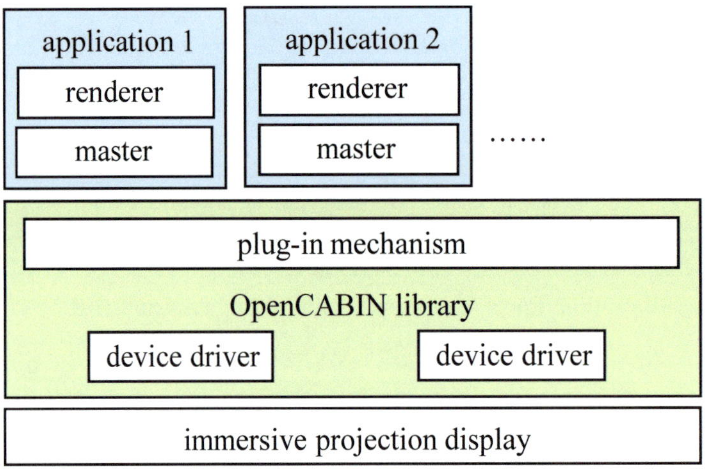

Fig. 4. Software structure of immersive visual data mining application.

The master-renderer programming is a style that constructs an application program consisting of a master part that calculates the state of the virtual world and renderer parts that render the image of the virtual world. This software configuration is effective to construct the network application that needs to access to the database or needs to transmit data to other system through the network, because master process has only to communicate with the remote processes.

On the other hand, the plug-in mechanism is a method to construct an application program in the form of dynamically loaded library. When API of the usual library is used, it is necessary to rewrite the source code of the program to add a certain function to improve it. For example, in order to construct an application program that visualizes several kinds of data simultaneously, the integrated visualization program must be developed specially besides the visualization program for each data. However, the plug-in mechanism can add a visualization function for necessary data to the application program that is being executed. Namely, the integrated visualization environment for several kinds of data can be constructed, by executing several visualization programs for each data simultaneously by using the plug-in mechanism.

4. Data representation ability of 4K stereo image

In the data visualization using the 4K image, detailed information can be represented based on the high resolution image compared with the conventional visualization using the SXGA or WUXGA resolution image. Particularly, when the 4K stereo image is used, it is expected that the detailed three-dimensional information can be displayed with high accuracy in the three-dimensional virtual space. In this study, the representation ability of the 4K stereo image in the immersive visual data mining was examined.

4.1 Perception of spatial resolution

First, the spatial resolution with which the visualized data can be perceived in the three-dimensional space was experimentally measured. In this experiment, the subjects sat at a position 3m away from the screen, and two vertical parallel lines with the gaps of 0.5mm, 1mm, 2.5mm, 5mm, or 10mm were displayed randomly in the direction from the front to left as shown in figure 5. The subjects were asked to move the parallel lines in the depth direction and to stop them at the boundary position where they can recognize the displayed image as two lines by using the USB game controller. The boundary positions of the parallel lines with various gaps and in various directions were recorded.

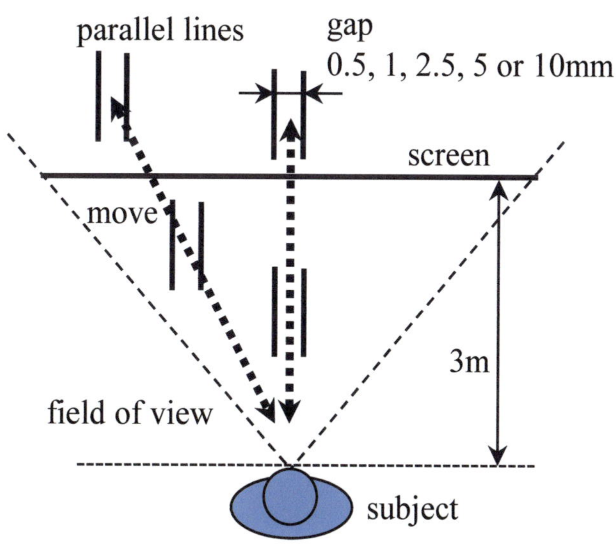

Fig. 5. Condition of experiment on the perception of spatial resolution.

Figure 6 shows the result of the experiment for five subjects with visual acuity of more than 1.0. In this graph, the contour lines are drawn by connecting the average values of the boundary positions for each direction and for each gap of the parallel lines. From this graph, we can see that the subjects could recognize 0.5mm gaps between lines when the parallel lines were displayed at the distance of about 50cm, and they could recognize 10mm gaps between lines when they were displayed at the distance of about 10m. This recognition ability is equivalent to visual acuity of about 0.3, and it is a little bad compared with the visual acuity (more than 1.0) of the subjects. From this result, we can consider that the effect of stereo image caused the decrease of the visual acuity in the visualization environment. However, the resolution of the parallel lines recognition at near distance (0.5mm) was higher than the pixel width (0.97mm) of the projected image. We can consider that this result is also caused by the effect of high resolution stereo image.

Therefore, it is understood that the 4K stereo display can represent the detailed information with high accuracy, though the recognized spatial resolution of the displayed image depends on the distance and direction from the user. Namely, this means that the visual data mining using the super high-definition stereo image has an ability to transmit a large amount of information from the computer to the user with high accuracy.

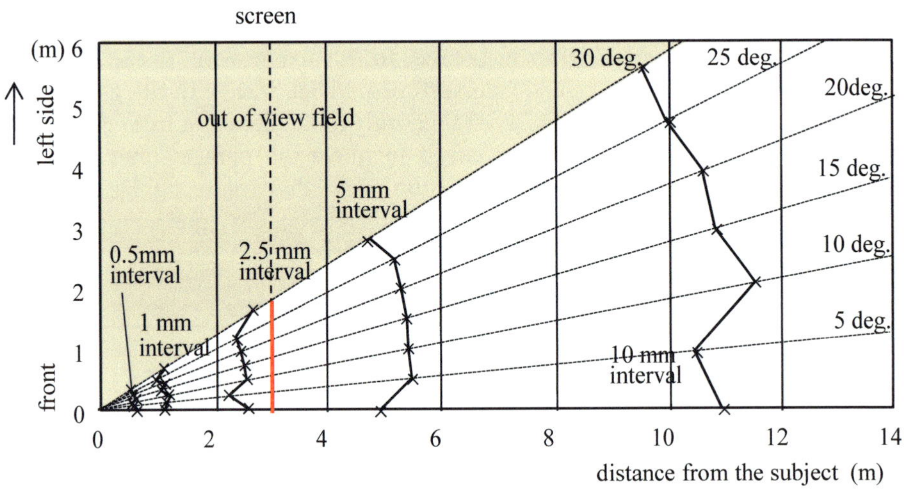

Fig. 6. Result of experiment on perception of spatial resolution.

4.2 Representation of point cloud data

Though this system can visualize detailed data with high accuracy using the super high-definition stereo image, it has a limitation in transmitting large amount of information from the computer to the user. Next, in this study, the ability of representing three-dimensional information in the visualization of large amount of point cloud data was experimentally examined.

In the experiment, the subjects stood at the position 3m away from the screen and the image of the colored point cloud that was distributed uniformly in the rectangular solid area was displayed. In this case, the number of point cloud data was changed up to 500,000 points, and the distance to the near side of the rectangular solid area was changed among 1m, 2m and 3m. In addition, the depth of the volume of the rectangular solid area was changed among 1.0m, 1.5m, 2.0m, and 2.5m, as shown in figure 7. Then, the subjects were asked to evaluate the three-dimensional sensation that was felt from the displayed image using the three-grade system (2: clear three-dimensional sensation, 1: unclear three-dimensional sensation, 0: no three-dimensional sensation).

Figure 8 shows the result of this experiment for nine subjects. Each plotted point means average value of the evaluation for each depth condition and for each near distance condition. From the results, there was significant difference among the condition of the distance to the near side at 1% level, though there was no significant difference among the condition of the depth of volume. From the graph, we can see that the evaluation of the depth sensation felt by the subjects decreased according to the increase of the number of the displayed points. This means that the subjects could not recognize the three-dimensional scene from the left eye image and the right eye image when too many point clouds were displayed. Namely, the representation ability of the super high definition display for the three-dimensional point cloud image would decrease when a large amount of point data are displayed simultaneously. In addition, the ability of representing three-dimensional point

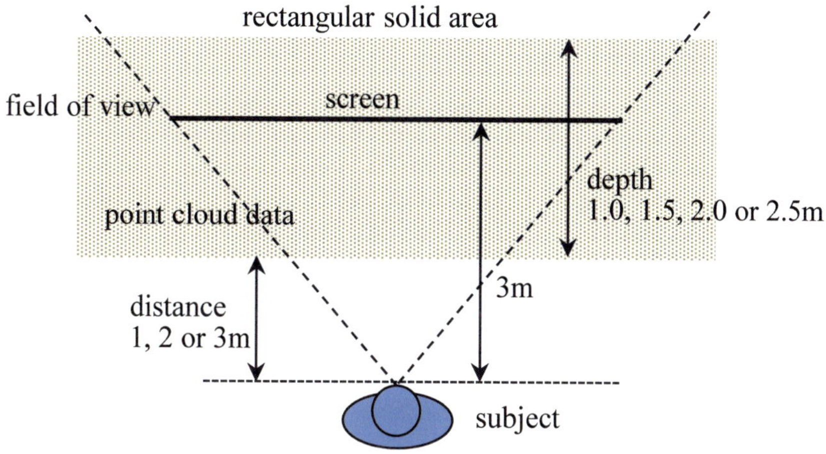

Fig. 7. Condition of experiment on representation of point cloud data.

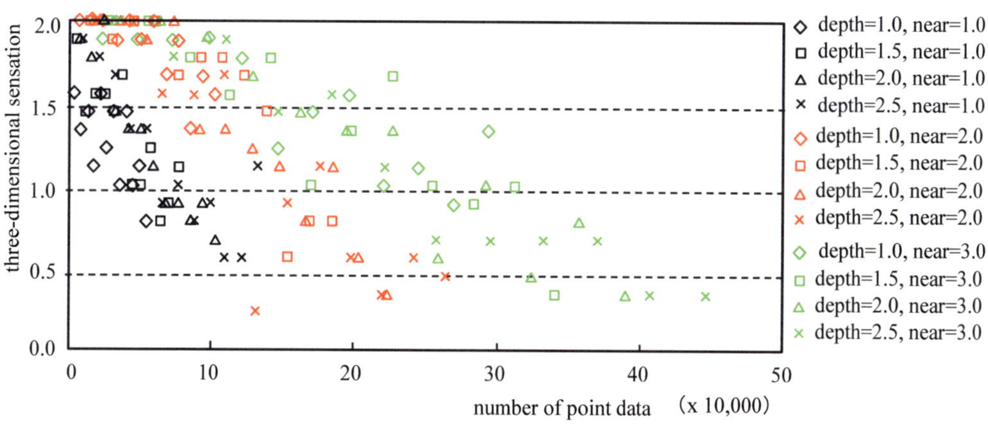

Fig. 8. Result of experiment on representation of point cloud data.

cloud image decreased steeply when the data were displayed near the subjects. We can consider that this is because the binocular parallax was large when the point image was displayed close to the subject in front of the screen. Therefore, we can understand that the control of the number of the visualized data is very important when a large amount of point cloud data are visualized.

5. Visual data mining platform

In general, effective visualization method used in visual data mining depends on the visualized data or the purpose of data analysis. In particular, in the early phase of the data mining, visualization method or visualization parameter are often changed in trials and errors. Therefore, the development of the platform of immersive visual data mining in which the user can easily analyze data by changing the visualization method or visualization parameter interactively is required. In this study, the platform of immersive visual data mining for the point cloud data was developed, because the super high-definition display can be used effectively to represent the point data.

5.1 Process of visual data mining

In the platform of immersive visual data mining, multi-dimensional data that is stored in the database table managed by RDBMS (relational database management system) can be visualized. This database table consists of ID field and eight floating point number fields (d_1, d_2, ..., d_8). Then, data in various application fields can be visualized in the immersive visual data mining environment by storing them in the database table.

Figure 9 shows the data flow in the process of immersive visual data mining. In order to visualize the data in the three-dimensional space, several attributes such as the three-dimensional position, color, and filtering condition should be specified. In this system, five visualization parameters such as the position (X, Y, Z), color (C) and reference parameter for filtering (R) are made from the values in the floating point number fields of the database table, and the data is visualized based on the five parameters. Thus, the user can perform the visual data mining independently from the domain or type of the target data.

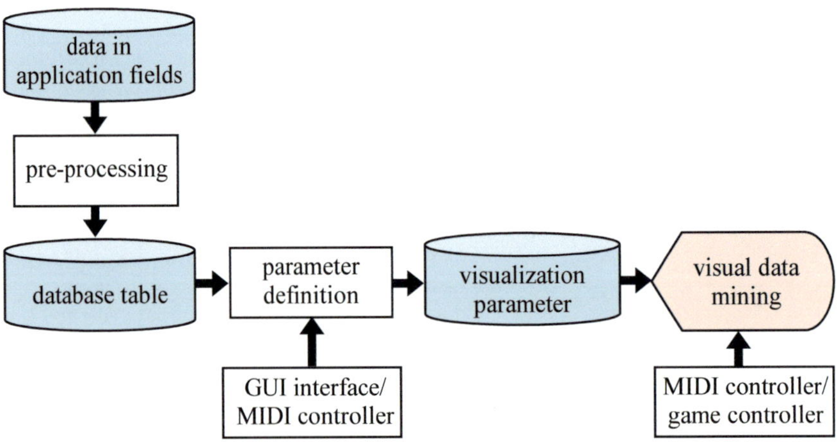

Fig. 9. Data flow of visual data mining in platform.

5.2 Interface

In the data visualization, it is important that the user can interact intuitively with the visualized data to recognize the phenomenon. In addition, in the visual data mining, it is also important that the user can operate the visualized data precisely. Therefore, in this system, GUI interface and physical USB controller are used to realize the intuitive and precise operation.

Fig. 10 shows the screen image of the GUI interface. The visualization parameters X, Y, Z, C, and R are defined using the linear equation,

$$X=a_{11}d_1+a_{12}d_2++a_{13}d_3+a_{14}d_4+a_{15}d_5+a_{16}d_6+a_{17}d_7+a_{18}d_8$$

$$Y=a_{21}d_1+a_{22}d_2++a_{23}d_3+a_{24}d_4+a_{25}d_5+a_{26}d_6+a_{27}d_7+a_{28}d_8$$

$$Z=a_{31}d_1+a_{32}d_2++a_{33}d_3+a_{34}d_4+a_{35}d_5+a_{36}d_6+a_{37}d_7+a_{38}d_8$$

$$C=a_{41}d_1+a_{42}d_2++a_{43}d_3+a_{44}d_4+a_{45}d_5+a_{46}d_6+a_{47}d_7+a_{48}d_8$$

$$R=a_{51}d_1+a_{52}d_2++a_{53}d_3+a_{54}d_4+a_{55}d_5+a_{56}d_6+a_{57}d_7+a_{58}d_8$$

where d_1,.., d_8 are data values in the floating point number fields of the database table, and a_{11},…, a_{58} are coefficients that are specified by the user. Each tab in the right side on the GUI screen corresponds to the visualization parameter, and the user can define these visualization parameters by moving the sliders to adjust the coefficients.

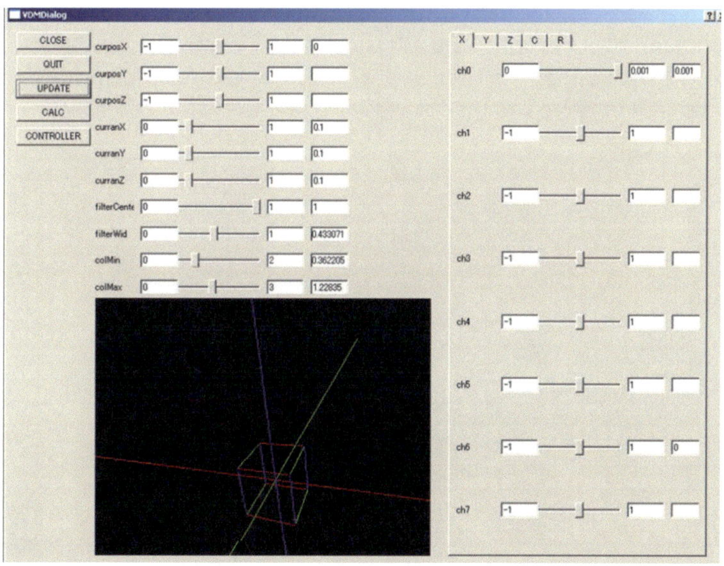

Fig. 10. GUI interface.

The data is displayed at the position specified by parameters of X, Y, Z. In this case, visualized data can be selected by specifying the rectangular region in the three-dimensional space. This area is defined by giving the center position of the rectangular region and the width along each axis using the sliders displayed on the left side of the GUI interface.

Point cloud data can be displayed in various colors according to the value of the color parameter C. In this system, the color of the displayed data is defined by specifying minimum value and maximum value of the color parameter using the sliders, and the value of the color parameter is mapped to the displayed color. In this case, when the color value is less than minimum value, the data is visualized with gray color, and when the color value exceeds the maximum value, the data is visualized with white color.

The displayed data can be filtered using the value of the reference parameter R. When the center value and the range are specified using the sliders on the left side of the GUI screen, the visualized data is filtered by comparing the value of reference parameter with the filtering range.

In addition, the view point for the visualization image in the three-dimensional space can be controlled by dragging the cursor in the lower left area of the GUI interface. This function supports the rotation of the view point around the arbitrary axis as well as the movement along the screen and perpendicular to the screen. Then, the user's view point can be controlled minutely using the GUI interface as well as the user can walk through the visualization space using the game controller.

Though the parameter values are controlled using the sliders on the GUI interface, these sliders are assigned to the MIDI control channels. Then, the parameter values can also be controlled by using the physical MIDI controller connected to the interface PC shown in Figure 11. Since the MIDI controller communicates with the interface PC using USB protocol, the control data are sent to the visual data mining system through the interface PC. Therefore, the user can control the plural parameter values interactively in the immersive virtual environment by operating the physical MIDI controller without looking at the console. Figure 12 shows that the user is operating the platform of immersive visual data mining using the GUI interface on the interface PC and the MIDI controller.

Fig. 11. Physical MIDI controller.

Fig. 12. Operation using GUI interface and physical MIDI controller.

6. Application to seismic data analysis

In this study, in order to evaluate the effectiveness of the developed system, the platform of immersive visual data mining was applied to the seismic data analysis. In Japan, a lot of earthquakes occur every year. Then, it is important to analyze large amount of past data to predict next earthquake and estimate damage (Furumura, 2005). Particularly, this problem has been very important after Great East Japan Earthquake on March 11, 2011. As original data for the immersive visual data mining, the seismic hypocenter data in last five years that is stored in Hi-net system (Okada, 2004) constructed by National Research Institute for Earth Science and Disaster Prevention was used.

6.1 Visualization of hypocenter data

In the visualization using the conventional two-dimensional display, it is difficult to observe both the individual location and the overall distribution of the hypocenter data and to understand the feature of three-dimensional distribution of the earthquake. Therefore, first, the seismic hypocenter data was visualized using the platform of representing point cloud data in the super high-definition immersive visual data mining environment. In this system, about 600,000 seismic hypocenter data with magnitude and occurrence time were stored in the database table and they were visualized as point clouds. From the hypocenter data, statistical data of b-value in Gutenberg-Richter (GR) relation were calculated. GR relation is a typical model to represent the distribution of magnitude of the earthquakes. In this case, more than 2,000,000 b-value data were calculated in the area specified by time and place, and they were stored in another database table to visualize them in the platform. In this application, these data were visualized overlapped with the coastal line of Japan using the plug-in function of Open CABIN Library.

Figure 13 shows the visualization image of the seismic hypocenter data that is colored according to the magnitude value. From the high resolution stereo image, the user can recognize the tendency of the earthquake distribution. Figure 14 shows another example of the visualization image in which the occurrence time of the earthquake is mapped to the z-axis. From this image, the user can see how long a lot of small aftershocks continued after big earthquake.

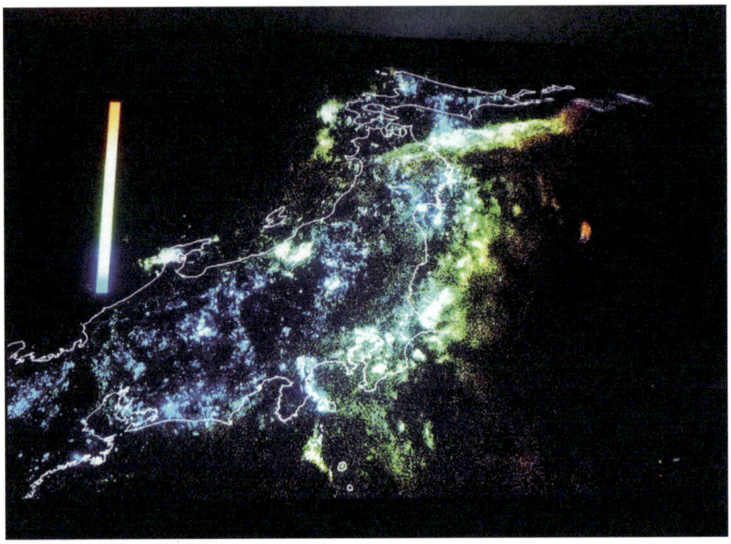

Fig. 13. Visualization of seismic hypocenter data

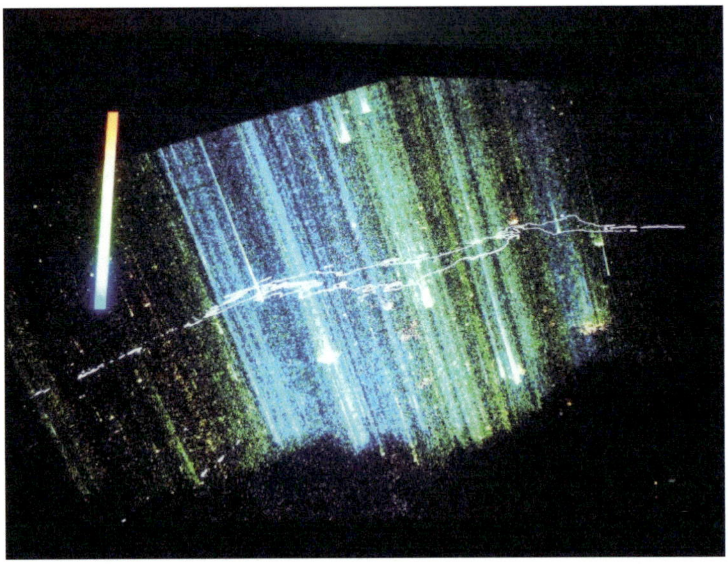

Fig. 14. Visualization of seismic hypocenter data by mapping occurrence time to z-axis

Figure 15 shows the visualization of b-values calculated from the seismic hypocenter data. In this case, it was difficult for the user to recognize the distribution of the visualized b-value data, because too many point clouds were visualized simultaneously. Figure16 shows the visualization image of b-value data filtered by time parameter interactively. With the reduction of the number of displayed point data, the users can recognize the feature of spatially distributed data. These visualization images were rendered in real time through the user's interactive operation using the physical MIDI controller. Thus, in this application, the user could effectively examine the feature of the distribution of the earthquakes interactively.

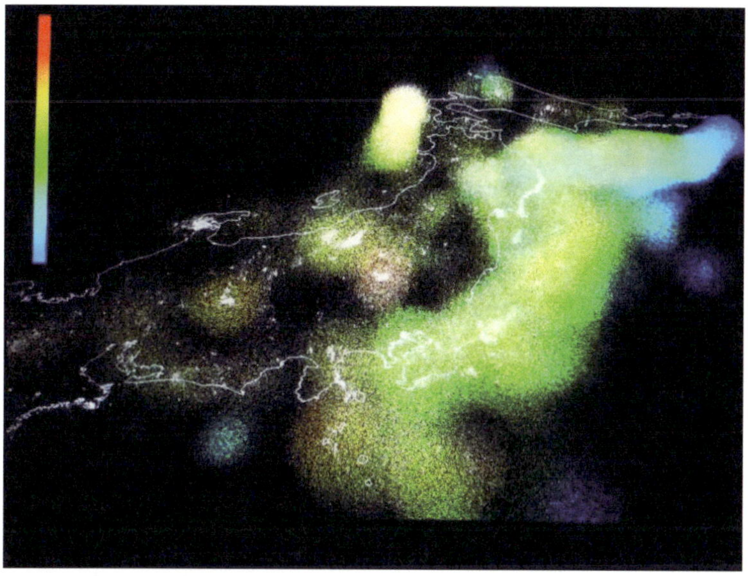

Fig. 15. Visualization of b-value data

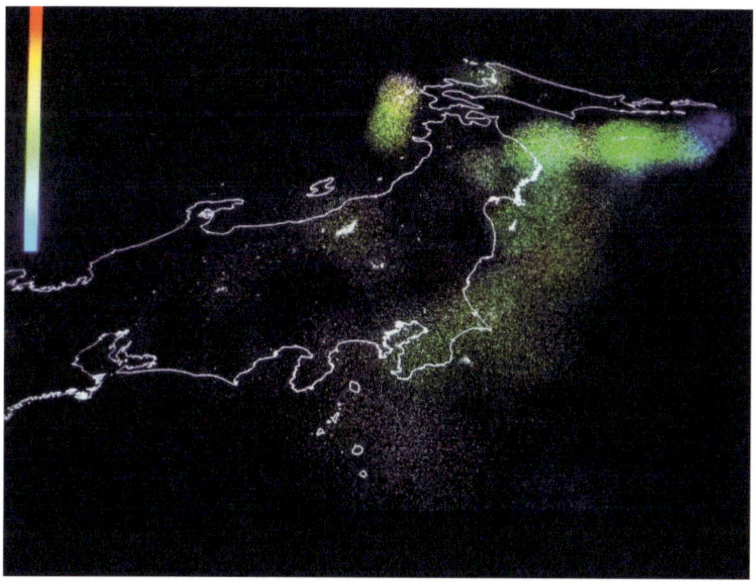

Fig. 16. Visualization of b-value data filtered by time

6.2 Visualization of integrated data

Next, this system was applied to analyze the relationship between several kinds of data by visualizing integrated image. In this case, several application programs that visualize hypocenter data, terrain data, basement depth data and plate structure data were integrated in the super high-definition immersive visual data mining environment. Though these data are stored in different database, every data has location information. Therefore, they can be related with each other using the location information as a reference key. Table 1 to Table 4 show the database table used in this system. Though the terrain data originally consist of altitude information corresponding to the latitude and longitude on the lattice, they are stored as data sets for the divided areas in the database.

latitude	longitude	depth	magnitude	date
36.3005	139.9837	40.68	0.8	2003-01-01
36.0927	138.7390	153.97	1.7	2003-01-01
36.2901	139.6655	121.42	1.3	2003-01-01
…..	…..	…..	…..	…..

Table 1. Database table of hypocenter data.

latitude	longitude	depth
36. 505	138.510	3.057
36.505	138.515	2.801
36.505	138.520	2.661
…..	…..	…..

Table 2. Database table of basement structure data.

latitude	longitude	depth
36.510	138.460	151.827
36.510	138.465	151.103
36.510	138.470	151.371
…..	…..	…..

Table 3. Database table of plate depth data.

north edge in latitude	west edge in latitude	south edge in latitude	east edge in latitude	filename
36.6051	139.8046	36.5895	139.8202	N36.6051_E139.8046.dat
36.6051	139.8202	36.5895	139.8358	N36.6051_E139.8202.dat
36.6051	139.8358	36.5895	139.8514	N36.6051_E139.8358.dat
.....	.....	.....	.....	.....

Table 4. Database table of terrain data

In this system, the user can access these databases from the virtual environment and visualize the retrieved data by specifying the condition. Thus, this system enables the user to understand the relationship among the hypocenter, terrain, basement depth, and plate structure data intuitively, and to analyze the feature of the earthquake phenomenon, by overlapping these data in the three-dimensional visualization environment.

As for the mechanism of integrating the visualized data in the virtual space, the plug-in function of the OpenCABIN library was used. In this system, each data is visualized by different application programs and they are integrated in the three-dimensional space in the runtime. Figure 17 and figure 18 show that several visualization data are integrated in the same space. In these examples, visualization programs for hypocenter data, terrain data, basement depth data and plate structure data are plugged-in to represent the relation among the data. When the hypocenter data were visualized using the sphere, the

Fig. 17. Visualization of relationship between terrain data and hypocenter data

size of it indicates the magnitude of the earthquake. The terrain data is created by mapping the texture image captured from the satellite onto the shape model. And the basement depth and the plate structure data are represented using the colors that indicate the depth values.

Fig. 18. Visualization of relationship among hypocenter data, basement depth data and plate structure data.

In this system, when the several visualization programs are plugged-in, the toggle buttons that show the conditions of each data are displayed. The user can switch the visible condition of each data by using the toggle button in the virtual space. For example, the user can change the visualization data from the combination of hypocenter data and basement depth data to the combination of hypocenter data and plate structure data, while running the application programs in the visualization environment. By using this method, the user could intuitively understand the feature of the distribution of hypocenter and the relation with other data. For example, the user could see whether the attention data of the earthquake occurred on the plate or in the plate structure. Thus, this system could be effectively used to represent the relationship among several kinds of data in the three-dimensional space and to analyze the earthquake phenomenon.

7. Conclusion

In this study, the super high-definition immersive visual data mining environment that uses 4K stereo projectors was constructed. In this system, it is expected that the effect of visual data mining is greatly improved, since the super high-definition stereo image transmits a large amount of information from the computer to the user and the interactive interface enables the user to explore the data space. However, the result of the experiments also suggested the limitations of representation ability of the super high-definition image. Therefore, the platform of immersive visual data mining for point cloud data was developed so that the user can easily visualize the data by changing the visualization method and visualization parameter in trials and errors. This platform was applied to the seismic data analysis, and several kinds of data such as map, terrain model, depth of basement and plate structure were visualized overlapped with the hypocenter data. Then, the effectiveness and possibility of the intuitive and accurate analysis in the immersive visual data mining environment were confirmed through the interaction with the visualized data.

Future research will include developing more effective visual data mining method through the collaboration with the earthquake experts and applying this technology to other application fields.

8. Acknowledgment

This study was partially supported by Keio University Global COE program (Center for Education and Research of Symbiotic, Safe and Secure System Design). And we would like to thank Takashi Furumura, Shoji Itoh, Kengo Nakajima, Takahiro Katagiri (The University of Tokyo), Hanxiong Chen, Osamu Tatebe, Atsuyuki Morishima, Hiroto Tadano (University of Thsukuba) for their supports.

9. References

Ammoura, A., Zaiane, O.R., Ji, Y. (2001). Immersed Visual Data Mining: Walking the Walk, Lecture Notes in Computer Science, Proc. of BNCOD 2001 (18th British National Conference on Databases), pp.202-218

Ferey, N., Gros, P.E., Herisson, J., Gherbi, R. (2005). Visual Data Mining of Genomic Databases by Immersive Graph-Based Exploration, *Proc. of 3rd International Conference on Computer Graphics and Interactive Techniques in Australasia and South East Asia*, pp.143-146

Furumura, T., Kennett, B.L.N. (2005). Subduction Zone Guided Waves and the Heterogeneity Structure of the Subducted Plate: Intensity anomalies in northern Japan, *Journal of Geophysical Research*, Vol.110, B10302.1-B10302.27

Kantardzie M. (2002). *Data Mining: Concepts, Models, Methods, and Algorithms*, Wiley-IEEE Press

Keim, D.A. (2002). Information Visualization and Visual Data Mining, *IEEE Transactions on Visualization and Computer Graphics*, Vol.7, No.1, pp.100-107

Nagel, H.R., Granum, E., Bovbjerg, S., Vittrup, M. (2008). Immersive Visual Data Mining: The 3DVDM Approach, *Visual Data Mining: Theory, Techniques and Tools for Visual Analytics*, Springer-Verlag, pp.281-311

Ogi, T., Daigo, H., Sato, S., Tateyama, Y., Nishida, Y. (2008). Super High Definition Stereo Image Using 4K Projection System, *ICAT 2008 (Proceedings of 18th International Conference on Artificial Reality and Telexistence)*, pp.365-366

Okada, Y., Kasahara, K., Hori, S., Obara, K., Sekiguchi, S., Fujiwara, H. Yamamoto, A. (2004). Recent progress of seismic observation networks in Japan -Hi-net, F-net, K-NET and KiK-net, *Earth Planets Space*, 56, xv-xxviii

Renambot, L., Jeong, B., Jagodic, R., Johnson, A., Leigh, J., Aguilera, J. (2006). Collaborative Visualization using High-Resolution Tiled Displays, *CHI 06 Workshop on Information Visualization and Interaction Techniques for Collaboration Across Multiple Displays*

Tateyama, Y., Oonuki, S., Ogi, T. (2008). K-Cave Demonstration: Seismic Information Visualization System Using the OpenCABIN Library, *ICAT 2008 (Proceedings of 18th International Conference on Artificial Reality and Telexistence)*, pp.363-364

Wegman, E.J., Symanzik, J. (2002). Immersive Projection Technology for Visual Data Mining, *Journal of Computational and Graphical Statistics*, Vol.11, pp.163-188

Wong, P.C. (1999). Visual Data Mining, *Computer Graphics and Applications*, Vol.19, No.5, pp.20-21

9

Realizing Semantic Virtual Environments with Ontology and Pluggable Procedures

Yu-Lin Chu and Tsai-Yen Li
Department of Computer Science, National Chengchi University, Taipei Taiwan, ROC

1. Introduction

Multi-User Virtual Environment (MUVE) has attracted much attention recently due to the increasing number of users and potential applications. Fig. 1 shows the common components that a MUVE system may provide. Generally speaking, a MUVE refers to a virtual world that allows multiple users to log in concurrently and interact with each other by texts or graphics provided by the system. On-line games can be considered as a special kind of virtual environment with specific characters, episode, and ways of interactions. Other MUVE systems such as SecondLife provide a general framework for users to design their own 3D contents and interact with other users through their avatars in a more general way. Although the users are allowed to build their own world, the animations that can be displayed are limited to those that have been prepared by the system. In addition, due to the lack of semantic information, it is not feasible to design virtual avatars that are controlled by the computer to interact with other avatars.

Under the concept of web 2.0, we think future virtual environments will also depend on how easily the users can share their own designs of procedures for customized animations and high-level behaviours. However, it is a great challenge to design an extensible virtual environment system that allows the users to write their own customized procedures that can dynamically acquire the information of the virtual environment and other users. In our previous work, we have succeeded in extending a MUVE system developed by ourselves, called IMNET (Li et al., 2005), to allow user-defined animation procedures to be specified, downloaded, and executed on the fly (Chu et al., 2008). However, in order to enable these user-defined procedures to create richer animations for interactions, we must be able to describe the semantics of the objects in the world in a standard way accessible to all potential animation/behaviour designers.

In this paper, we aim to make use of ontology to describe the semantics of the objects in the virtual environment such that users can design their own animation procedures based on the information. For examples, if we can acquire object information such as 3D geometry, height, and 2D approximation, we can design a motion planning procedure that can generate a collision-free path for the avatar to walk to a given destination. In addition, we have also designed the ontology for information exchange between avatars and added a new information query mechanism to facilitate the communication between avatars. These new functions will be demonstrated through several examples where the user-designed programs acquire application-specific semantics in the standard ontology format after the programs have been deployed dynamically to other clients' machines.

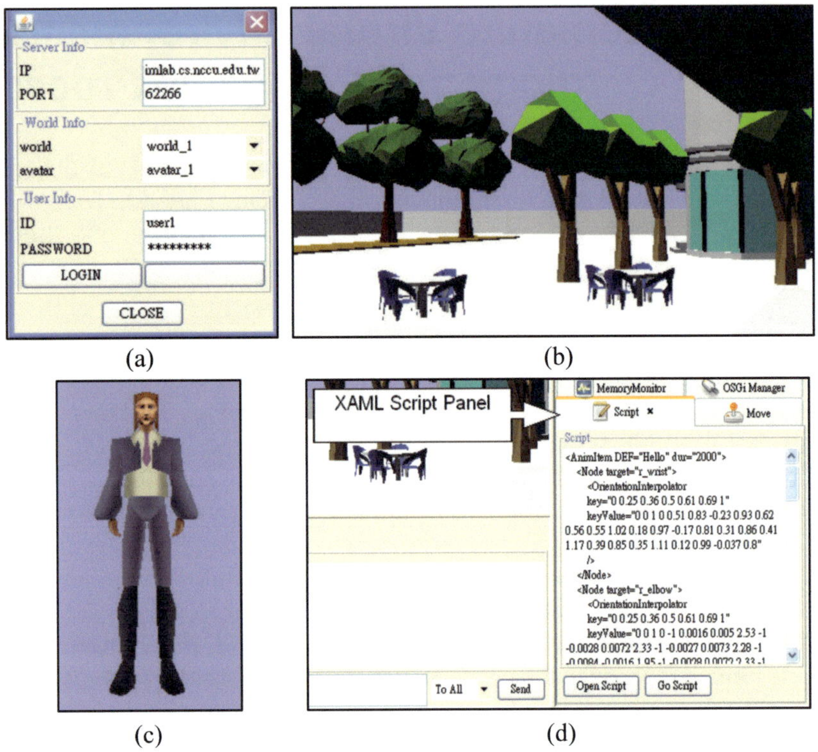

Fig. 1. Common components in a multi-user virtual environment: (a) login; (c) choose an avatar; (b) interact with virtual world; (d) a scripting interface (optional)

The remaining of the paper is organized as follows. In the next section, we will review the research related to our work. In the third section, we will describe the example design of ontology for the objects in the virtual worlds and for the avatars. In Section 4, we will describe the improved communication protocol allowing on-demand query of information among avatars. Then, in the following two sections, we will give examples of how to design animation components that can take advantage of the semantic information to generate richer user behaviours. Finally, we will conclude the paper with future directions.

2. Related work

In this work, we aim to provide a smart virtual environment that can enable richer contents and interactions. Before the concept of semantic virtual environment emerges, there has been much research about how to integrate AI technologies into a virtual environment system. R. Aylett et al. (2001) found that this type of virtual environments have several common features. For example, these systems added components for solving problems such as configuration, scheduling, and interaction. These systems constructed knowledge-level representation of the virtual scene and supported high-level processing with a natural language interface. These systems also used causal behaviours to replace the simulation of physical features.

The concept of semantic virtual environment was proposed to facilitate advanced applications that allow better communications between agents and the environment (Otto, 2005; Kleinermann et al., 2007). Unlike traditional virtual environments that were designed mainly for visual effects, semantic virtual environments are designed to contain richer structural semantic information adequate for a computer to process (Otto, 2005). For example, a plate on top of four sticks may be easily interpreted as a table by a human but it will be more difficult for a machine to infer its function from low-level geometry reasoning. An analogy of this unstructured information for visual interpretation is the vast home pages on the web. This is also why semantic web was proposed to facilitate automatic processing and communication among web servers. Similarly, in order to facilitate the reuse of 3D design and animation procedures, it is crucial to annotate the objects in a virtual world with semantic information in a standard format such that the same contents can be reused in different worlds or in different MUVE systems.

The idea of SVE has been realized from various aspects by much work in the literature. For example, the SEVEN system was proposed by Otto (2005) as an example of SVE with the concept of software components. It focuses more on the reusability of system components on different MUVE systems instead of components designed by the users. Gutierrez et al. (2005) also have proposed an ontology for virtual human by incorporating semantics into human shapes. They also regarded that the design of ontology is a continuous process where richer semantic information about human attributes should be added in a collaborative fashion. Instead of dealing with human shapes, Abaci et al. (2005) focused on adding action semantics in smart objects to facilitate the interaction between the avatars and with the objects in the virtual environment. Garcia-Rojas et al. (2006) also proposed to add semantic information, such as emotion and expressiveness, to animations in order to facilitate the selection of appropriate animations for a specific scenario.

3. Ontology design in IMNET

For developing and sharing animation procedures in the IMNET system, we will describe our ontology design for virtual objects and avatars in IMNET in this section. The topology described here is to serve as a demonstration example for potential applications; therefore, the design is by no means complete.

3.1 Ontology design of virtual environment

The objective of ontology design for virtual environment in this work is two-fold. First, we would like to keep the information that exists in the original IMNET such as object geometry and transformation. Second, we hope to use an example to show that more semantic information about the virtual objects can facilitate the computation of advanced reasoning procedures such as a path planner that may be designed by the users.

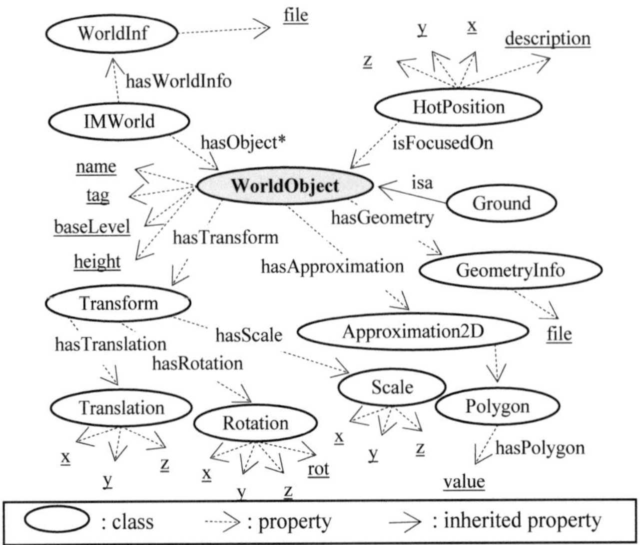

Fig. 2. Ontology design for virtual world

Our ontology design of the virtual environment is shown in Fig. 2. The root of the world document is the IMWorld node, which contains world information (WorldInfo) and all the virtual objects (WorldObject) in the world. In order to retain the semantic information of the virtual objects existing in the original IMNET, we have designed the GeometryInfo and Transform nodes. Each object also has some additional attributes such as name, tag, baseLevel, and height. The tag attribute is designed for the user to denote application-specific properties for virtual objects. For example, in the example of path planning, one can tag certain objects as sidewalk and crosswalk such that these regions can be treated appropriately by the path planner according to their meanings in the world. Each object may also have the attribute of Approximation2D, which is a polygon that can be used to define 2D approximation of obstacles in the environment for the path planner. In addition, if 2D approximation is over simplified for the application, one can also use the baseLevel and height attributes to define 3D approximation regions where the obstacles are located. If these attributes are not available for some objects, they still can be computed from the given 3D geometry and transformation of the objects. Some objects may also serve as the ground of the world through the node of Ground to define the boundary of the world. In addition, some objects could also be treated as HotPosition when they are the foci of interest in the application.

3.2 Ontology design for avatars

In MUVE's, an avatar could be controlled by a real user or by a computer program (called virtual user) if the system provides such a function. Virtual users can be used to by the designer of the virtual world to perform simple tasks such as a watching a gate or offering guided tours. In this section, we describe the basic ontology classes and attributes (as shown in Fig. 3) that we have designed for the applications of avatar interactions. Although an avatar is also an object in a virtual world, they have more active and complicated roles to play. For example, a user may choose to use his/her own animation for a specific behaviour by using the hasBehaviour property to connect to the Behaviour class. This Behaviour class defines the procedure (with name, package, and codebase) in order to generate the desired animation. In addition, an avatar may contain some basic attributes such as name, geometryInfo, and status. We also use the hasFriend and hasPosition properties to get the friendship and current position information of the avatars.

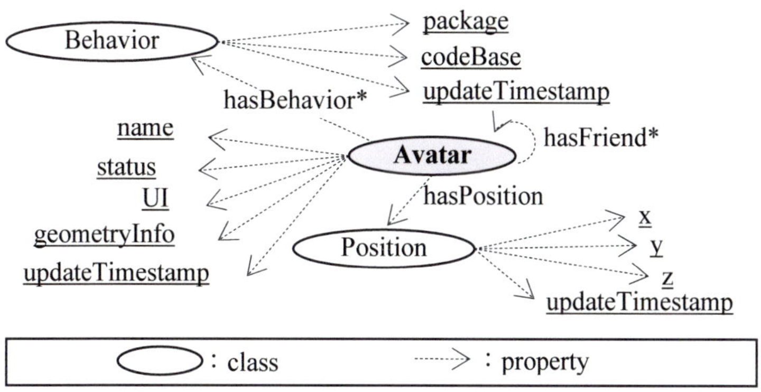

Fig. 3. Ontology design for avatars

3.3 Using ontology to load the virtual world

In the two subsections above, we have defined an ontology for the objects and avatars in the virtual world. However, in the original IMNET system, the geometry of the virtual world is loaded from a single VRML file. The geometry is parsed and converted into the underlying format for 3D display by a module called VRMLModelFactory as shown in Fig. 4. In order to augment the system with semantic information, we have split the geometry into several VRML files with one file for each object. This file is specified in the geometryInfo attribute of every worldObject. We have adopted the Web Ontology Language (OWL) established by W3C as the file format for the ontology of the virtual world. As shown in Fig. 5, the system

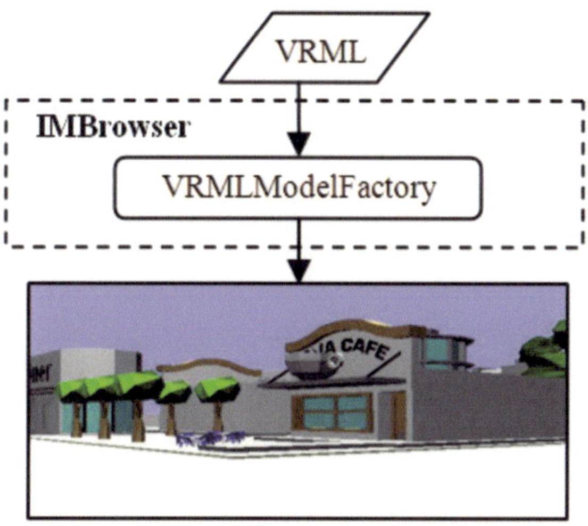

Fig. 4. Processing a single VRML file to generate the virtual world

first loads and parses the OWL file into an object format through the automatic generated Java class and the Protégé API. The geometry file for each object is then retrieved from the ontology and loaded into the system by the VRMLModelFactory module.

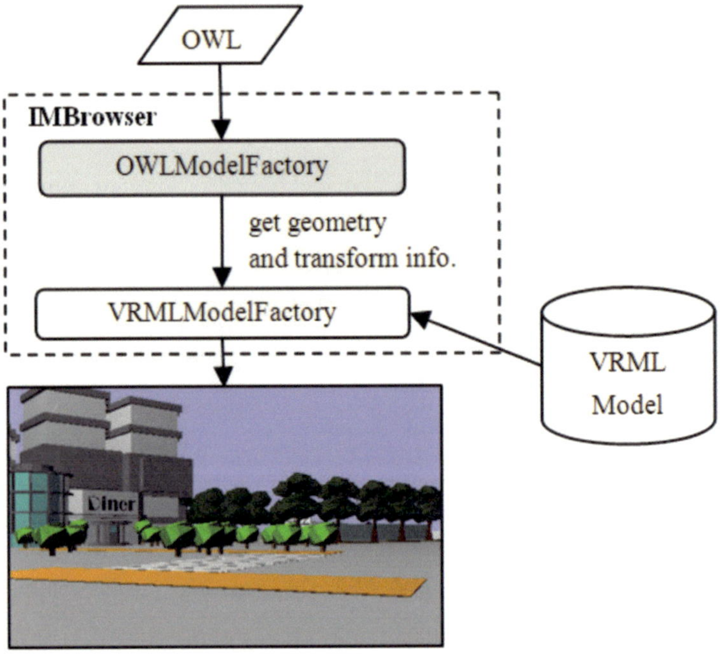

Fig. 5. Processing an OWL file and loading multiple VRML files to generate the virtual world

4. Communication protocol for information query

In a semantic virtual environment, we think semantic information should not only be used by internal modules, but should also be accessible to other clients through user-defined pluggable modules. In the previous section, we have described the ontology of the world and how it is loaded into the IMNET system. However, the clients are not required to specify all attributes defined in the ontology of the avatar. In addition, not all information described in the ontology will be broadcast to all clients. Therefore, we need to have a flexible way for the avatars to communicate semantic information with each other. In this subsection, we will describe how we modify the current communication protocol of IMNET to take information query into account.

```
<IMNET from="user1" to="user2">
 <Chat> Hello, How are you? </Chat>
</IMNET>
```

Fig. 6. An example of IMNET message

The application protocol in the original IMNET is similar to other MUVE's that only encapsulates predefined message types in the XML format. The underlying animation scripting language, XAML, is an example of message type (Li, et al., 2004). Another example is the message for textual information used in the chat module. For instance, in Fig. 6, we show an example where User1 wants to send a <Chat> message to user2. However, in the original design there is no way for the clients to query the information of other avatars that may be defined by the avatar designers instead of the system. This function is crucial for the avatars to exchange information for richer interactions in a semantic virtual environment.

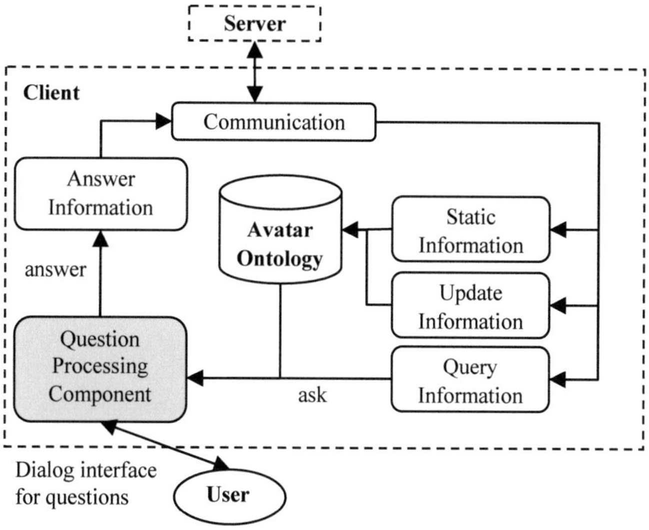

Fig. 7. Client architecture for the processing of three types of information

In the work, we have enhanced the communication protocol of IMNET to incorporate a broader range of message types. We distinguish three types of information exchange between avatars and have designed their processing flow in IMNET as shown in Fig. 7. The first one is static information, such as the id and name properties that are delivered only once at the beginning when a user logs in. The second type is update information, such as the position of an avatar, which is voluntarily pushed to all clients in a more frequent way. An example of update information is shown in Fig. 8. The third type is query information, such as optional attributes or questions, which are sent to the inquirer only upon requests. We have integrated these three types of messages with the tag <Info> and distinguish their types in an internal tag. For example, in Fig. 9, we show a scenario where user1 asks user2 if user2 wants to be a friend of user1. The message is sent with a <queryInfo> internal tag and with a timestamp property. This timestamp property can be used as the id of the query. The query processing component in Fig. 7 may prompt user2 (if user2 is a real user) with a dialog box or evoke an auto-responding component (if user2 is a virtual user) for a response. Then he/she can use this id to indicate this query (askId) in his/her reply message to user1 as shown in Fig. 10.

```
<Info from= "user2" to="all" timestamp="1215476355">
  <updateInfo position="20 34"/>
</Info>
```

Fig. 8. An example of message for update information

```
<Info from="user1" to="user2" timestamp="1215476323">
 <queryInfo ask="make friend"/>
</Info>
```

Fig. 9. An example of query message

```
<Info from="user2" to="user1" timestamp="1215476330">
 <queryInfo askId="1215476323"  answer="yes"/>
</Info>
```

Fig. 10. An example of responding message

5. Demonstrative examples

In this section, we will give two examples of using semantic information in the virtual world to enhance the functions and behaviours of the avatars.

5.1 Example 1: Motion planning for avatars

A common way for a user to navigate in a virtual environment is by controlling his/her avatar by input devices such as keyboard or mouse. However, it is a low-level task that may not be easy for a novice user to control his/her avatar to reach a destination. There has been much research that proposed to use motion planning techniques to generate collision-free navigation paths for the avatar to follow (Salomon et al., 2003). However, in order to define a motion planning problem, we need to obtain the geometric information of the objects in the environment such that we know where the boundary of the world is and which of the objects needs to be treated as an obstacle.

In this subsection, we will use a motion planning component as an example to illustrate how a user-defined animation procedure can be installed dynamically and retrieve necessary world information for the needs of the application. A user first prepares the procedure as a software bundle according to the specification of OSGi . Then he/she can use a XAML script, such as the one shown in Fig. 11, to indicate where he/she wants to move to. In this script, he/she needs to specify the name of the package, the initial (optional) and goal locations, and the URL for downloading the bundle if it is not already installed. In this case, the bundle will be installed dynamically and evoked through the OSGi mechanism (Chu et al., 2008).

```
<MoPlan package='imlab.osgi.bundle.interfaces'
   codebase='http://imlab.cs.nccu.edu.tw/plan.jar'>
   <param name="-s" value="1.1  2.3"/>
   <param name="-g" value="5.2  3.8"/>
</MoPlan>
```

Fig. 11. An example of specifying a motion planning problem in a user-defined component, MoPlan

In order to generate a collision-free path, a motion planner needs to acquire obstacle information from the world. In our system, the motion planning component obtains this semantic information through the ontology of the virtual world defined in Section 3. According to the obtained obstacle information, the planner first converts the obstacle information into a 2D bitmap and then computes a potential field that is commonly used in a motion planner. And then the planner performs a best-first search to find a feasible path to the goal according to the potential field. Finally, the planner component translates the path to a XAML script and assigns it to the avatar to generate the walking animation as depicted in Fig. 12.

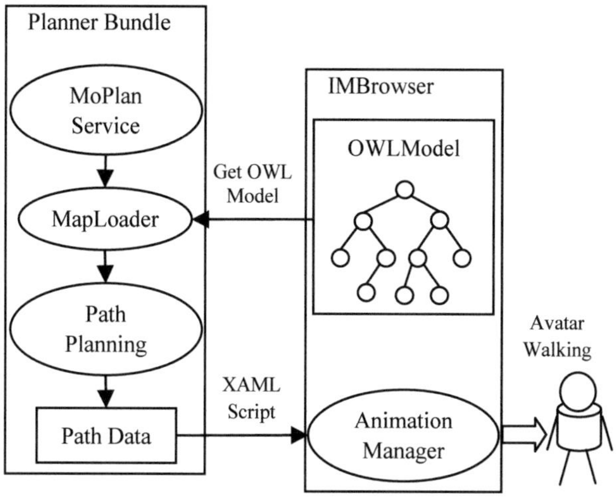

Fig. 12. The process of how to generate animations through the motion planning component

Obstacle information can not only be inferred from low-level geometry but also be given as approximation by the scene designer. In Section 3, we have designed an optional attribute called Ap-proximation2D in the ontology of a virtual object. In Fig. 13, we show an example of the collision-free path generated by the planner by the use of the 2D approximation of the objects in the world. If the planner can find this 2D approximation for an object, it will use it to build the 2D bitmap needed in the planner. If not, it still can build the convex hull of the 3D geometry and project it into the ground to form a 2D approximation. In other words, semantic information could be designed to facilitate automatic reasoning but it is not mandatory. The designers of virtual objects are not obligated to define all attributes in an ontology that could be large in collaborative creation. In addition, the user-defined animation procedures do not easily break down in such a loosely coupled distributed environment either since they can take this into account in the design stage.

However, some semantic information cannot be inferred directly from geometry. For example, in the virtual environment, there could be some crosswalk or sidewalk regions that need to be used whenever possible. One can tell this kind of objects from their appearance but it would be difficult for the machine to infer their functions through geometry. In this case, the planner has to acquire this information through the semantics defined in the ontology of the virtual world. In the example shown in Fig. 14, the planner knows where the sidewalk and crosswalk through object tagging in the ontology and makes the regions occupied by these objects a higher priority when planning the path for the avatar. The potential values in these regions are lowered to increase the priority during the search for a feasible path. Consequently, a path passing through these regions was generated in the example shown in Fig. 14. In addition, according to this semantic information, appropriate animations, such as looking around before moving onto the crosswalk region, could be inserted into the motion sequence of walking to the goal, as shown in Fig. 14(c).

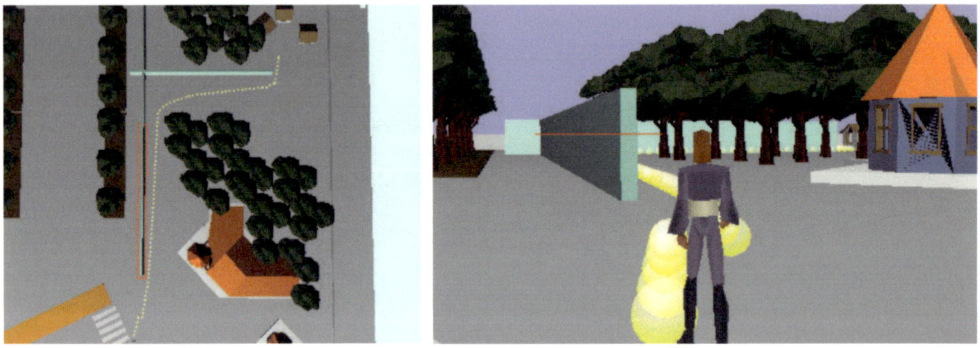

(a) (b)

Fig. 13. An example path generated by the path planner: (a) avoiding the obstacles described by the 2D approximation in semantics; (b) a snapshot of the scene from the avatar's view.

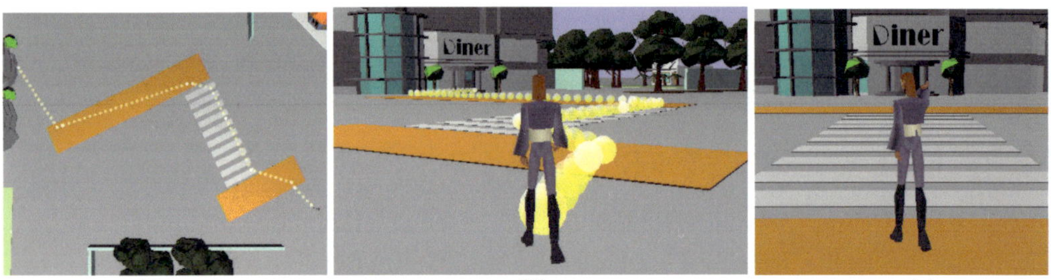

(a) (b) (c)

Fig. 14. Another example path generated by the path planner: (a) the path generated by taking crosswalk and sidewalk into account; (b) a snapshot of the scene from the avatar's view; (c) special animation can be inserted before crossing the crosswalk.

5.2 Example 2: Interaction between avatars

An objective of this work is to allow different animation components owned by different clients to interact with each other. The users can communicate through customized tags to acquire the avatar ontology of each other and use this information to perform specific interactions. The user behind an avatar can actually be a real user or a virtual user controlled by a computer program. In this subsection, we will use two scenarios to illustrate these two types of interactions. The first scenario is to demonstrate the interaction between two real users, and the second scenario is for the interaction between a real user and a virtual user.

To facilitate the interaction between the avatars, we have designed a component called SocialService. There are three steps for initiating an interaction between avatars as shown in Fig. 15. A user who would like to initiate the interaction first sends a customized XAML script shown in Fig. 16 to the other avatar (step 1) for it to install this social interaction component (step 2). Once the component has been installed, interaction queries related to social activities can be delivered through the communication protocol described in Section 4 and processed by the SocialService component (step 3).

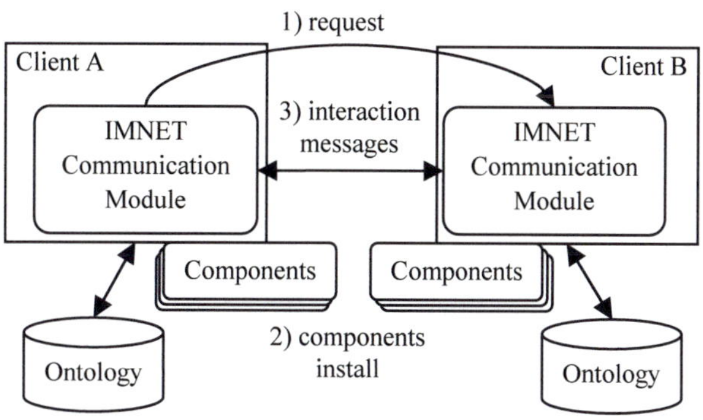

Fig. 15. The steps for initiating an interaction between avatars

```
<SocialService package='imlab.osgi.bundle.interfaces'
  codebase='http://imlab.cs.nccu.edu.tw/social.jar'/>
```

Fig. 16. Starting the mechanism of the interaction between avatars through XML script

In the first scenario, both users are real users. First, user1 would like to invite user2 to be his friend (Fig. 17(a)). Therefore, a query message: "'User1' added you to his friend list. Do you want to invite 'user1' to be your friend as well?" appeared in user2's interface (Fig. 17(b)). If user2 choose 'yes', user1 would be added into her friend list and a confirmation message would be sent back to user1 (Fig. 17(c)). Through the interaction between the two real users, the friend information was updated into the ontology of both avatars.

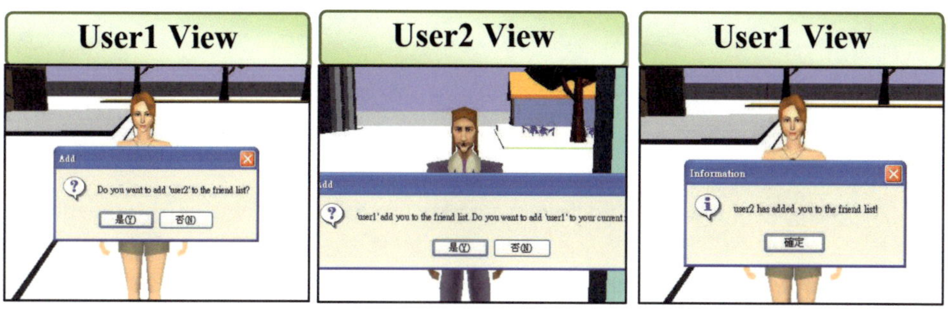

(a) (b) (c)

Fig. 17. An example of interaction between the real users

In the second scenario, user1 arranged a virtual user called door-keeper to watch the door and provide information to potential guests (Fig. 18(1~2)). When user2 entered a designated region, the doorkeeper would turn to face user2 and ask: "May I help you?" At the first encounter, user2 just entered this area by accident and therefore chose the answer: "Just look around." The doorkeeper replied: "Have a good day!" (Fig. 18(3~5)) The state of the doorkeeper in this interaction was then set to FINISH. After user2 left the area, the state was restored to IDLE (Fig. 18(6)). Assume that after some period of time, user2 approached the doorkeeper again for the second time. This time user2 chose: "I'm looking for my friend." The doorkeeper replied: "Who's your friend?" Then user2 answered: "Jerry." At this moment, the doorkeeper queried the avatar ontology of user1 (named Jerry) to see if user2 is in his friend list. If so, the doorkeeper would inform user2 the current position of user1. Otherwise, the doorkeeper would answer: "Sorry, Jerry does not seem to know you." If there is no such a user called Jerry, the doorkeeper would answer: "Jerry is not in this world." (Fig. 18(7~9))

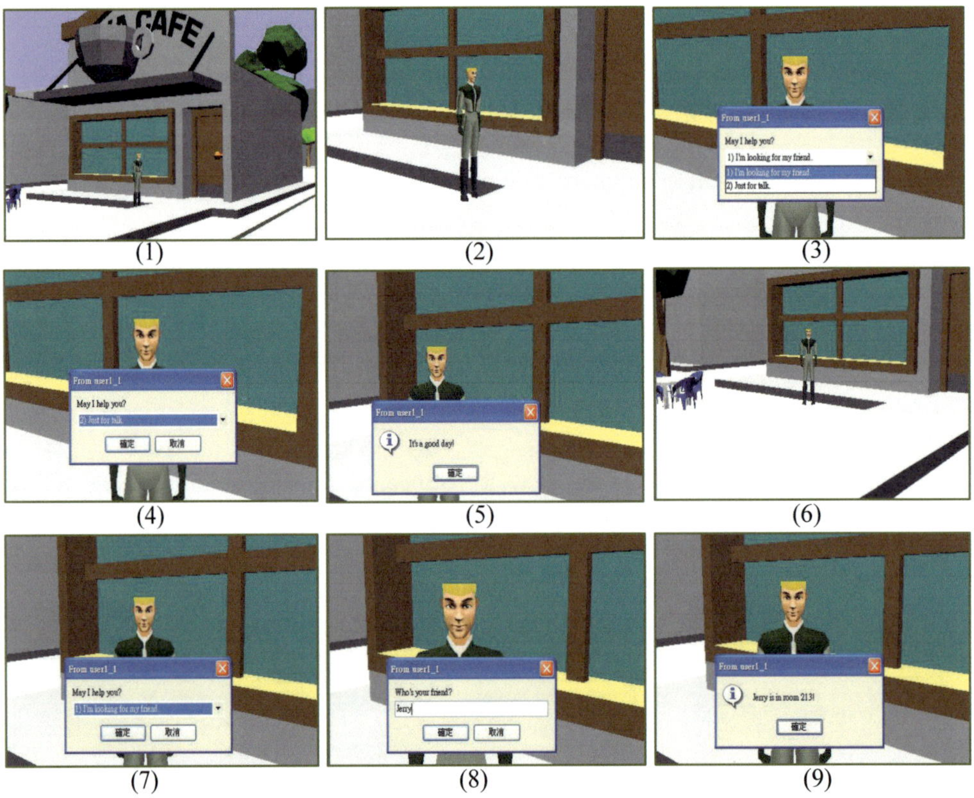

Fig. 18. An example of interaction between a real users and a virtual user (doorkeeper)

6. Conclusions and future work

It is crucial to be able to share user-designed software components to enable richer contents and behaviours in the future development of MUVE systems. In previous work, we have designed a mechanism under OSGi to facilitate dynamic installation of user-designed software components in IMNET. In this work, we have extended the MUVE system to allow the semantics of the objects and avatars in the virtual environment to be described in the form of ontology. This provides a standard way for the software components to acquire semantic information of the world for further reasoning. We have used two types of examples: path planning and social interaction, to show how users can design their own code to facilitate richer or autonomous behaviours for their avatars (possibly virtual). We hope that these examples will shed some lights on the further development of object ontology and more sophisticated applications.

7. Acknowledgement

This research was funded in part by the National Science Council of Taiwan, R.O.C., under contract No. NSC96-2221-E-004-008. The paper is extended from a conference paper published in the International Conference on Virtual Reality Continuum and Its Applications in Industry (VRCAI2008)

8. References

Abaci, T.; C'iger, J. & Thalmann, D. (2005). Action semantics in Smart Objects. *Proc. of Workshop towards Semantic Virtual Environments*

Aylett, R. & Cavazza, M. (2001). Intelligent Virtual Environments - A State-of-the-art Report. *Proc. of Eurographics*

Chu, Y.L.; Li, T.Y. & Chen, C.C. (2008). User Pluggable Animation Components in Multi-user Virtual Environment. *Proc. of the Intl. Conf. on Intelligent Virtual Environments and Virtual Agents*, China

Garcia-Rojas, A.; Vexo, F.; Thalmann, D.; Raou-Zaiou, A.; Karpouzis, K. & Kollias, S. (2006). Emotional Body Expression Parameters In Virtual Human Ontology. *Proc. of the 1st Intl. Workshop on Shapes and Semantics*, pp. 63-70, Matsushima, Japan

Guti'errez, M.; Garcia-Rojas, A.; Thalmann, D.; Vexo, F.; Moc-Cozet, L.; Magnenat-Thalmann, N.; Mortara, M. & Spag-Nuolo, M. (2005). An Ontology of Virtual Humans: incorporating semantics into human shapes. *Proc. of the Workshop towards Semantic Virtual Environments*

Kleinermann, F.; Troyer, O.D.; Creelle, C. & Pellens, B. (2007). Adding Semantic Annotations, Navigation paths and Tour Guides to Existing Virtual Environments. *Proc. of the 13th Intl. Conf. on Virtual Systems and Multimedia (VSMM'07)*, Brisbane, Australia.

Li, T.Y.; Liao, M.Y. & Liao, J.F. (2004). An Extensible Scripting Language for Interactive Animation in a Speech-Enabled Virtual Environment. *Proc. of the IEEE Intl. Conf. on Multimedia and Expo (ICME2004)*, Taipei, Taiwan.

Li, T.Y.; Liao, M.Y & Tao, P.C. (2005). IMNET: An Experimental Testbed for Extensible Multi-user Virtual Environment Systems. *Proc. of the Intl. Conf. on Computational Science and its Applications, LNCS 3480*, O. Gervasi et al. (Eds.), Springer-Verlag Berlin Heidelberg, pp. 957-966.

Otto, K.A. (2005). The Semantics of Multi-user Virtual Environments. *Proc. of the Workshop towards Semantic Virtual Environments*

Salomon, B.; Garber, M.; Lin, M. C. & MANOCHA, D. (2003). Interactive Navigation in Complex Environment Using Path Planning. *Proc. of the 2003 Symposium on Interactive 3D graphics.*

10

An Overview of Interaction Techniques and 3D Representations for Data Mining

Ben Said Zohra[1], Guillet Fabrice[1], Richard Paul[2], Blanchard Julien[1] and Picarougne Fabien[1]
[1]*University of Nantes*
[2]*University of Angers*
France

1. Introduction

Since the emergence of databases in the 1960s, the volume of stored information has grown exponentially every year (Keim (2002)). This information accumulation in databases has motivated the development of a new research field: Knowledge Discovery in Databases (KDD) (Frawley et al. (1992)) which is commonly defined as the extraction of potentially useful knowledge from data. The KDD process is commonly defined in three stages: pre-processing, Data Mining (DM), and post-processing (Figure 1). At the output of the DM process (post-processing), the decision-maker must evaluate the results and select what is interesting. This task can be improved considerably with visual representations by taking advantage of human capabilities for 3D perception and spatial cognition. Visual representations can allow rapid information recognition and show complex ideas with clarity and efficacy (Card et al. (1999)). In everyday life, we interact with various information media which present us with facts and opinions based on knowledge extracted from data. It is common to communicate such facts and opinions in a virtual form, preferably interactive. For example, when watching weather forecast programs on TV, the icons of a landscape with clouds, rain and sun, allow us to quickly build a picture about the weather forecast. Such a picture is sufficient when we watch the weather forecast, but professional decision-making is a rather different situation. In professional situations, the decision-maker is overwhelmed by the DM algorithm results. Representing these results as static images limits the usefulness of their visualization. This explains why the decision-maker needs to be able to interact with the data representation in order to find relevant knowledge. Visual Data Mining (VDM), presented by Beilken & Spenke (1999) as an interactive visual methodology "to help a user to get a feeling for the data, to detect interesting knowledge, and to gain a deep visual understanding of the data set", can facilitate knowledge discovery in data.

In 2D space, VDM has been studied extensively and a number of visualization taxonomies have been proposed (Herman et al. (2000), Chi (2000)). More recently, hardware progress has led to the development of real-time interactive 3D data representation and immersive Virtual Reality (VR) techniques. Thus, aesthetically appealing element inclusion, such as 3D graphics and animation, increases the intuitiveness and memorability of visualization. Also, it eases the perception of the human visual system (Spence (1990), Brath et al. (2005)). Although there is still a debate concerning 2D vs 3D data visualization (Shneiderman (2003)), we believe that

3D and VR techniques haves a better potential to assist the decision-maker in analytical tasks, and to deeply immerse the user's in the data sets. In many cases, the user needs to explore data and/or knowledge from the inside-out and not from the outside-in, like in 2D techniques (Nelson et al. (1999)). This is only possible in using VR and Virtual Environment (VEs). VEs allow users to navigate continuously to new positions inside the data sets, and thereby obtain more information about the data. Although the benefits offered by VR compared to desk-top 2D and 3D still need to be proven, more and more researchers is investigating its use with VDM (Cai et al. (2007)). In this context, we are trying to develop new 3D visual representations to overcome some limitations of 2D representations. VR has already has been studied in different areas of VDM such as pre-processing (Nagel et al. (2008), Ogi et al. (2009)), classification (Einsfeld et al. (2006)), and clustering (Ahmed et al. (2006)).

In this context, we review some work that is relevant for researchers seeking or intending to use 3D representation and VR techniques for KDD. We propose a table that summarizes 14 VDM tools focusing on 3D - VR and interaction techniques based on 3 dimensions:

- Visual representations;
- Interaction techniques;
- Steps in the KDD process.

This paper is organized as follows: firstly, we introduce VDM. Then we define the terms related to this field of research. In Section 3, we explain our motivation for using 3D representation and VR techniques. In Section 4, we provide an overview of the current state of research concerning 3D visual representations. In Section 5, we present our motivation for interaction techniques in the context of KDD. In Section 6, we describe the related work about visualization taxonomy and interaction techniques. In Section 7, we propose a new classification for VDM based on both 3D representations and interaction techniques. In addition, we survey representative works on the use of 3D and VR interaction techniques in the context of KDD. Finally, we present possible directions for future research.

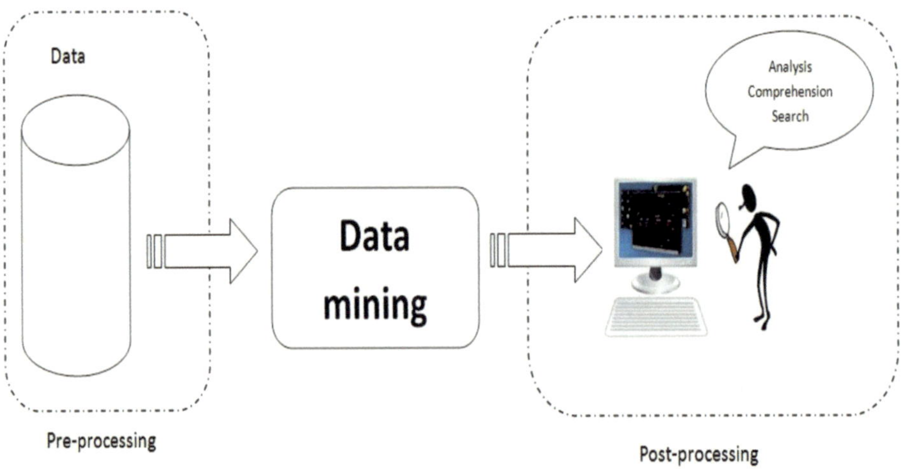

Fig. 1. The KDD process

2. Visual Data Mining

Historically, VDM has evolved from the fields of scientific visualization and information visualization. Both visualizations forms create visual representations from data that support user interaction with the aim to find useful information in the data. In scientific visualization, visual representations are typically constructed from measured or simulated data which represent objects or concepts of the physical world. Figure 2(a) shows an application that provides a VR interface to view the flow field around a space shuttle. In information visualization, graphic models present abstract concepts and relationships that do not necessarily have a counterpart in the physical world. For instance, figure 2(b) shows a 3D tree representation to visualize data clusters.

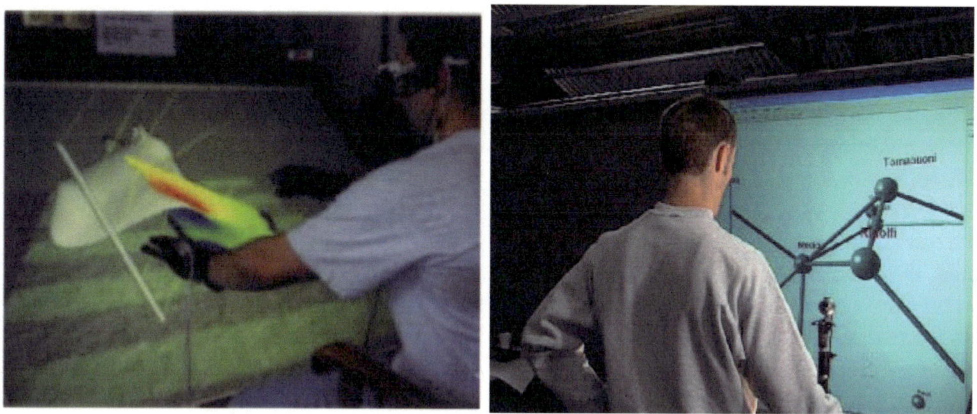

(a) (b)

Fig. 2. Scientific visualization and information visualization examples: (a): visualization of the flow field around a space shuttle (Laviola (2000)) (b): GEOMIE (Ahmed et al. (2006))information visualization framework

Beilken & Spenke (1999) presented the purpose of VDM as a way to "help a user to get a feeling for the data, to detect interesting knowledge, and to gain a deep visual understanding of the data set". Niggemann (2001) looked at VDM as a visual representation of the data close to the mental model. In this paper we focus on the interactive exploration of data and knowledge that is built on extensive visual computing(Gross (1994)).

As humans understand information by forming a mental model which captures only the main information, in the same way, data visualization, similar to the mental model, can reveal hidden information encoded in the data. In addition to the role of the visual data representation, Ankerst (2001) explored the relation between visualization and the KDD process. He defined VDM as "a step in the KDD process that utilizes visualization as a communication channel between the computer and the user to produce novel and interpreted patterns". He also explored three different approaches to VDM, two of which affect the final or intermediate visualization results. The third approach involves the interactive manipulation of the visual representation of the data rather than the results of the KDD methods. The three definitions recognize that VDM relies heavily on human perception capabilities and the use of interactivity to manipulate data representations. The three definitions also emphasize the key importance of the following three aspects of VDM: visual representations; interaction processes; and KDD tasks.

In most of the existing KDD tools, VDM is only used during two particular steps of the KDD process: in the first step (pre-processing) VDM can play an important role since analysts need tools to view and create hypotheses about complex (i.e. very large and / or high-dimensional) original data sets. VDM tools, with interactive data representation and query resources, allow domain experts to explore quickly the data set (de Oliveira & Levkowitz (2003)). In the last step (post-processing) VDM can be used to view and to validate the final results that are mostly multiple and complex. Between these two steps, an automatic algorithm is used to perform the DM task. Some new methods have recently appeared which aim at involving the user more significantly in the KDD process; they use visualization and interaction more intensively, with the ultimate goal of gaining insight into the KDD problem described by vast amounts of data or knowledge. In this context, VDM can turn the information overload into an opportunity by coupling the strengths of machines with that of humans. On the one hand, methods from KDD are the driving force of the automatic analysis side, while on the other hand, human capabilities to perceive, relate and make conclusions turn VDM into a very promising research field. Nowadays, fast computers and sophisticated output devices can create meaningful visualization and allow us not only to visualize data and concepts, but also to explore and interact with this data in real-time. Our goal is to look at VDM as an interactive process with the visual representation of data allowing KDD tasks to be performed. The transformation of data / knowledge into significant visualization is not a trivial task. Very often, there are many different ways to represent data and it is unclear which representations, perceptions and interaction techniques needs to be applied. This paper seeks to facilitate this task according to the data and the KDD goal to be achieved by reviewing representation and interaction techniques used in VDM. KDD tasks have different goals and diverse tasks need to be applied several times to achieve a desired result. Visual feedback has a role to play, since the decision-maker needs to analyze such intermediate results before making a decision. We can distinguish two types of cognitive process within which VDM assists users to make a decision:

- Exploration: the user does not know what he/she is looking for (discovery).
- Analysis: the user knows what he/she is looking for in the data and tries to verify it (visual analysis).

3. From 2D to 3D visualization and virtual reality

There is a controversial debate on the use of 2D versus 3D and VR for information visualization. In order to justify our choice of 3D and VR, we first review the difference between 3D visualizations and VR techniques:

- 3D visualization is a representation of an object in a 3D space by showing length, width and height coordinates on a 2D surface such as a computer monitor. 3D visual perception is achieved using visual depth cues such as lighting, shadows and perspective.
- VR techniques enable user immersion in a multi-sensorial VE and user interaction devices and stereoscopic images to increase depth perception and the relative 3D position of objects.

3.1 2D versus 3D

Little research has been dedicated to the comparison of 2D and 3D representations. Concerning the non-interactive visualization of static graphs, 3D representations have generally not been advised ever since the publications by Tufte (1983) and Cleveland & McGill (1984). Nevertheless, the experiments of Spence (1990) and Carswell et al. (1991) show that there is no significant difference of accuracy between 2D and 3D for the comparison of numerical values. In particular, Spence (1990) pointed out that it is not the apparent dimensionality of visual structures that counts but rather the actual number of parameters that show variability. Under some circumstances, information may be processed even faster when represented in 3D rather than in 2D. Concerning the perception of global trends in data, experimental results of Carswell et al. (1991) also show an improvement in answer times using 3D but to the detriment of accuracy. Other works compare 2D and 3D within the framework of interactive visualization. Ware & Franck (1994) indicated that displaying data in 3D instead of 2D can make it easier for users to understand the data. Finally, Tavanti & Lind (2001) pointed out that realistic 3D displays could support cognitive spatial abilities and memory tasks, namely remembering the place of an object, better than with 2D.

On the other hand, several problems arise such as intensive computation, more complex implementations than 2D interfaces, and user adaptation and disorientation. The first problem can be addressed by using powerful and specialized hardware. However, one of the main problems of 3D applications is user adaptation. In fact, most users just have experience with classical windows, icons, menu pointing devices (WIMP) and 2D-desktop metaphors. Therefore, interaction with 3D presentations and possibly the use of special devices demand considerable adaptation efforts to use this technology. There is still no commonly-accepted standard for interaction with 3D environments. Some research has shown that it takes users some time to understand what kind of interaction possibilities they actually have (Baumgärtner et al. (2007)). In particular, as a consequence of a richer set of interactions and a higher degree of freedom, users may be disoriented.

3.2 Toward virtual reality

To overcome limitations of interaction with 3D representations, VR interfaces and input devices have been proposed. These interfaces and devices offer simpler and more intuitive interaction techniques (selection, manipulation, navigation, etc.), and more compelling functionality (Shneiderman (2003)). In VR, the user can always access external information without leaving the environment and the context of the representation. Also, the user's immersion in the data allows him to take advantage of stereoscopic vision that enables him to disambiguate complex abstract representations (Maletic et al. (2001)). Ware & Franck (1996), compared the visualization of 2D and 3D graphs. Their work shows a significant improvement in *intelligibility* when using 3D. More precisely, they found that the ability to decide if two nodes are connected or not is improved by a factor 1.6 when adding stereo cues, by 2.2 when using motion parallax depth cues, and by a factor of 3 when using stereoscopic as well as motion parallax depth cues. Aitsiselmi & Holliman (2009), found that the participants obtained better scores if they were doing a mental rotation task on a stereoscopic screen instead of a 2D screen. This result demonstrates the *efficiency* of VR and shows that the extra depth information given by stereoscopic display makes it easier to move a shape mentally. It is generally considered that only stereoscopy allows one to fully exploit the characteristics of the 3D representations. It helps the viewer to judge the relative size of objects and the distances between them. It also helps him to mentally move a shape in the 3D visualization area. Finally, Cai et al. (2007), found that visualization increases *robustness* in object tracking and positive detection accuracy in object prediction. They also found that the interactive method enables the user to process the image data 30 times faster than manually. As a result, they suggested that human interaction may significantly increase overall productivity.

We can therefore conclude that stereoscopy and interaction are the two most important components of VE and the most useful to users. Therefore, the equipment used should be taken into account from the very beginning of application design, and consequently be taken into account as a part of VDM techniques taxonomy.

4. Visual representations for Visual Data Mining

One of the problems that VDM must address is to find an effective representation of something that has no inherent form. In fact, it is crucial not only to determine which information to visualize but also to define an effective representation to convey the target information to the user. The design of a visualization representation must address a number of different issues: what information should be presented? How this should be done? What level of abstraction to support? etc. For example, a user tries to find out interesting relations between variables in large databases. This information may be visualized as a graph (Pryke & Beale (2005)) or as an abstract representation based on a sphere and cone (Blanchard et al. (2007)).

Many representations for VDM have been proposed. For instance, some visual representations are based on *abstract representations*, such as graphs (Ahmed et al. (2006)), trees (Einsfeld et al. (2007), Buntain (2008)), and geometrical shapes (Ogi et al. (2009), Nagel et al. (2008), Meiguins et al. (2006)) and others on *virtual worlds objects* (Baumgärtner et al. (2007)). The classification proposed in this chapter provides some initial insight into which techniques are oriented to certain data types, but does not assert that one visual representation is more suitable than others to explore a particular data set. Selecting a representation depends largely on the task being supported and is still a largely intuitive process.

4.1 Abstract visual representations

3D representations are still abstract and require the user to learn certain conventions, because they do not look like what they refer to or they do not have a counterpart in the real-world. There are 3 kinds of abstract representations: graphs, trees, and geometrical shapes.

1. Graphs

A graph (Figure.3) is a network of nodes and arcs, where the nodes represent entities while the arcs represent relationships between entities. For a review on the state of the art in graph visualization see Herman et al. (2000).

At the beginning, graph visualization was used in 2D space to represent components around simple boxes and lines. However, several authors think that larger graph structures can be viewed in 3D (Parker et al. (1998)). In the empirical study of Ware & Franck (1996), which measured path-tracing ability in 3D graphs, they suggested that the amount of information that can be displayed in 3D with stereoscopic and motion depth cues exceeds 2D representations by a factor of 3. Another experiment with new display technologies confirmed the previous experiment and showed much greater benefits than previous studies. Ware & Mitchell (2008) experiments showed that the use of stereoscopic display, kinetic depth and 3D tubes was much more beneficial than using lines to display the links as in previous studies.

A technique based on the hyper system (Hendley et al. (1999)) for force-based visualization can be used to create a graph representation. The visualization consists of nodes and links whose properties are given by the parameters of the data. Data elements affect parameters such as node size and color, link strength and elasticity. The dynamic graphs algorithm enables the self-organization of nodes in the visualization area by the use of a force system in order to find a steady state, and determine the position of the nodes. For example, Beale (2007) proposed a Haiku system (Figure.3(b)) which provides an abstract 3D perspective of clustering algorithm results based on the hyper system. One of the characteristics of this system is that the user can choose which parameters are used to create the distance metrics (distance between two nodes), and which ones affect the other characteristics of the visualization (node size, link elasticity, etc.). Using the hyper system allows related things (belonging to the same cluster) to be near to each other, and unrelated things to be far away.

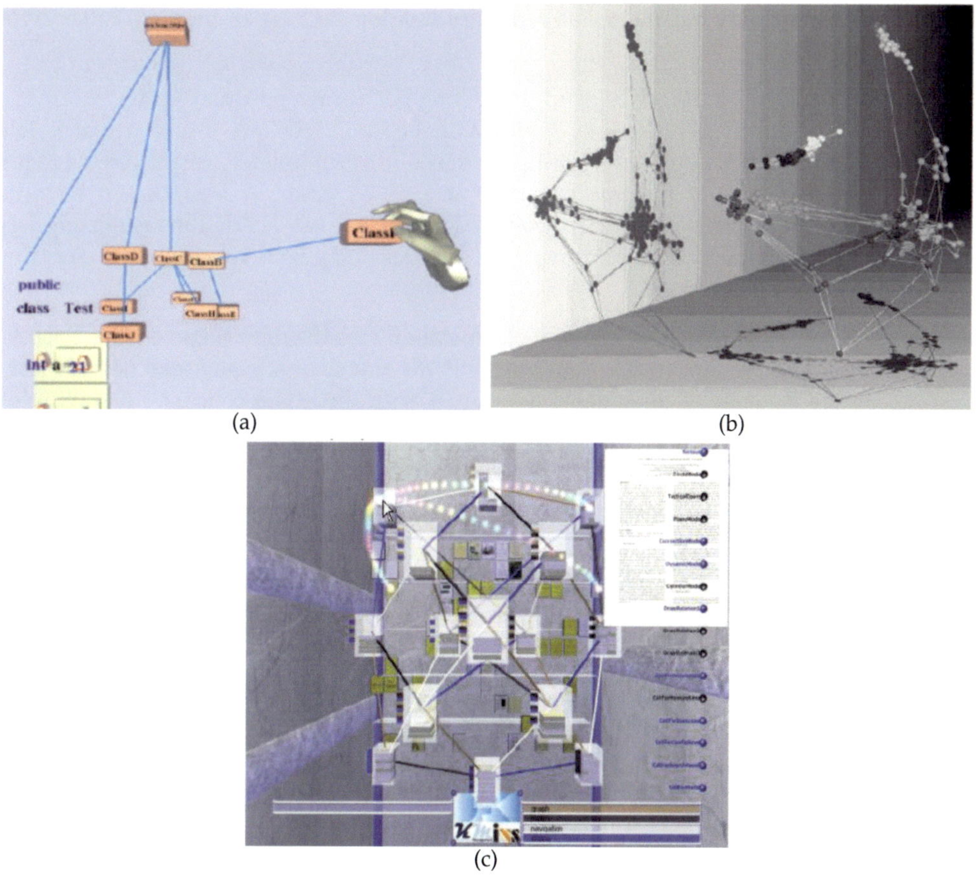

Fig. 3. An example of graph representations: (a) Source code Ougi (Osawa et al. (2002)), (b) Association rules: Haiku (Beale (2007)), (c) DocuWorld (Einsfeld et al. (2006))

2. 3D trees

3D trees (Figure.4) is a visualization technique based on the hierarchical organization of data. A tree can represent many entities and the relationships between them. In general, the visualization of hierarchical information structures is an important topic in the information visualization community (Van Ham (2002)). Because trees are generally easy to layout and interpret (Card et al. (1999)), this approach finds many applications in classification visualization (Buntain (2008)). 3D trees were designed to display a larger number of entities than in 2D representations, in a comprehensible form (Wang et al. (2006)). Various methods have been developed for this purpose, among which, space-filling techniques and node-link techniques.

Space-filling techniques (Van Ham (2002), Wang et al. (2006)) based upon 2D tree-maps visualization proposed by Johnson & Shneiderman (1991) have been successful for visualizing trees that have attributes values at the node level. Space-filling techniques are particularly useful when users care mostly about nodes and their attributes but do not need to focus on the topology of the tree, or consider that the topology of the tree is trivial (e.g 2 or 3 levels). The users of space-filling techniques also require training because of the unfamiliar layout (Plaisant et al. (2002)).

Node-link techniques, on the other hand, have long been frowned upon in the information visualization community because they typically make inefficient use of screen space. Even trees of a hundred nodes often need multiple screens to be completely displayed, or require scrolling since only part of the tree is visible at a given time. A well-known node-link representation in cone trees was introduced by Robertson et al. (1991) for visualizing large hierarchical structures in a more intuitive way. 3D trees may be displayed vertically (Cone Tree) or horizontally (Cam Tree).

Buntain (2008) used 3D trees for ontology classification visualization (Figure.4(a)). Each leaf represents a unique concept in the ontology, and the transparency and size of each leaf is governed by the number of documents associated with the given concept. A molecule is constructed by clustering together spheres that share common documents, and surrounds the leaves with a semi transparent shell (Figure.4(b)).

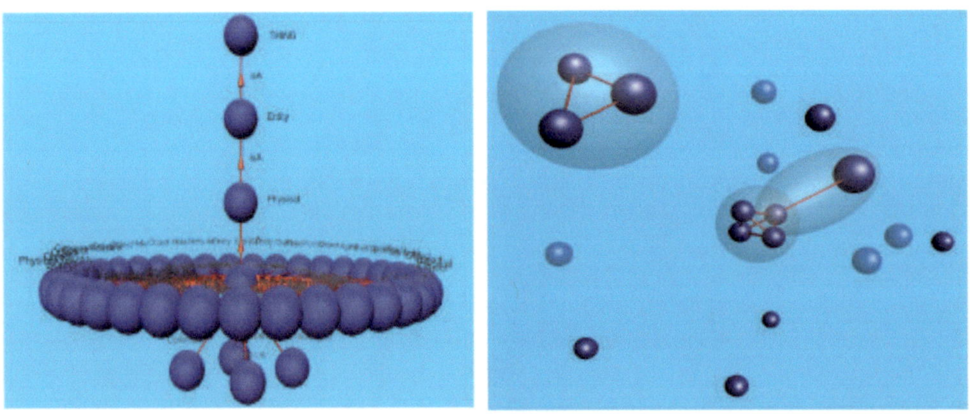

(a) (b)

Fig. 4. An example of trees representing ontology classification: SUMO (Buntain (2008))

3. Geometric shapes

In this technique, 3D objects with certain attributes are used to represent data and knowledge. The 3D scatter-plot visualization technique (Nagel et al. (2001)) is one of the most common representations based on geometric shapes (Figure.5). The main innovation compared to 2D visualization techniques is the use of volume rendering which is a conventional technique used in scientific visualization. 3D rendering techniques use voxels (instead of pixels in 2D) to present a certain density of the data. 3D scatter-plot has been adapted by Becker (1997), making the opacity of each voxel a function of points density. Using scatter-plots is intuitive since each data is faithfully displayed. Scatter-plots have been used successfully for detecting relationships in two dimensions (Bukauskas & Böhlen (2001), Eidenberger (2004)). This technique hit limitations if the dataset is large, noisy, or if it contains multiple structures. With large amounts of data, the amount of displayed objects makes it difficult to detect any structure at all.

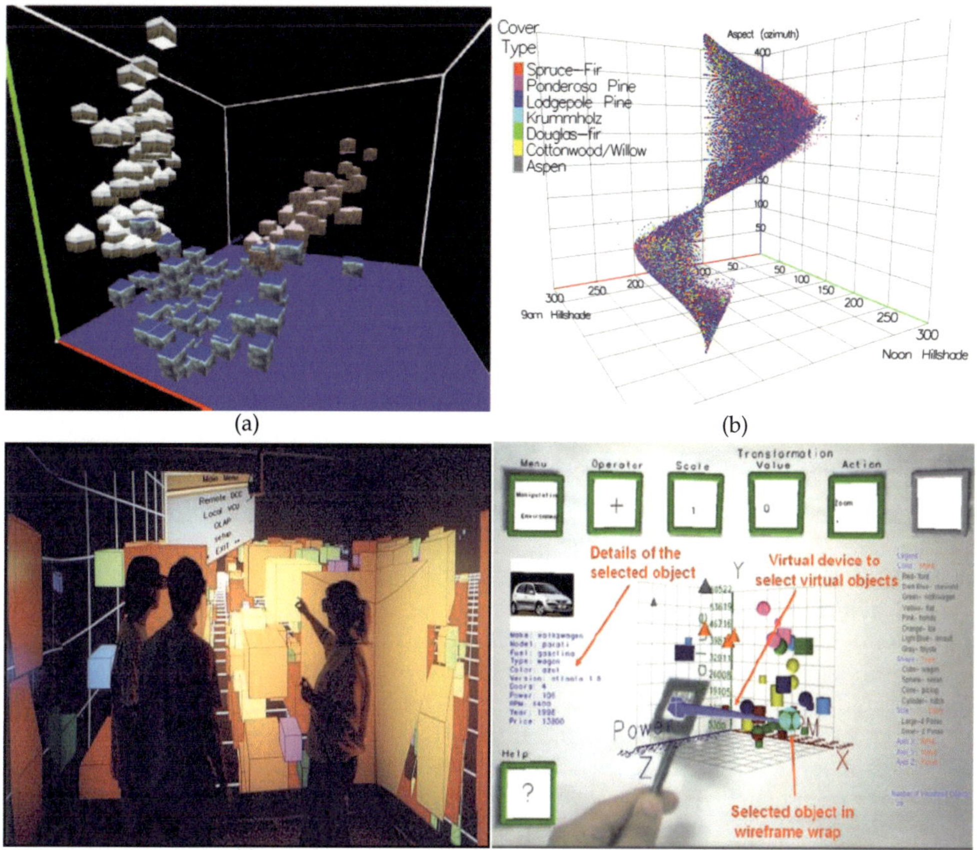

Fig. 5. Different 3D scatter plot representations: (a) VRMiner (Azzag et al. (2005)), (b) 3DVDM (Nagel et al. (2008)), (c) DIVE-ON (Ammoura et al. (2001)), (d) Visualization with augmented reality (Meiguins et al. (2006))

4.2 Virtual worlds

Trying to find easily-understandable data representations, several researchers proposed the use of real-world metaphors. This technique uses elements of the real-world to provide insights about data. For example, some of these techniques are based on a city abstraction

(Figure.6). The virtual worlds (sometimes called cyber-spaces) for VDM are generally based either on the information galaxy (Krohn (1996)) or the information landscape metaphor (Robertson et al. (1998)). The difference between the two metaphors is that in the information landscape, the elevation of objects is not used to represent information (objects are placed on a horizontal floor). The specificity of virtual worlds is that they provide the user with some real world representations.

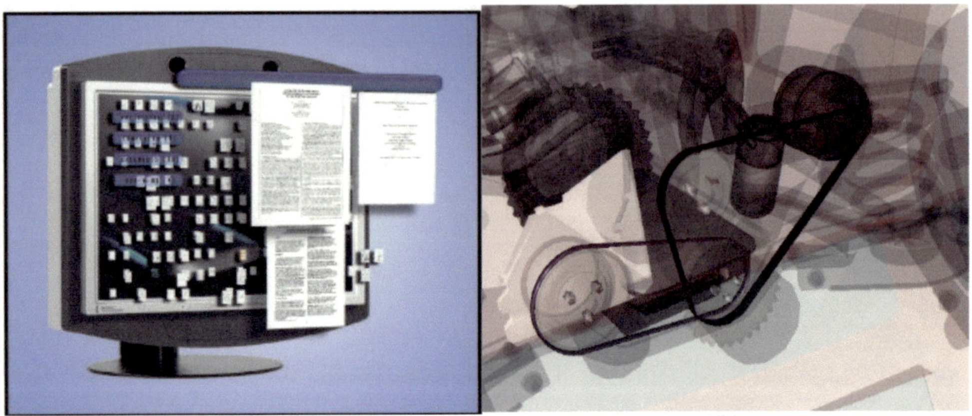

(a) (b)

Fig. 6. Example of virtual world representation (a) faults projected onto a car model in (Götzelmann et al. (2007)) (b) documents classification in @VISOR Baumgärtner et al. (2007)

5. Interaction techniques for Visual Data Mining

Interaction techniques can empower the user's perception of information when visually exploring a data set (Hibbard et al. (1995)). The ability to interact with visual representations can greatly reduce the drawbacks of visualization techniques, particularly those related to visual clutter and object overlap, providing the user with mechanisms for handling complexity in large data sets. Pike et al. (2009) explored the relationship between interaction and cognition. They consider that the central percept of VDM is that the development of human insight is aided by interaction with a visual interface. As VDM is concerned with the relationship between visual displays and human cognition, merely developing only novel visual metaphors is rarely sufficient to make new discoveries provide or confirmation or negation of a prior belief.

Interaction also allows the integration of the user in the KDD process. KDD is not a completely human-guided process, since DM algorithms analyze a data set searching for useful information and statistically valid knowledge. The degree of automation of the KDD process actually varies considerably since different levels of humans guidance and interaction are usually required. But it is still the algorithm, and not the user, that is looking for knowledge. In this context, de Oliveira & Levkowitz (2003) suggested that VDM should have a greater role than a traditional application of visualization techniques to support the non-analytic stages of a KDD process. It is through the interactive manipulation of a visual interface that knowledge is constructed, tested, refined and shared.

We can distinguish 3 different interaction categories: exploration, manipulation and human-centered approaches.

5.1 Visual exploration

Visual exploration techniques are designed to take advantage of the considerable visual capabilities of human beings, especially when users try to analyze tens or even hundreds of graphic variables in a particular investigation. Visual exploration allows the discovery of data trends, correlations and clusters, to take place quickly, and can support users in formulating hypotheses about the data. It is essential in some situations to allow the user to simply look at the visual representation in a passive sense. This may mean moving around the view point in order to reveal structure in the data that may be otherwise masked and overlooked . In this way, exploration provides the means to view information from different perspectives to avoid occlusion and to see object details. It can be very useful to have the ability to move the image to resolve any perceptual ambiguities that exist in a static representation when a large amount of information is displayed at once. The absence of certain visual cues (when viewing a static image) can mask important results (Kalawsky & Simpkin (2006)).

Navigation is often the primary task in 3D worlds and refers to the activity of moving through the scene. The task of navigation presents challenges such as supporting spatial awareness and providing efficient and comfortable movements between distant locations. Some systems enable users to navigate without constraint through the information space (Nagel et al. (2008), Einsfeld et al. (2006), Azzag et al. (2005)). Other systems restrict movement in order to reduce possible user disorientation (Ahmed et al. (2006)). As an illustration, in VRMiner (Azzag et al. (2005)) a six-degree freedom sensor is fixed to the user's hand (Figure.7) allowing him/her to easily define a virtual camera in 3D space. For example, when the user moves his hand forward in the direction of the object, he/she may zoom in or out. The 3DVDM system (Nagel et al. (2008)) allows the user to fly around and within the visualized scatter-plot. The navigation is controlled by the direction of a "wanda" device tracked with 6 degrees of freedom. Dissimilarly, in GEOMI (Ahmed et al. (2006)), the user can only rotate the representation along the X and Y axes but not along the Z axis.

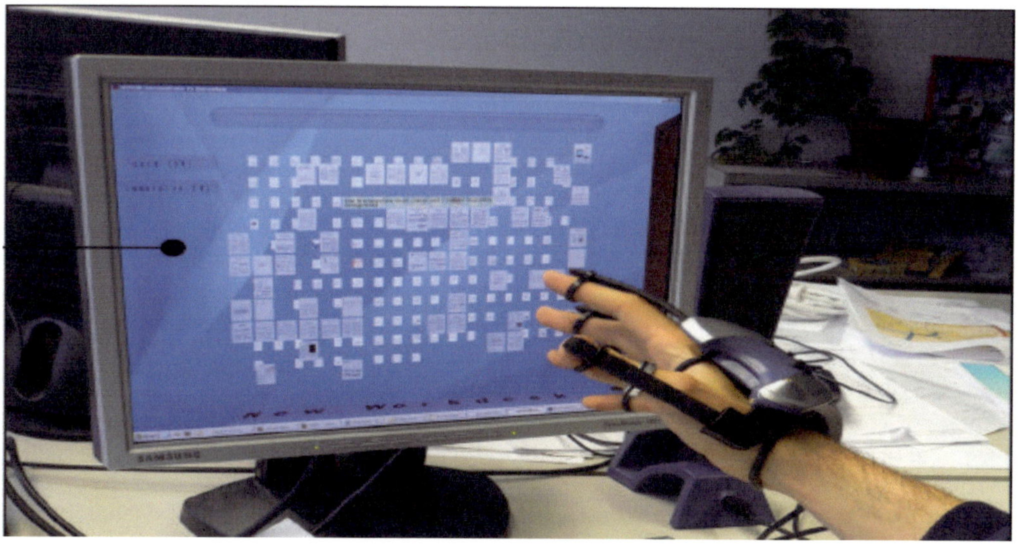

Fig. 7. Illustration of navigation through a virtual environment with data-glove (Baumgärtner et al. (2007))

In visual exploration, the user can also manipulate the objects in the scene. In order to do this, interaction techniques provide means to select and zoom-in and zoom-out to change the scale of the representation. Beale (2007) has demonstrated that using a system which supports the free exploration and manipulation of information delivers increased knowledge even from a well know dataset. Many systems provide a virtual hand or a virtual pointer (Einsfeld et al. (2007)), a typical approach used in VE, which is considered as being intuitive as it simulates real-world interaction (Bowman et al. (2001)).

- Select: this technique provides users with the ability to mark interesting data items in order to keep track of them when too many data items are visible, or when the perspective is changed. In these two cases, it is difficult for users to follow interesting items. By making items visually distinctive, users can easily keep track of them even in large data sets and/or with changed perspectives.
- Zoom: by zooming, users can simply change the scale of a representation so that they can see an overview (context) of a larger data set (using zoom-out) or the detailed view (focus) of a smaller data set (using zoom-in). The essential purpose is to allow hidden characteristics of data to be seen. A key point here is that the representation is not fundamentally altered during zooming. Details simply come into focus more clearly or disappear into context.

Visual exploration (as we can see in Section.7) can be used in the pre-processing of the KDD process to identify interesting data (Nagel et al. (2008)), and in post-processing to validate DM algorithm results (Azzag et al. (2005)). For example, in VRMiner (Azzag et al. (2005)) and in ArVis (Blanchard et al. (2007)), the user can point to an object to select it and then obtain informations about it.

5.2 Visual manipulation

In KDD, the user is essentially faced with a mass of data that he/she is trying to make sense of. He/she should look for something *interesting*. However, *interest* is an essentially human construct, a perspective of relationships among data that is influenced by tasks, personal preferences, and past experience. For this reason, the search for knowledge should not only be left to computers; the user has to guide it depending upon what he/she is looking for, and hence which area to focus computing power on. Manipulation techniques provide users with different perspectives of the visualized data by changing the representation. On of this techniques is the capability of changing the attributes presented in the representation. For example, in the system shown by Ogi et al. (2009), the user can change the combination of presented data. Other systems have interaction techniques that allow users to move data items more freely in order to make the arrangement more suitable for their particular mental model (Einsfeld et al. (2006)). Filter interaction techniques enable users to change the set of data items being presented on some specific conditions. In this type of interaction, the user specifies a range or condition, so that only data meeting those criteria are presented. Data outside the range or not satisfying the conditions are hidden from the display or shown differently; even so, the actual data usually remain unchanged so that whenever users reset the criteria, the hidden or differently-illustrated data can be recovered. The user is not changing data perspectives, just specifying conditions within which data are shown. ArVis (Blanchard et al. (2007)), allows the user to look for a rule with a particular item in it. To do this, the user can search for it in a menu which lists all the rule items and allows the wanted object to be shown.

5.3 Human-centered approach

In most existing KDD tools, interaction can be used in two different ways: exploration and manipulation. Some new methods have recently appeared (Baumgärtner et al. (2007), Poulet & Do (2008)), trying to involve the user in the DM process more significantly and using visualization and interaction more intensively. In this task, the user manipulates the DM algorithm and not only the graphical representation. The user sends commands to the algorithm in order to manipulate the data to be extracted. We speak here about local knowledge discovery. This technique allows the user to focus on interesting knowledge from user's point of view, in order to make the DM tool more generically useful to the user. It is also necessary for the user to either change the view point or manipulate a given parameter of the knowledge discovery algorithm and observe its effect. There must therefore be some way in which the user can indicate what it is considered interesting and what is not, and to do this the KDD tool needs to be dynamic and versatile (Ceglar et al. (2003)). The human-centered process should be iterative since it is repeated until the desired results are obtained. From a human interaction perspective, a human-centered approach closes the loop between the user and the DM algorithm in a way that allows them to respond to results as they occur by interactively manipulating the input parameters (Figure.8).

With the purpose of involving the user more intensively in the KDD process, this new kind of approach has the following advantages (Poulet & Do (2008))

- The quality of the results is improved by the use of human-knowledge recognition capabilities;
- Using the domain knowledge during the whole precess (and not only in the interpretation of the results) allows guided searching for knowledge.
- The confidence in the results is improved as the DM process gives more comprehensible results.

In Arvis (Blanchard et al. (2007)), the user can navigate among the subsets of rules via a menu providing neighborhood relations. By applying a neighborhood relation to a rule, the mining algorithm extracts a new subset of rules. The previous subset is replaced by the new subset in the visualization area.

6. Related work on taxonomies of visual representations and interaction techniques

Many researchers have attempted to construct a taxonomy for visualization. Chi (2000) used the Data State Model (Chi & Riedl (1998)) to classify information visualization techniques. This model is composed of 3 dimensions with categorical values: data stages (value, analytical abstraction, visualization abstraction, and view), transformation operators (data transformation, visualization transformation, and visual mapping transformation), and within-stage operators (value stage, analytical stage, visualization stage, and view stage). This model shows how data change from one stage to another requiring one of the three types of data transformation operators. This state model helps implementers understand how to apply and implement information visualization techniques. Tory & Moller (2004), present a high-level taxonomy for visualization which classifies visualization algorithms rather than data. Algorithms are categorized according to the assumption that they make about the data being visualized. Their taxonomy is based on 2 dimensions:

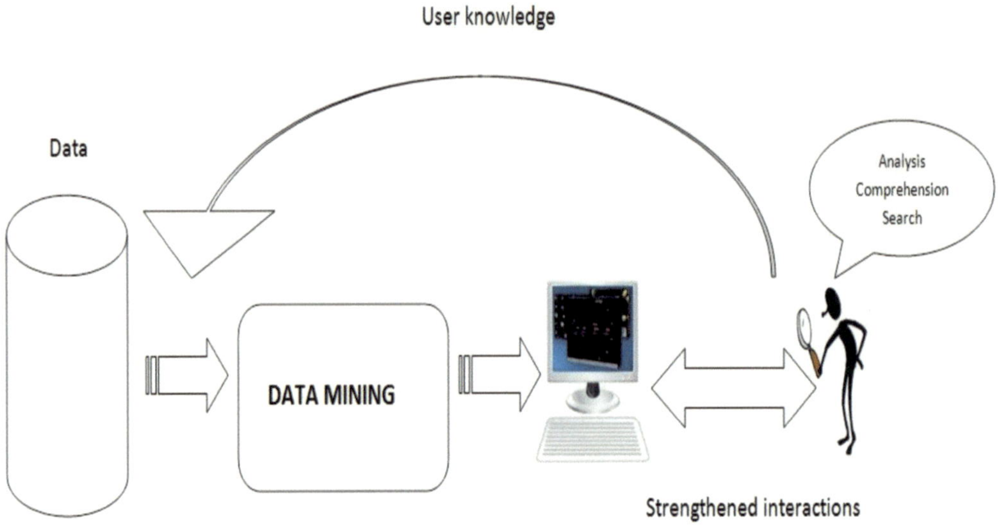

Fig. 8. The human-centered approach

- Data values: discrete or continuous
- How the algorithm designer chooses to display attributes: specialization, timing, color, and transparency.

Another area of related research is interaction and user interfaces. In this area, (Bowman et al. (2001)) present an overview of 3D interaction and user interfaces (3DUI). This paper also discuses the effect of common VE hardware devices on user interaction, as well as interaction techniques for generic 3D tasks and the use of traditional WIMP styles in 3D environments. They divide most user interaction tasks into three categories: navigation, selection/manipulation and system control. Arns (2002) thinks that Bowman's taxonomy is general and can encompass too many parts of a VR system. For that reason, she created a classification for virtual locomotion (travel) methods. This classification includes information on display devices, interaction devices, travel tasks, and the two primary elements of virtual travel: translation and rotation. Dachselt & Hinz (2005) have proposed a classification of 3D-widget solutions by interaction purpose/intention of use, e.g, direct 3D object interaction, 3D scene manipulation, exploration and visualization. Finally, Teyseyre & Campo (2009) presented an overview of 3D representations for visualizing software, describing several major aspects such as visual representations, interaction issues, evaluation methods, and development tools.

7. A new classification of Visual Data Mining based on visual representations and interaction techniques

In this section, we present a new classification of VDM tools composed of 3 dimensions: visual representations, interaction techniques, and KDD tasks. Table.1 presents the different modalities of each of the three dimensions. The proposed taxonomy takes into account both the representation and the interaction technique. In addition, many visualization

Dimension	Modalities
Visual representation	Graphs, 3D trees, geometrical shapes, virtual worlds
Interaction techniques	Visual exploration, visual manipulation, human-centered
KDD tasks	Pre-processing, classification, clustering, association rules

Table 1. Dimension modalities

design taxonomies include only a small subset of techniques (e.g., locomotion Arns (2002)). Currently, visualization tools have to provide not only effective visual representations but also effective interaction metaphors to facilitate the exploration and help users achieve insight. Having a good 3D representation without a good interaction technique does not mean having a good tool. This classification looks at some representative tools for doing different KDD tasks, e.g., pre-processing and post-processing (classification, clustering and association rules). Different tables summarize the main characteristics of the reported VDM tools with regard to visual representations and interaction techniques. Other relevant information such as interaction actions (navigation, selection and manipulation, and system control), input-output devices (CAVE, mouse, hand tracker, etc.) presentation (3D representation or VR representation) and year of creation is also reported.

7.1 Pre-processing

Pre-processing (in VDM) is the task of data visualization before the DM algorithm is used. It is generally required as a starting point of KDD projects so that analysts may identify interesting and previously unknown data by the interactive exploration of graphical representations of a data set without heavy dependence on preconceived assumptions and models. The basic visualization technique used for data pre-processing is the 3D scatter-plots method, where 3D objects with attributes are used as markers. The main principle behind the design of traditional VDM techniques, such as The Grand Tour (Asimov (1985)), the parallel coordinate (Inselberg & Dimsdale (1990)), etc., is that they are viewed from the outside-in. In contrast to this, VR lets users explore the data from inside-out by allowing users to navigate continuously to new positions inside the VE in order to obtain more information about the data. Nelson et al. (1999) demonstrated through comparisons between 2D and VR versions of the VDM tool XGobi that the VR version of XGobi performed better.

In the Ogi et al. (2009) system, the user can see several data set representations integrated in the same space. The user can switch the visible condition of each data set. This system could be used to represent the relationships among several data sets in 3D space, but it does not allows the user to navigate through the data set and interact with it. The user can only change the visual mapping of the data set. However, the main advantage of this system is that the data can be presented with a hight degree of accuracy using hight-definition stereo-images that can be beneficial especially when visualizing a large amount of data. This system has been applied to the visualization and analysis of earthquake data. Using the 3rd dimension has allowed the visualization of both the overall distribution of the hypocenter data and the individual location on any earthquake, which is not possible with the conventional 2D display. Figure 9 shows hypocenter data recorded over 3 years. The system allows the visualization of several databases at the same time e.g. map data, terrain data, basement depth, etc and the user can switch the visible condition of each data in the VE. For example, the user can change the visualization data from the combination of hypocenter data and basement depth

System	Visual Representation	Interaction techniques	Interaction actions			Input-Output devices	3D/ VR	year
			Navigation	Selection and Manipulation	System control			
Ogi et al. (2009)	Geometric shape	Visual manipulation	-	-	Graphical menu	CAVE	VR	2009
3DVDM Nagel et al. (2008) (Fig.5(c))	Geometric shape	Visual exploration	Manual view point manipulation + thought wizard metaphor	-	-	Three-button 'wand' + CAVE	VR	2008
Nested circles Wang et al. (2006)	Visual exploration and visual manipulation	Tree	-	Object selection + virtual pointer	Graphic menus	Mouse + 2D screen	3D	2006
Visualization with augmented reality Meiguins et al. (2006) (Fig.5(e))	Geometric shape	Visual manipulation	-	Object selection + virtual hand	Graphical menus	Hand tracker	VR	2006
Dive-On Ammoura et al. (2001) (Fig.5(d))	Geometric shape	Visual exploration and manipulation	Physical movement + steering + target-based travel	Object selection	Graphical menus	Hand + head tracker + CAVE	VR	2001

Table 2. 3D VDM tool summary for pre-processing KDD task

data to the combination of hypocenter data and terrain data. Thus, the system can shows the relationships between only any two data sets among the others.

As a result of using VR, the 3DVDM system (Nagel et al. (2008)) is capable of providing real-time user response and navigation as well as showing dynamic visualization of large amounts of data. Nagel et al. (2008) demonstrated that the 3DVDM visualization system allows faster detection of non-linear relationships and substructures in data than traditional methods of data analysis. An alternative proposal is available with DIVE-ON (Data mining in an Immersed Visual Environment Over a Network) system, proposed by Ammoura et al. (2001). The main idea of DIVE-ON is visualizing and interacting with data from distributed data warehouses in an immersed VE. The user can interact with such sources by walking or flying toward's them. He/she also can pop up a menu, scroll through it and execute all environment, remote, and local functions. Thereby, DIVE-ON makes intelligent use of the natural human capability of interacting with spatial objects and offers considerable navigation possibilities e.g. walking, flying, transporting and climbing.

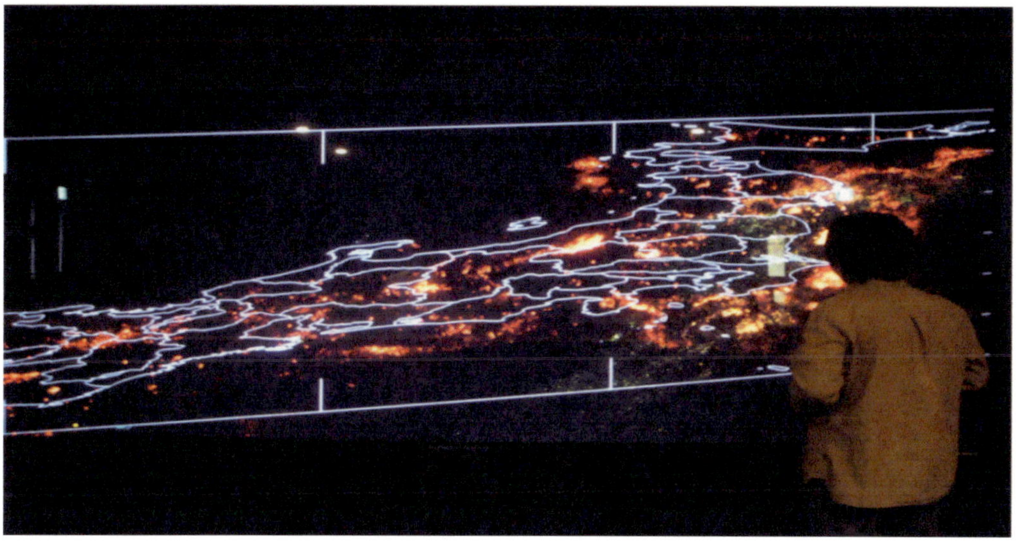

Fig. 9. Visualization of earthquakes data using a 4K stereo projection system (Ogi et al. (2009))

Inspired by treemaps Wang et al. (2006) presented a novel space-filling approach for tree visualization of file systems (Figure.10). This system provides a good overview for a large hierarchical data set and uses nested circles to make it easier to see groupings and structural relationships. By clicking on an item (a circle), the user can see the associated sub-items represented by the nested circles in a new view. The system provides the user with a control panel allowing him/her to filter files by types; by clicking on one file type, the other files types are filtered out. A zoom-in/zoom-out function allows the user to see folder or file characteristics such as name, size, and date. A user-feedback system means that user interaction techniques are friendly and easy to use.

Fig. 10. Representation of a file system with 3D-nested cylinders and spheresWang et al. (2006)

Meiguins et al. (2006) presented a tool for multidimensional VDM visualization in an augmented-reality environment where the user may visualize and manipulate information in real time VE without the use of devices such as a keyboard or mousse and interact simultaneously with other users in order to make a decision related to the task being analyzed. This tool uses a 3D scatter-plot to visualize the objects. Each visualized object has specific characteristics of position (x, y and z axes), color, shape, and size that directly represent data item values. The main advantages of this tools is that provide users with a dynamic menu which is displayed in an empty area when the user wants to execute certain actions. The tool also allows users to perform many manipulation interactions tasks such as real-time filter attributes, semantic zoom, rotation and translation of objects is the visualization area. A detailed comparison of these techniques is presented in Table.2.

7.2 Post-processing

Post-processing is the final step of the KDD process. Upon receiving the output of the DM algorithm, the decision-maker must evaluate and select the interesting part of the results.

7.2.1 Clustering

Clustering is used for finding groups of items that are similar. Given a set of data items, this set can be partitioned into a set of classes, so that items with similar characteristics are grouped together.

The GEOMI system proposed by Ahmed et al. (2006) is a visual analysis tool for the visualization of clustered graphs or trees. The system implements block model methods to associate each group of nodes to corresponding cluster. Two nodes are in the same cluster if they have the same neighbor set. This tool allows immersive navigation in the data using 3D head gestures instead of the classical mouse input. The system only allows the user visual exploration. Users can walk into the network, move closer to nodes or clusters by simply aiming in their direction. Nodding or tilting the head rotates the entire graph along the X and Y axes respectively, which provides users with intuitive interaction.

The objective of @VSIOR (Baumgärtner et al. (2007)), which is a human-centered approach, is to create a system for interaction with document, meta-data, and semantic relations. Human capabilities in this context are spatial memory and the fast visual processing of attributes and patterns. Artificial intelligence techniques assist the user, e.g. in searching for documents and calculating document similarities.

Otherwise, VRMiner (Azzag et al. (2005)) uses stereoscopic and intuitive navigation; these allow the user to easily select the interesting view point. VRMiner users have found that using this tool helps them solve 3 major problems: detecting correlation between data dimensions, checking the quality of discovered clusters, and presenting the data to a panel of experts. In this context, the stereoscopic display plays a crucial role in addition to the intuitive navigation which allows the user to easily select the interesting view point.

A detailed comparison of these techniques is presented in Table.3.

7.2.2 Classification

Given a set of pre-defined categorical classes, determine which of these classes a specific data item belongs to.

System	Visual Represen tation	Interaction techniques	Interaction actions			Input-Output devices	3D/ VR	year
			Navigation	Selection and Manipulation	System control			
@VISOR Baumgärtner et al. (2007) (fig.6(b))	Graph	Human-centered	-	Object selection + object positioning+ virtual hand	Graphical menu + gestural interaction	Tablet PC(2D) + Data glove + sterioscopic	VR	2007
GEOMI Ahmed et al. (2006)	Graph + tree	Visual exploration	Steering	-	Gestural interaction	Head tracker + stereoscopic	VR	2006
VRMiner Azzag et al. (2005) (Fig.5(b))	Abstract geometrical shape	Visual exploration	Manual view point manipulation	Object selection	Gestural interaction	Data glove + stereoscopic	VR	2005

Table 3. 3D VDM tool summary for clustering KDD task

In SUMO (Figure.4), a tool for document-class visualization is proposed (Buntain (2008)). The structure classes and relations among those classes can be presented to the user in a graphic form to facilitate understanding of the knowledge domain. This view can then be mapped onto the document space where shapes, sizes, and locations are governed by the sizes, overlaps, and other properties of the document classes. This view provides a clear picture of the relations between the resulting documents. Additionally, the user can manipulate the view to show only those documents that appear in a list of a results from of a query. Furthermore, if the results view includes details about subclasses of results and "near miss" elements in conjunction with positive results, the user can refine the query to find more appropriate results or widen the query to include more results if insufficient information is forthcoming. The third dimension allows the user a more expressive space, complete with navigation methods such as rotation and translation. In 3D, overlapping lines or labels can be avoided by rotating the layout to a better point of view.

DocuWorld (Einsfeld et al. (2006)), is a prototype for a dynamic semantic information system. This tool allows computed structures as well as documents to be organized by users. Compared to the web Forager (Card et al. (1996)), a workspace to organize documents with different degrees of interest at different distances to the user, DocuWorld provides the user with more flexible possibilities to store documents at locations defined by the user and visually indicates cluster-document relations (different semantics of connecting clusters to each other).

A detailed comparison of these techniques is presented in Table.4.

7.2.3 Association rules

On account of the enormous quantities of rules that can be produced by DM algorithms, association rule post-processing is a difficult stage in an association rule discovery process.

System	Visual Representation	Interaction techniques	Interaction actions			Input-Output devices	3D/VR	year
			Navigation	Selection and Manipulation	System control			
SUMO Buntain (2008) (Fig.4)	Tree	Visual exploration	Manual view point manipulation	-	-	2D Mouse + 2D screen	3D	2008
DocuWorld Einsfeld et al. (2006) (Fig.3(c))	Graph	human-centred	Thought wizard metaphor	Object selection + object positioning + virtual pointer	Gestural interaction + voice commands	Mouse + stereoscopic	VR	2006

Table 4. 3D VDM tool summary for classification KDD task

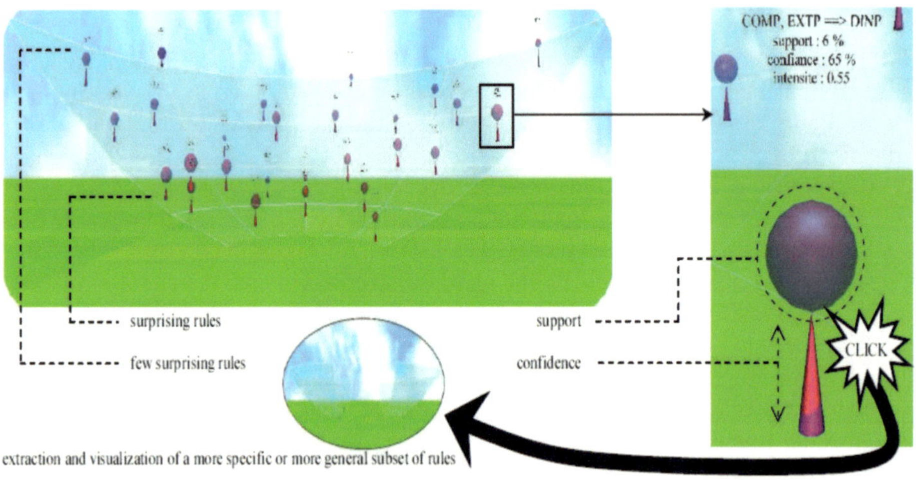

Fig. 11. ArVis a tool for association rules visualization Blanchard et al. (2007)

In order to find relevant knowledge for decision-making, the user needs to rummage through the rules.

ArVis proposed by Blanchard et al. (2007) is a human-centred approach. This approach consists of letting the user navigate freely inside the large set of rules by focusing on successive limited subsets via a visual representation of the rules (Figure.11). In other words, the user gradually drives a series of visual local explorations according to his/her interest for the rules. This approach is original compared to other rule visualization methods (Couturier et al. (2007), Gordal & Demiriz (2006), Zhao & Liu (2005)). Moreover, ARVis generates the rules dynamically during exploration by the user. Thus, the user's guidance during association rule

System	Visual Represen tation	Interaction techniques	Interaction actions			Input-Output devices	3D/ VR	year
			Navigation	Selection and Manipulation	System control			
ARVis Blanchard et al. (2007) (Fig.11)	Geometric shape	Human-centered	Manual view point manipulation	Object selecting + virtual pointer	Graphical menus	Mouse + 2D screen	3D	2007
3D spatial data mining on document sets (Fig.6(a)) Götzelmann et al. (2007)	Virtual world	Visual navigation and isual manipulation	-	Object selection	Graphical menus	-	3D	2006

Table 5. 3D VDM tool summary for association rules KDD task

post-processing is also exploited during association rule mining to reduce the search space and avoid generating huge amounts of rules.

Götzelmann et al. (2007) proposed a VDM system to analyze error sources of complex technical devices. The aims of the proposed approach is to extract association rules from a set of documents that describe malfunctions and errors for complex technical devices, followed by a projection of the results on a corresponding 3D model. Domain experts can evaluate the results gained by the DM algorithm by exploring a 3D model interactively in order to find spatial relationships between different components of the product. 3D enables a flexible spatial mapping of the results of statistical analysis. The visualization of statistical data on their spatial reference object by modifying visual properties to encode data (Figure.6(a)) can reveal apriori unknown facts, which where hidden in the database. By interactively exploring the 3D model, unknown sources and correlations of failures can be discovered that rely on the spatial configuration of several components and the shape of complex geometric objects.

A detailed comparison of these techniques is presented in Table.5.

7.2.4 Combining several methods

The Haiku tool (Figure.3(b)) combines several DM methods: clustering, classification and association rules (Beale (2007)). In this tool, the use of 3D graphs allows the visualization of high-dimensional data in a comprehensible and compact representation. The interface provides a large set of 3D manipulation feature of the structure, such as zooming in and out, moving through the representation (flying), rotating, jumping to specific location, viewing data details, and defining an area of interest . The only downside is that the control is done using a mouse. A detailed presentation is shown in Table.6.

System	Visual Representation	Interaction techniques	Interaction actions			Input-Output devices	3D/ VR	year
			Navigation	Selection and Manipulation	System control			
Heiku Pryke & Beale (2005) (Fig.3(b))	Graph	Human-centred	Manual view point manipulation + target based	Object selection	-	Mouse + 2D screen	3D	2005

Table 6. 3D VDM tool combining several methods

8. Conclusion

A new classification of VDM tools composed of 3 dimensions: visual representations; interaction techniques; and DM tasks, has been presented along with a survey of visual representations and interaction techniques in VDM. We can see that most of the recent VDM tools still rely on interaction metaphors developed more than a decade ago, and do not take into account the new interaction metaphors and techniques offered by VR technology. It is questionable whether these classical visualization/interaction techniques are able to meet the demands of the ever-increasing mass of information, or whether we are losing ground because we still lack the possibilities to properly interact with the databases to extract relevant knowledge. Devising intuitive visual interactive representations for DM and providing real-time interaction and mapping techniques that are scalable to the huge size of many current databases, are some of the research challenges that need to be addressed. In answer to this challenge, Mackinlay (1986) proposes two essential criterias to evaluate data mapping by visual representation: expressiveness and effectiveness. Firstly, expressiveness criteria determine whether a visual representation can express the desired information. Secondly, effectiveness criteria determine whether a visual representation exploits the capabilities of the output medium and the human visual system. Although the criteria were discussed in a 2D-graphic context, they can be extended to 3D and VR visualization. Finally, VDM is inherently cooperative requiring many experts to coordinate their activities to make decisions. Thus, collaborative research visualization may help to improve VDM processes. For example, current technology provided by 3D collaborative virtual worlds for gaming and social interaction, may support new methods of KDD.

9. References

Ahmed, A., Dwyer, T., Forster, M., Fu, X., Ho, J., Hong, S.-H., Koschutzki, D., Murray, C., Nikolov, N. S., Tarassov, R. T. A. & Xu, K. (2006). Geomi: Geometry for maximum insight, *Graph Drawing* 3843: 468–479.

Aitsiselmi, Y. & Holliman, N. S. (2009). Using mental rotation to evaluate the benefits of stereoscopic displays, *Proceedings of SPIE, the International Society for Optical Engineering*, pp. 1–12.

Ammoura, A., Zaïane, O. R. & Ji, Y. (2001). Immersed visual data mining: Walking the walk, *Proceedings of the 18th British National Conference on Databases*, pp. 202–218.

Ankerst, M. (2001). *Visual Data Mining*, PhD thesis, Institute for Computer Science Database and Information Systems, University of Munich.

Arns, L. L. (2002). *A new taxonomy for locomotion in virtual environments*, PhD thesis, Iowa State University, USA.

Asimov, D. (1985). The grand tour: a tool for viewing multidimensional data, *SIAM Journal on Scientific and Statistical Computing* 6(1): 128–143.

Azzag, H., Picarougne, F., Guinot, C. & Venturini, G. (2005). Vrminer: a tool for multimedia databases mining with virtual reality, *in* J. Darmont & O. Boussaid (eds), *Processing and Managing Complex Data for Decision Support*, pp. 318–339.

Baumgärtner, S., Ebert, A., Deller, M. & Agne, S. (2007). 2d meets 3d: a human-centered interface for visual data exploration, *Extended abstracts on Human factors in computing systems*, pp. 2273–2278.

Beale, R. (2007). Supporting serendipity: Using ambient intelligence to augment user exploration for data mining and web browsing, *International Journal of Human-Computer Studies* 65(5): 421–433.

Becker, B. (1997). Volume rendering for relational data, *Proceedings of the IEEE Symposium on Information Visualization*, pp. 87–91.

Beilken, C. & Spenke, M. (1999). Interactive data mining with infozoom : the medical data set, *Workshop Notes on Discovery Challenge, at the 3rd European Conference on Principles and Practice of Knowledge Discovery in Databases*, pp. 49–54.

Blanchard, J., Guillet, F. & Briand, H. (2007). Interactive visual exploration of association rules with rule-focusing methodology, *Knowledge and Information Systems* 13(1): 43–75.

Bowman, D. A., Kruijff, E., LaViola, J. J. & Poupyrev, I. (2001). An introduction to 3-d user interface design, *Presence: Teleoper. Virtual Environ.* 10(1): 96–108.

Brath, R., Peters, M. & Senior, R. (2005). Visualization for communication: The importance of aesthetic sizzle, *Proceedings of the 9th International Conference on Information Visualisation*, pp. 724–729.

Bukauskas, L. & Böhlen, M. (2001). Observer relative data extraction, *In Proceedings of the International Workshop on Visual Data Mining*, pp. 1–2.

Buntain, C. (2008). 3d ontology visualization in semantic search, *Proceedings of the 46th Annual Southeast Regional Conference*, pp. 204–208.

Cai, Y., Stumpf, R., Wynne, T., Tomlinson, M., Chung, D. S. H., Boutonnier, X., Ihmig, M., Franco, R. & Bauernfeind, N. (2007). Visual transformation for interactive spatiotemporal data mining, *Knowledge and Information Systems* 13(2): 119–142.

Card, S. K., Mackinlay, J. D. & Schneiderman, B. (1999). *Readings in information visualization : using vision to think*, Morgan Kaufmann publishers.

Card, S. K., Robertson, G. G. & York, W. (1996). The webbook and the web forager: an information workspace for the world-wide web, *Proceedings of the SIGCHI conference on Human factors in computing systems*, pp. 416–417.

Carswell, C. M., Frankenberger, S. & Bernhard, D. (1991). Graphing in depth: Perspectives on the use of three-dimensional graphs to represent lower-dimensional data., *Behaviour & Information Technology.* 10(6): 459–474.

Ceglar, A., Roddick, J. F. & Calder, P. (2003). *Managing data mining technologies in organizations*, IGI Publishing, chapter Guiding knowledge discovery through interactive data mining, pp. 45–87.

Chi, E. (2000). A taxonomy of visualization techniques using the data statereference model, *Proceedings of IEEE Symposium on Information Visualization*, pp. 69–75.

Chi, E. H. & Riedl, J. T. (1998). An operator interaction framework for visualization systems, *Proceedings of IEEE Symposium on Information Visualization*, pp. 63–70.

Cleveland, W. S. & McGill, R. (1984). Graphical perception: Theory, experimentation, and application to the development of graphical methods., *Journal of the American Statistical Association* 79(387): 531–554.

Couturier, O., Rouillard, J. J. L. & Chevrin, V. (2007). An interactive approach to display large sets of association rules, *Proceedings of the 2007 conference on Human interface*, pp. 258–267.

Dachselt, R. & Hinz, M. (2005). Three-dimensional widgets revisited: towards future standardization, *in* K. Y. Bowman D, Froehlich B & S. W (eds), *New directions in 3D user interfaces*, pp. 89 – 92.

de Oliveira, M. C. F. & Levkowitz, H. (2003). From visual data exploration to visual data mining: A survey, *Visualization and Computer Graphic* 9(3): 378–394.

Eidenberger, H. (2004). Visual data mining, *SPIE Information Technology and Communication Symposium*, pp. 121–132.

Einsfeld, K., Agne, S., Deller, M., Ebert, A., Klein, B. & Reuschling, C. (2006). Dynamic visualization and navigation of semantic virtual environments, *Proceedings of the conference on Information Visualization*, pp. 569–574.

Einsfeld, K., Ebert, A. & Wolle, J. (2007). Hannah: A vivid and flexible 3d information visualization framework, *Proceedings of the 11th International Conference on Information Visualization*, pp. 720–725.

Frawley, W. J., Piatetsky-Shapiro, G. & Matheus, C. J. (1992). Knowledge discovery in databases: An overview, *AI Magazine* 13(3): 57–70.

Gordal & Demiriz, A. (2006). A framework for visualizing association mining results, *Lecture Notes in Computer Science* 4263/2006: 593–602.

Götzelmann, T., Hartmann, K., Nürnberger, A. & Strothotte, T. (2007). 3d spatial data mining on document sets for the discovery of failure causes in complex technical devices, *Proceedings of the I2nd Int. Conf. on Computer Graphics Theory and Applications*, pp. 137–145.

Gross, M. (1994). *Visual computing : the integration of computer graphics, visual perception and imaging*, Springer-Verlag.

Hendley, R. J., Drew, N. S., Wood, A. M. & Beale, R. (1999). Narcissus: visualising information, *Proceedings of the IEEE Symposium on Information Visualization*, pp. 90 – 96.

Herman, I., , Melancëon, G. & Marshall, M. S. (2000). Graph visualization and navigation in information visualization: A survey, *IEEE Transactions on Visualization and Computer Graphics* 6(1): 24–43.

Hibbard, W., Levkowitz, H., Haswell, J., Rheingans, P. & Schroeder, F. (1995). Interaction in perceptually-based visualization, *Perceptual Issues in Visualization* IFIP Series on Computer Graphics: 23–32.

Inselberg, A. & Dimsdale, B. (1990). Parallel coordinates: a tool for visualizing multi-dimensional geometry, *Proceedings of the 1st conference on Visualization*, pp. 361–378.

Johnson, B. & Shneiderman, B. (1991). Tree-maps: a space-filling approach to the visualization of hierarchical information structures, *Proceedings of the 2nd conference on Visualization*, pp. 284–291.

Kalawsky, R. & Simpkin, G. (2006). Automating the display of third person/stealth views of virtual environments, *Presence: Teleoper. Virtual Environ.* 15(6): 717–739.

Keim, D. A. (2002). Information visualization and visual data mining, *IEEE Transactions on Visualization and Computer Graphics* 8(1): 1–8.

Krohn, U. (1996). Vineta: navigation through virtual information spaces, *Proceedings of the workshop on Advanced visual interfaces*, pp. 49–58.

Laviola, J. J. (2000). Msvt: A multimodal scientific visualization tool, *the 3ed IASTED International Conference on Computer Graphics and Imaging*, pp. 1–17.

Mackinlay, J. (1986). Automating the design of graphical presentations of relational information, *ACM Transactions on Graphics* 5(2): 110–141.

Maletic, J. I., Marcus, A., Dunlap, G. & Leigh, J. (2001). Visualizing object-oriented software in virtual reality, *Proceedings of the 9th International Workshop on Program Comprehension (IWPC'01)*, pp. 26–38.

Meiguins, B. S., Melo, R., do Carmo, C., Almeida, L., Gonćalves, A. S., Pinheiro, S. C. V. & de Brito Garcia, M. (2006). Multidimensional information visualization using augmented reality, *Proceedings of ACM international conference on Virtual reality continuum and its applications*, pp. 391 – 394.

Nagel, H. R., Granum, E., Bovbjerg, S. & Vittrup, M. (2008). *Visual Data Mining*, Springer-Verlag, chapter Immersive Visual Data Mining: The 3DVDM Approach, pp. 281–311.

Nagel, H. R., Granum, E. & Musaeus, P. (2001). Methods for visual mining of data in virtual reality, *Proceedings of the International Workshop on Visual Data Mining in conjunction with 2nd European Conference on Machine Learning and 5th European Conference on Principles and Practice of Knowledge Discovery in Databases*, pp. 13–27.

Nelson, L., Cook, D. & Cruz-Neira, C. (1999). Xgobi vs the c2: Results of an experiment comparing data visualization in a 3-d immersive virtual reality environement with a 2-d workstation display, *computational statistics* 14: 39–51.

Niggemann, O. (2001). *Visual Data Mining of Graph-Based Data*, PhD thesis, Department of Mathematics and Computer Science of the University of Paderborn, Germany.

Ogi, T., Tateyama, Y. & Sato, S. (2009). Visual data mining in immersive virtual environment based on 4k stereo images, *Proceedings of the 3rd International Conference on Virtual and Mixed Reality*, pp. 472 – 481.

Osawa, K., Asai, N., Suzuki, M., Sugimoto, Y. & Saito, F. (2002). An immersive programming system: Ougi, *Proceedings of the 12th International Conference on Artificial Reality and Telexistence*, pp. 36 – 43.

Parker, G., Franck, G. & Ware, C. (1998). Visualization of large nested graphs in 3d: Navigation and interaction, *Journal of Visual Languages & Computing* 9(3): 299–317.

Pike, W. A., Staskob, J., Changc, R. & O'Connelld, T. A. (2009). The science of interaction, *Information Visualization* 8(4): 263–274.

Plaisant, C., Grosjean, J. & Bederson, B. B. (2002). Spacetree: Supporting exploration in large node link tree, design evolution and empirical evaluation, *Proceedings of the IEEE Symposium on Information Visualization*, pp. 57–64.

Poulet, F. & Do, T. N. (2008). *Visual Data Mining*, Springer-Verlag, chapter Interactive Decision Tree Construction for Interval and Taxonomical Data, pp. 123–135.

Pryke, A. & Beale, R. (2005). Interactive comprehensible data mining, *Ambient Intelligence for Scientific Discovery* 3345/2005: 48–65.

Robertson, G., Czerwinski, M., Larson, K., Robbins, D. C., Thiel, D. & van Dantzich, M. (1998). Data mountain: using spatial memory for document management, *Proceedings of the 11th annual ACM symposium on User interface software and technology*, pp. 153–162.

Robertson, G. G., Mackinlay, J. D. & Card, S. K. (1991). Cone trees: animated 3d visualizations of hierarchical information, *Proceedings of the SIGCHI conference on Human factors in computing systems: Reaching through technology*, pp. 189 – 194.

Shneiderman, B. (2003). Why not make interfaces better than 3d reality?, *IEEE Computer Graphics and Applications* 23(6): 12–15.

Spence, I. (1990). Visual psychophysics of simple graphical elements., *Journal of Experimental Psychology: Human Perception and Performance.* 16(4): 683–692.

Tavanti, M. & Lind, M. (2001). 2d vs 3d, implications on spatial memory, *Proceedings of the IEEE Symposium on Information Visualization*, p. 139.

Teyseyre, A. R. & Campo, M. R. (2009). An overview of 3d software visualization, *IEEE Transactions on Visualization and Computer Graphics* 15(1): 87–105.

Tory, M. & Moller, T. (2004). Rethinking visualization: A high-level taxonomy, *Proceedings of IEEE Symposium on Information Visualization*, pp. 151–158.

Tufte, E. R. (1983). *The Visual Display of Quantitative Information*, Graphics Press.

Van Ham, F. van Wijk, J. (2002). Beamtrees: compact visualization of large hierarchies, *Proceedings of IEEE Symposium on Information Visualization* pp. 93– 100.

Wang, W., Wang, H., Dai, G. & Wang, H. (2006). Visualization of large hierarchical data by circle packing, *Proceedings of SIGCHI conference on Human Factors in computing systems*, pp. 517–520.

Ware, C. & Franck, G. (1994). Viewing a graph in a virtual reality display is three times as good as a 2d diagram, *Proceedings of IEEE Visual Languages*, pp. 182–183.

Ware, C. & Franck, G. (1996). Evaluating stereo and motion cues for visualizing information nets in three dimensions, *ACM Transactions on Graphics* 15(2): 121–140.

Ware, C. & Mitchell, P. (2008). Visualizing graphs in three dimensions, *ACM Transactions on Applied Perception* 5(1): 1–15.

Zhao, K. & Liu, B. (2005). *Opportunity Map: A Visualization Framework for Fast Identification of Actionable Knowledge*, PhD thesis, University of Illinois at Chicago.